Citizens of
the World

SELECTED AND EDITED BY

Nancy Carr

Joseph Coulson

Anne Gendler

Mike Levine

Judith McCue

EXPANDED EDITION EDITED BY

Donald H. Whitfield

INTERIOR DESIGN

Studio Blue, Chicago

studioblueinc.com

Citizens of the World

Readings in Human Rights

EXPANDED EDITION

The Great Books Foundation

A nonprofit educational organization

With generous support from Harrison Middleton University,
a Great Books distance-learning college

Published and distributed by
The Great Books Foundation
A nonprofit educational organization

35 East Wacker Drive, Suite 400
Chicago, IL 60601
www.greatbooks.org

With generous support from
Harrison Middleton University,
a Great Books distance-learning college
www.chumsci.edu

First printing
9 8 7 6 5 4 3 2 1

The Library of Congress has cataloged the first edition as follows:

Citizens of the world: readings in human rights/[selected and edited by
    Nancy Carr, senior editor...et al.].
        p. cm.
    ISBN 0-945159-36-6 (pbk. : alk. paper)
      1. Human rights. I. Carr, Nancy. II. Great Books Foundation (U.S.)

JC571.C585 2004
323—dc22

                                              2004052294

I am not an Athenian or a Greek,
but a citizen of the world.

—attributed to SOCRATES

About the Great Books Foundation

The Great Books Foundation is an independent, nonprofit educational organization whose mission is to empower readers of all ages to become more reflective and responsible thinkers. To accomplish this, we teach the art of civil discourse through the Shared Inquiry™ method and publish enduring works across the disciplines.

The Great Books Foundation was established in 1947 to promote liberal education for the general public. In 1962, the Foundation extended its mission to children with the introduction of Junior Great Books®. Since its inception, the Foundation has helped thousands of people throughout the United States and in other countries begin their own discussion groups in schools, libraries, and community centers. Today, Foundation instructors conduct hundreds of workshops each year, in which educators and parents learn to lead Shared Inquiry discussion.

The Great Books Foundation's workshops in Shared Inquiry help people get the most from discussion. Participants learn how to read actively, pose fruitful questions, and listen and respond to others effectively in discussion. All participants also practice leading a discussion and have an opportunity to reflect on the process with others. For more information about Great Books materials or workshops, call the Great Books Foundation at 800-222-5870 or visit our website at www.greatbooks.org.

Contents

Preface to the Expanded Edition

This book brings into sharp focus some of the critical questions about human rights that have emerged in the course of history. By means of key documents—declarations, essays, stories, and personal narratives—it traces the development of the concept of human rights throughout the world. Certainly, concern about securing wider recognition of human rights and limiting their abuse is nothing new. Still, it can be argued that in recent times jarring historical events have brought discussions about human rights to an urgent pitch. This expanded edition of *Citizens of the World* seeks to address some of the issues that have been raised, especially in the wake of the traumatic events of September 11, 2001.

Repeatedly throughout the twentieth century, in times of war and in times of relative peace and across the spectrum of political regimes, individuals and groups of people have been denied the right to provide for their own basic needs, to flourish, and even to live. Throughout the last century, international and civil wars and acts of genocide have been the extreme flash points that repeatedly refocused our attention on the urgent need for a deeper understanding of the nature of human rights and the means for promoting—and guaranteeing—them. Without any doubt, the terrorist attacks of September 11 and the ensuing consequences, not just in places like Iraq, Afghanistan, and the Guantánamo Bay detention center, but throughout the world, have helped ignite new debates about what human rights are and how they can be observed and enforced.

Human rights issues that have come to the fore in the wake of September 11 include the surge of transnational organizations dedicated to acts of terrorism, the ongoing debate on how to balance national security with the preservation of civil rights, the detention of suspects by Western democracies without due process of law, the blurring of standards about torture and interrogation, and widely differing national and international concepts of justice with respect to securing human rights.

This expanded edition of *Citizens of the World: Readings in Human Rights* includes selections by noted authors such as Hannah Arendt, Alan Dershowitz, and Michael Ignatieff, offering provocative and multifaceted perspectives on these urgent matters.

Introduction

In *Citizens of the World: Readings in Human Rights*, voices speak against injustice—a jailed dissident, a concentration camp inmate, a girl imprisoned in her home under the rule of religious extremists. We see families torn apart, a man arrested in the middle of the night because of a poem he wrote, peaceful demonstrators flattened by the tanks of their own government's military.

The experiences of these people raise urgent questions about human rights. Our sense of what human rights are and how they should be protected is always evolving and always subject to debate. Rather than attempt to survey the history of human rights, the selections in *Citizens of the World* suggest a way of thinking about human rights, with each representing a moment in its history. In addition to foundational documents, this anthology includes memoirs, letters, speeches, fiction, and poetry from different periods and parts of the world. The range of readings shows how the struggle for human rights is driven by the efforts, and affects the lives, of individuals. Some selections mark great advances in the cause of human rights; others depict horrific human rights abuses.

The idea that each individual possesses a set of rights that society and government are obligated to respect and protect took shape in Europe in the seventeenth and eighteenth centuries; and so, the history traced here is primarily Western. Although the concept of human rights has become more deeply rooted in some parts of the world than in others, it is important to note that, in theory, human rights are independent of geography, political borders, or cultural heritage. The fact that forty-eight nations have signed the Universal Declaration of Human Rights shows that the idea of human rights has been embraced by many diverse populations, but it also shows that, for a significant number of people, human rights are still not assured.

Although the idea of human rights is only a few centuries old, the selections from ancient Greece and Rome indicate that societies have always confronted issues that involve human rights: What should people be free to do? What should they be forbidden to do? What does a society owe its individual members and what do they owe it? Giving her impassioned (and unauthorized) speech in the Roman Forum in 42 BCE, Hortensia argues that making Rome's richest women pay a war tax is unjust. She does not say that the tax would violate women's rights, but her argument is essentially the same as that of the American colonists in the 1770s when they refused to submit to British taxation without representation.

While issues pertaining to human rights are always with us, the way a society thinks about them changes with its circumstances. For example, when national security becomes a primary concern—as in a time of war— ideas about the relative importance of individual rights may change. Should citizens be willing to give up part of their right to privacy, if doing so may help protect them against their nation's enemies? Similarly, the rights of individuals can come into conflict with one another. The First Amendment in the Bill of Rights guarantees U.S. citizens freedom of speech and the right to assemble peaceably. Should these rights be extended to those who assemble for the purpose of expressing their hatred of other citizens? Even in a society that places a consistently high value on human rights, decisions about which rights should take precedence will depend on what else it values.

Just as there is always debate about which rights should be protected, there is also disagreement about how best to protect them. This issue became especially acute in the twentieth century, with its two world wars and the rise of totalitarian governments. What recourse is available to citizens whose rights are not respected by their government? Ensuring the rights of such citizens, or of people who have no citizenship anywhere, is an exceedingly difficult problem. The formation of the United Nations in 1945, tribunals set up for those accused of "crimes against humanity," and the creation of the International Criminal Court all intended to guarantee human rights on an international scale. But all are still subject to intense debate both in terms of their authority and their effectiveness.

The history of human rights has shaped the world in which we live and reminds us that the freedoms many of us take for granted are recent and fragile. Some freedoms still spark bitter controversy, in the United States and elsewhere. Listening to the many voices in this anthology can help us better understand both the experiences of those whose rights have been violated and the victories of those who have fought against injustice. Reading and discussing what they have to say prepares us to join the ongoing public discussion of human rights and to participate in the effort to extend them to everyone.

About Shared Inquiry

SHARED INQUIRY™ is the effort to achieve a more thorough understanding of a text by discussing questions, responses, and insights with others. For both the leader and the participants, careful listening is essential. The leader guides the discussion by asking questions about specific ideas and problems of meaning in the text, but does not seek to impose his or her own interpretation on the group.

During a Shared Inquiry discussion, group members consider a number of possible ideas and weigh the evidence for each. Ideas that are entertained and then refined or abandoned are not thought of as mistakes, but as valuable parts of the thinking process. Group members gain experience in communicating complex ideas and in supporting, testing, and expanding their thoughts. Everyone in the group contributes to the discussion, and while participants may disagree with each other, they treat each other's ideas respectfully.

This process of communal discovery is vital to developing an understanding of important texts and ideas, rather than merely cataloging knowledge about them. By reading and thinking together about important works, you and the other members of your group are joining a great conversation that extends across the centuries.

GUIDELINES FOR LEADING
AND PARTICIPATING IN DISCUSSION

Over the past sixty years, the Great Books Foundation has developed guidelines that distill the experience of many discussion groups, with participants of all ages. We have found that when groups follow the procedures outlined below, discussions are most focused and fruitful:

1. *Read the selection before participating in the discussion.* This ensures that all participants are equally prepared to talk about the ideas in the work.

2. *Support your ideas with evidence from the text.* This keeps the discussion focused on understanding the selection and enables the group to weigh textual support for different.

3. *Discuss the ideas in the selection and try to understand them fully before exploring issues that go beyond the selection.* Reflecting on the ideas in the text and the evidence to support them makes the exploration of related issues more productive.

4. *Listen to other participants and respond to them directly.* Directing your comments and questions to other group members, not always the leader, will make the discussion livelier and more dynamic.

5. *Expect the leader to only ask questions.* Effective leaders help participants develop their own ideas, with everyone gaining a new understanding in the process. Participants should look to leaders for questions, not answers.

HOW TO MAKE DISCUSSIONS
MORE EFFECTIVE

• *Ask questions when something is unclear.* Simply asking someone to explain what he or she means by a particular word, or to repeat a comment, can give everyone in the group time to think about the idea in depth.

• *Ask for evidence.* Asking "What in the text gave you that idea?" helps everyone better understand the reasoning behind an answer, and it allows the group to consider which ideas have the best support.

• *Ask for agreement and disagreement.* "Does your idea agree with hers, or is it different?" Questions of this kind help the group understand how ideas are related or distinct.

• *Reflect on discussion afterward.* Sharing comments about how the discussion went and ideas for improvement can make each discussion better than the last.

ROOM ARRANGEMENT
AND GROUP SIZE

Ideally, everyone in a discussion should be able to see and hear everyone else. When it isn't possible to arrange the seating in a circle or horseshoe, encourage group members to look at the person talking, acknowledging one another and not just the leader.

In general, Shared Inquiry discussion is most effective in groups of ten to twenty participants. If a group is much bigger than twenty, it is important to ensure that everyone has a chance to speak. This can be accomplished either by dividing the group in half for discussion or by setting aside time at the end of discussion to go around the room and give each person a chance to make a brief final comment.

Using the Questions for Each Reading

FOR DISCUSSION

These questions ask about the meaning of a selection and may be reasonably answered in different ways. Interpretive questions offer you the opportunity to weigh evidence, listen to the perspectives of others, and synthesize different points of view to reach a deeper, more informed understanding of the selection.

FOR FURTHER REFLECTION

These questions ask your opinion about some aspect of a selection. Your answers will be based on your own experience and knowledge, rather than evidence from the selection. Evaluative questions help you to see how issues raised in a selection may be relevant to your particular time and place.

FOR RESEARCH

Researching topics related to a selection provides opportunities to consider the larger context. Obtaining more information about the historical circumstances in which something was written, its immediate effects, or the ways in which it remains influential will give you a broader picture of human rights history and its ongoing debates.

How to Keep a Slave

CATO THE ELDER (234–149 BCE)

Marcus Porcius Cato, known as Cato the Elder, was a Roman soldier, censor, statesman, and orator who wrote Origenes, *the first Latin history of Rome. Deeply conservative, he fought against what he considered the corrupting influence of Greek thought and culture on traditional Roman beliefs and values. Cato opposed the decadence and laziness he saw among Rome's elite, even passing a law to limit the size of Roman feasts. To protect his sons from being contaminated by the ideas of Aristotle, Socrates, and Plato, he educated them himself in the Roman tradition. Cato's wealth included land and slaves, but he was known to be very frugal, eating only simple, coarse food. Cato's only surviving complete work,* De agri cultura, *from which this selection is taken, is a treatise on farming that includes much practical advice. Most slaves in ancient Rome came from other countries, from which they were kidnapped or captured in war; native Romans could also be enslaved if they fell into debt. Most slaves worked as domestic servants, agricultural laborers, or in secretarial or managerial positions.*

How to Keep a Slave

from De Agri cultura

THE FOLLOWING ARE the duties of the overseer: He must show good management. The feast days must be observed. He must withhold his hands from another's goods and diligently preserve his own. He must settle disputes among the slaves, and if anyone commits an offense, he must punish him properly in proportion to the fault. He must see that the servants are well provided for and that they do not suffer from cold or hunger. Let him keep them busy with their work—he will more easily keep them from wrongdoing and meddling. If the overseer sets his face against wrongdoing, they will not do it; if he allows it, the master must not let him go unpunished. He must express his appreciation of good work, so that others may take pleasure in well-doing. The overseer must not be a gadabout; he must always be sober and must not go out to dine. He must keep the servants busy and see that the master's orders are carried out. . . .

Rations for the hands: Four modii of wheat in winter, and in summer, four and a half for the field hands. The overseer, the housekeeper, the foreman, and the shepherd should receive three. The chain gang should have a ration of four pounds of bread through the winter, increasing to five when they begin to work the vines, and dropping back to four when the figs ripen.

Wine ration for the hands: For three months following the vintage, let them drink after-wine. In the fourth month, issue a hemina a day, that is, two and a half congii a month; in the fifth, sixth, seventh, and eighth months a sextarius a day, that is, five congii a month; in the ninth, tenth, eleventh, and twelfth months three heminae a day, that is, an amphora a month. In addition, issue three and a half congii per person for the Saturnalia and the Compitalia. Total of wine for each person per year, seven quadrantals, and an additional amount for the chain gang proportioned to their work. Ten quadrantals of wine per person is not an excessive allowance for the year.

Relish for the hands: Store all the windfall olives you can and later the mature olives, which will yield very little oil. Issue them sparingly and make them last as long as possible. When they are used up, issue fish-pickle and vinegar, and a pint of oil a month per person. A modius of salt a year per person is sufficient.

Clothing allowance for the hands: A tunic three and a half feet long and a blanket every other year. When you issue the tunic or the blanket, first take up the old one and have patchwork made of it. A stout pair of wooden shoes should be issued every other year.

For Discussion

1. What does Cato's tone suggest about the way he views slavery?
2. What factors does Cato seem to have considered when deciding how much food, drink, and clothing different categories of slaves should receive?
3. In this selection, does Cato regard slaves more as possessions or as human beings?

For Further Reflection

1. Is Cato's concern for the welfare of slaves moral or purely practical?
2. Is it possible to be both a slave owner and a person of high moral principles?

For Research

1. Find a part of the world where slavery still exists. Why does slavery continue there?
2. What are some of the ways in which ancient Roman slavery was different from American slavery? How was it similar?

Hortensia's Protest

APPIAN OF ALEXANDRIA (*fl. second century* CE)

A Greek official from Alexandria, Appian moved to Rome after gaining citizenship and worked as a lawyer and procurator. He wrote a twenty-four volume history of the Roman conquests from the republican period to the second century CE. Only eleven volumes survive in their complete form. This account of Hortensia's speech comes from Appian's history of the Roman civil wars.

The daughter of a widely known orator, Hortensia (fl. first century BCE) was well educated and had been trained in the art of speech writing by her father. In her famous speech protesting taxation without representation, she argues against the imposition of a tax on some 1,400 of Rome's wealthiest women to raise money for a civil war against the assassins of Julius Caesar and their sympathizers. Hortensia gave her speech in the Roman Forum, the seat of government and a place from which women were legally barred. Her public address angered the ruling triumvirate—Mark Antony, Lepidus, and Octavian—who tried unsuccessfully to drive her and her followers out of the forum. Hortensia's cause won support from many present in the forum, and the next day the triumvirate lowered to four hundred the number of women to be taxed and also required a similar number of men to pay the tax.

Hortensia's Protest

THE TRIUMVIRS ADDRESSED the people on this subject and published an edict requiring 1,400 of the richest women to make a valuation of their property and to furnish for the service of the war such portion as the triumvirs should require from each. It was provided further that if any should conceal their property or make a false valuation they should be fined and that rewards should be given to informers, whether free persons or slaves. The women resolved to beseech the womenfolk of the triumvirs. With the sister of Octavian and the mother of Antony they did not fail, but they were repulsed from the doors of Fulvia, the wife of Antony, whose rudeness they could scarce endure. They then forced their way to the tribunal of the triumvirs in the forum, the people and the guards dividing to let them pass. There, through the mouth of Hortensia, whom they had selected to speak, they spoke as follows:

> As befitted women of our rank addressing a petition to you, we had recourse to the ladies of your households; but having been treated as did not befit us, at the hands of Fulvia, we have been driven by her to the forum. You have already deprived us of our fathers, our sons, our husbands, and our brothers, whom you accused of having wronged you; if you take away our property also, you reduce us to a condition unbecoming our birth, our manners, our sex. If we have done you wrong, as you say our husbands have, proscribe us as you do them. But if we women have not voted any of you public enemies, have not torn

down your houses, destroyed your army, or led another one against you; if we have not hindered you in obtaining offices and honors—why do we share the penalty when we did not share the guilt?

Why should we pay taxes when we have no part in the honors, the commands, the statecraft, for which you contend against each other with such harmful results? "Because this is a time of war," do you say? When have there not been wars, and when have taxes ever been imposed on women, who are exempted by their sex among all mankind? Our mothers did once rise superior to their sex and made contributions when you were in danger of losing the whole empire and the city itself through the conflict with the Carthaginians. But then they contributed voluntarily, not from their landed property, their fields, their dowries, or their houses, without which life is not possible to free women, but only from their own jewelry, and even these not according to fixed valuation, not under fear of informers or accusers, not by force and violence, but what they themselves were willing to give. What alarm is there now for the empire or the country? Let war with the Gauls or the Parthians come, and we shall not be inferior to our mothers in zeal for the common safety, but for the civil wars may we never contribute, nor ever assist you against each other! We did not contribute to Caesar or to Pompey. Neither Marius nor Cinna imposed taxes upon us. Nor did Sulla, who held despotic power in the state, do so, whereas you say that you are reestablishing the commonwealth.

While Hortensia thus spoke, the triumvirs were angry that women should dare to hold a public meeting when the men were silent, that they should demand from magistrates the reasons for their acts, and themselves not so much as furnish money while the men were serving in the army. They ordered the lictors to drive them away from the tribunal, which they proceeded to do until cries were raised by the multitude outside, when the lictors desisted and the triumvirs said they would postpone till the next day the consideration of the matter. On the following day they reduced the number of women who were to present a valuation of their property from 1,400 to 400, and decreed that all men who possessed more than 100,000 drachmas, both citizens and strangers, freedmen and priests, and men of all nationalities without a single exception, should (under the same dread of penalty and also of informers) lend them at interest a fiftieth part of their property and contribute one year's income to the war expenses.

For Discussion

1. What does Hortensia mean when she says that women "are exempted by their sex among all mankind" (18) from having taxes imposed on them?
2. Does Hortensia expect women and men to be treated alike by their government?
3. Under what conditions does Hortensia think that women should pay taxes?

For Further Reflection

1. Is an individual obligated to pay a tax even if she or he disagrees with how the money is spent by the government?
2. Should women and men always be treated alike by their government?

For Research

1. In the first century BCE, what rights did a freeborn Roman woman enjoy? What was her role and status in society?
2. Research a nineteenth- or twentieth-century example of refusal to pay a tax as a form of political protest. What was being protested? Was the goal of the protest achieved?

Letter XLVII

SENECA THE YOUNGER (C. 4 BCE–65 CE)

Lucius Annaeus Seneca, known as Seneca the Younger, was born in Cordoba, Spain. He became one of the most influential men in first-century Rome, serving as a statesman and an orator as well as writing works of literature and philosophy that are still read today. His most important works are the tragedies Oedipus, Phaedra, *and* Medea, *and* Epistulae morales ad Lucilium, *essays in the form of letters expounding the Stoic philosophy. Seneca's political career was filled with upheaval. Twice sentenced to death—by the emperors Caligula in 37 CE and Claudius in 41 CE—he was one of the virtual rulers of Rome from 54 to 62 CE. He served as tutor to the future emperor Nero and as one of his advisers during the early part of Nero's reign. Seneca committed suicide in 65 CE, ordered to do so along with others who were accused of plotting against Nero.*

In this selection, taken from Epistulae morales ad Lucilium, *Seneca expresses to his friend Lucilius his convictions about the treatment of slaves. Writing at a time when slaves were mostly captives taken in war or debtors, Seneca's warning to remember that only fortune separates the free from the enslaved is typical of Stoic philosophy.*

Letter XLVII

I'M GLAD TO HEAR, from these people who've been visiting you that you live on friendly terms with your slaves. It is just what one expects of an enlightened, cultivated person like yourself. "They're slaves," people say. No. They're human beings. "They're slaves." But they share the same roof as ourselves. "They're slaves." No, they're friends, humble friends. "They're slaves." Strictly speaking, they're our fellow slaves, if you once reflect that fortune has as much power over us as over them.

This is why I laugh at those people who think it degrading for a man to eat with his slave. Why do they think it degrading? Only because the most arrogant of conventions has decreed that the master of the house be surrounded at his dinner by a crowd of slaves, who have to stand around while he eats more than he can hold, loading an already distended belly in his monstrous greed until it proves incapable any longer of performing the function of a belly, at which point he expends more effort in vomiting everything up than he did in forcing it down. And all this time the poor slaves are forbidden to move their lips to speak, let alone to eat. The slightest murmur is checked with a stick; not even accidental sounds like a cough, or a sneeze, or a hiccup are let off a beating. All night long they go on standing about, dumb and hungry, paying grievously for any interruption.

The result is that slaves who cannot talk before his face talk about him behind his back. The slaves of former days, however, whose mouths were not sealed up like this, who were able to make conversation not only in the presence of their master but actually with him, were ready to bare their necks to the executioner for him, to divert on to themselves any danger that threatened him; they talked at dinner, but under torture they kept their mouths shut. It is just this high-handed treatment that is responsible for the frequently heard saying, "You've as many enemies as you've slaves." They are not our enemies when we acquire them; we make them so.

For the moment I pass over other instances, of our harsh and inhuman behavior: the way we abuse them as if they were beasts of burden instead of human beings; the way for example, from the time we take our places on the dinner couches, one of them mops up the spittle and another stationed at the foot of the couch collects up the "leavings" of the drunken diners. Another carves the costly game birds, slicing off choice pieces from the breast and rump with the unerring strokes of a trained hand—unhappy man, to exist for the one and only purpose of carving a fat bird in the proper style—although the person who learns the technique from sheer necessity is not quite so much to be pitied as the person who gives demonstrations of it for pleasure's sake. Another, the one who serves the wine, is got up like a girl and engaged in a struggle with his years; he cannot get away from his boyhood, but is dragged back to it all the time; although he already has the figure of a soldier, he is kept free of hair by having it rubbed away or pulled out by the roots. His sleepless night is divided between his master's drunkenness and sexual pleasures—boy at the table, man in the bedroom. Another, who has the privilege of rating each guest's character, has to go on standing where he is, poor fellow, and watch to see whose powers of flattery and absence of restraint in appetite or speech are to secure them an invitation for the following day. Add to these the caterers with their highly developed knowledge of their master's palate, the men who know the flavors that will sharpen his appetite, know what will appeal to his eyes, what novelties can tempt his stomach when it is becoming queasy, what dishes he will push aside with the eventual coming of sheer satiety, what he will have a craving for on that particular day.

These are the people with whom a master cannot tolerate the thought of taking his dinner, assuming that to sit down at the same table with one of his slaves would seriously impair his dignity. "The very idea!" he says. Yet have a look at the number of masters he has from the ranks of these very slaves.[1] Take Callistus's one-time master. I saw him once actually standing waiting at Callistus's door and being refused admission while others were going inside, the very master who had attached a price-ticket to the man and put him up for sale along with other rejects from his household staff. There's a slave who has paid his master back—one who was pushed into the first lot, too, the batch on which the auctioneer is merely trying out his voice! Now it was the slave's turn to strike his master off his list, to decide that *he*'s not the sort of person he wants in *his* house. Callistus's master sold him, yes, and look how much it cost him!

How about reflecting that the person you call your slave traces his origin back to the same stock as yourself, has the same good sky above him, breathes as you do, lives as you do, dies as you do? It is as easy for you to see in him a freeborn man as for him to see a slave in you. Remember the Varus disaster:[2] many a man of the most distinguished ancestry, who was doing his military service as the first step on the road to a seat in the Senate, was brought low by fortune, condemned by her to look after a steading, for example, or a flock of sheep. Now think contemptuously of these people's lot in life, in whose very place, for all your contempt, you could suddenly find yourself.

---

1. [Many ex-slaves had risen to high positions under Claudius and Nero. EDS.]
2. [Publius Quintilius Varus, a Roman civil administrator and military commander, intended to establish Rome's sovereignty over territory east of the Rhine River. In 9 CE, he lost every member of three legions of the Roman army to a trap laid by Germanic tribes in the Teutoburg Forest, after which he committed suicide. The disaster was a great shock to Rome.]

For Discussion

1. Is Seneca urging humane treatment of slaves mainly because he thinks that such treatment is their right or because it makes them more loyal to their masters?
2. Why does Seneca believe that masters and slaves are not natural enemies and can live together as friends?
3. Why does Seneca encourage his reader to reflect that "your slave traces his origin back to the same stock as yourself, has the same good sky above him, breathes as you do, lives as you do, dies as you do"? (25)

For Further Reflection

1. Why does Seneca argue for the humane treatment of slaves and not for the abolition of slavery?
2. Must a slave owner see himself or herself as in some way superior to a slave in order to justify the keeping of slaves?
3. Do you believe that it would be possible to reconcile behaving humanely with keeping slaves?
4. Respond to Seneca's letter as if you were a slave.

For Research

1. By what process could slaves become free citizens in ancient Rome?
2. Compare Seneca's statements about slavery to arguments for the abolition of slavery in the American South. What assumptions do these arguments make that lead to the conclusion that, no matter how slaves are treated by their owners, slavery is wrong?

Magna Carta

England's MAGNA CARTA, *or Great Charter, of civil liber-*
ties is one of the most famous documents in European history.
Since its signing in 1215, it has frequently been invoked as a
symbol of freedom from oppression. The actual circumstances
of the Charter's signing, and its effects, were less inspiring.
The document is a compromise between King John and English
barons dissatisfied with his rule, and it failed to produce the
peace that the signers had hoped for. Almost immediately after
it was signed, the barons and the king were embroiled in civil
war. Magna Carta did, however, formalize ideas of govern-
ment that secured England's commitment to basic civil rights,
and its provisions influenced other significant documents,
including the Constitution of the United States. Magna Carta
required that "freemen" be given trial by jury, be allowed to
enter and leave the country (except in wartime), be entitled to
meet and determine whether to consent to financial demands
from the king, and be safeguarded against government con-
fiscation of their property. The rights were guaranteed only
to wealthy and landowning men (the term freemen *referred*
specifically to this class) but the idea that the king and the gov-
ernment were answerable to the people in the form of the law
laid the foundation for England's constitutional monarchy and
representative government.

Magna Carta

John, by the grace of God, King of England, Lord of Ireland, Duke of Normandy and Aquitaine, and Count of Anjou, to the archbishop, bishops, abbots, earls, barons, justiciaries, foresters, sheriffs, stewards, servants, and to all his bailiffs and liege subjects, greetings. Know that, having regard to God and for the salvation of our soul, and those of all our ancestors and heirs, and unto the honor of God and the advancement of his holy church and for the rectifying of our realm, we have granted as underwritten by advice of our venerable fathers, Stephen, Archbishop of Canterbury, Primate of all England and Cardinal of the holy Roman Church, Henry, Archbishop of Dublin, William of London, Peter of Winchester, Jocelyn of Bath and Glastonbury, Hugh of Lincoln, Walter of Worcester, William of Coventry, Benedict of Rochester, bishops; Master Pandulf, subdeacon and member of the household of our lord the pope, of brother Aymeric (master of the Knights of the Temple in England), and of the illustrious men William Marshal, Earl of Pembroke, William, Earl of Salisbury, William, Earl of Warenne, William, Earl of Arundel, Alan of Galloway (constable of Scotland), Waren Fitz Gerold, Peter Fitz Herbert, Hubert De Burgh (seneschal of Poitou), Hugh de Neville, Matthew Fitz Herbert, Thomas Basset, Alan Basset, Philip d'Aubigny, Robert of Roppesley, John Marshal, John Fitz Hugh, and others, our liegemen.

1. In the first place we have granted to God, and by this our present charter confirmed for us and our heirs forever that the English Church shall be free, and shall have her rights entire and her liberties inviolate; and we will that it be thus observed; which is apparent from this that the freedom of elections, which is reckoned most important and very essential to the English Church, we, of our pure and unconstrained will, did grant, and did by our charter confirm and did obtain the ratification of the same from our lord, Pope Innocent III, before the quarrel arose between us and our barons: and this we will observe, and our will is that it be observed in good faith by our heirs forever. We have also granted to all freemen of our kingdom, for us and our heirs forever, all the underwritten liberties, to be had and held by them and their heirs, of us and our heirs forever.

2. If any of our earls or barons, or others holding of us in chief by military service shall have died, and at the time of his death his heir shall be full of age and owe relief, he shall have his inheritance by the old relief, to wit, the heir or heirs of an earl, for the whole baroncy of an earl by £100; the heir or heirs of a baron, £100 for a whole barony; the heir or heirs of a knight, 100s, at most, and whoever owes less let him give less, according to the ancient custom of fees.

3. If, however, the heir of any one of the aforesaid has been under age and in wardship, let him have his inheritance without relief and without fine when he comes of age.

4. The guardian of the land of an heir who is thus under age, shall take from the land of the heir nothing but reasonable produce, reasonable customs, and reasonable services, and that without destruction or waste of men or goods; and if we have committed the wardship of the lands of any such minor to the sheriff, or to any other who is responsible to us for its issues, and he has made destruction or waste of what he holds in wardship, we will take of him amends, and the land shall be committed to two lawful and discreet men of that fee, who shall be responsible for the issues to us or to him to whom we shall assign them; and if we have given or sold the wardship of any such land to anyone and he has therein made destruction or waste, he

shall lose that wardship, and it shall be transferred to two lawful and discreet men of that fief, who shall be responsible to us in like manner as aforesaid.

5. The guardian, moreover, so long as he has the wardship of the land, shall keep up the houses, parks, fishponds, stanks, mills, and other things pertaining to the land, out of the issues of the same land; and he shall restore to the heir, when he has come to full age, all his land, stocked with ploughs and wainage, according as the season of husbandry shall require, and the issues of the land can reasonably bear.

6. Heirs shall be married without disparagement, yet so that before the marriage takes place the nearest in blood to that heir shall have notice.

7. A widow, after the death of her husband, shall forthwith and without difficulty have her marriage portion and inheritance; nor shall she give anything for her dower, or for her marriage portion, or for the inheritance which her husband and she held on the day of the death of that husband; and she may remain in the house of her husband for forty days after his death, within which time her dower shall be assigned to her.

8. No widow shall be compelled to marry, so long as she prefers to live without a husband; provided always that she gives security not to marry without our consent, if she holds of us, or without the consent of the lord of whom she holds, if she holds of another.

9. Neither we nor our bailiffs will seize any land or rent for any debt, as long as the chattels[1] of the debtor are sufficient to repay the debt; nor shall the sureties of the debtor be distrained[2] so long as the principal debtor is able to satisfy the debt; and if the principal debtor shall fail to pay the debt, having nothing wherewith to pay it, then the sureties shall answer for the debt; and let them have the lands and rents of the

---

1. [Chattel—Personal property as opposed to real property. A personal object which can be transported. EDS.]
2. [Distrain—The act of taking as a pledge another's property to be used as an assurance of performance of an obligation. Also a remedy to ensure a court appearance or payment of fees, etc. EDS.]

debtor, if they desire them, until they are indemnified for the debt which they have paid for him, unless the principal debtor can show proof that he is discharged thereof as against the said sureties.

10. If one who has borrowed from the Jews any sum, great or small, dies before that loan be repaid, the debt shall not bear interest while the heir is under age, of whomsoever he may hold; and if the debt fall into our hands, we will not take anything except the principal sum contained in the bond.

11. And if anyone dies indebted to the Jews, his wife shall have her dower and pay nothing of that debt; and if any children of the deceased are left under age, necessaries shall be provided for them in keeping with the holding of the deceased; and out of the residue the debt shall be paid, reserving, however, service due to feudal lords; in like manner let it be done for debts due to others than Jews.

12. No scutage[3] or aid shall be imposed on our kingdom, unless by common counsel of our kingdom, except for ransoming our person, for making our eldest son a knight, and for once marrying our eldest daughter; and for these there shall not be levied more than a reasonable aid. In like manner, it shall be done concerning aids from the city of London.

13. And the city of London shall have all its ancient liberties and free customs, as well by land as by water; furthermore, we decree and grant that all other cities, boroughs, towns, and ports shall have all their liberties and free customs.

14. And for obtaining the common counsel of the kingdom anent the assessing of an aid (except in the three cases aforesaid) or of a scutage, we will cause to be summoned the archbishops, bishops, abbots, earls, and greater barons, severally by our letters; and we will moveover cause to be summoned generally, through our sheriffs and bailiffs, and others who hold of us in chief, for a fixed date, namely, after

---

3. [Scutage—Tax or contribution raised by someone holding lands by knight's service used to furnish the king's army. EDS.]

the expiry of at least forty days, and at a fixed place; and in all letters of such summons we will specify the reason of the summons. And when the summons has thus been made, the business shall proceed on the day appointed, according to the counsel of such as are present, although not all who were summoned have come.

15. We will not for the future grant to anyone license to take an aid from his own free tenants, except to ransom his person, to make his eldest son a knight, and once to marry his eldest daughter; and on each of these occasions there shall be levied only a reasonable aid.

16. No one shall be distrained for performance of greater service for a knight's fee, or for any other free tenement, than is due therefrom.

17. Common pleas shall not follow our court, but shall be held in some fixed place.

18. Inquests of *novel disseisin*, of *mort d'ancestor*, and of *darrein present-ment*[4] shall not be held elsewhere than in their own county courts, and that in manner following: We, or, if we should be out of the realm, our chief justiciar, will send two justiciaries through every county four times a year, who shall alone with four knights of the county chosen by the county, hold the said assizes[5] in the county court, on the day and in the place of meeting of that court.

19. And if any of the said assizes cannot be taken on the day of the county court, let there remain of the knights and freeholders, who were present at the county court on that day, as many as may be required for the efficient making of judgments, according as the business be more or less.

---

4. [Novel Disseisin—Writ of Assize for the recovery of lands and tenements. Mort d'Ancestor—Real action to recover a person's lands of which he had been deprived on the death of his ancestor by the abatement of intrusion of a stranger. Darrein Present-ment—Writ of Assize when a man or his ancestors under whom he claimed presented a clerk to a benefice, who was instituted, and afterward, upon the next avoidance, a stranger presented a clerk and thereby disturbed the real patron. EDS.]

5. [Assize—A court, usually but not always, consisting of twelve men, summoned together to try a disputed case. They performed the functions of jury, except the verdict was rendered from their own investigation and knowledge and not from evidence adduced. EDS.]

20. A freeman shall not be amerced[6] for a slight offense, except in accordance with the degree of the offense; and for a grave offense he shall be amerced in accordance with the gravity of the offense, yet saving always his livelihood; and a merchant in the same way, saving his merchandise; and a villein shall be amerced in the same way, saving his wainage if they have fallen into our mercy: and none of the aforesaid amercements shall be imposed except by the oath of honest men of the neighborhood.

21. Earls and barons shall not be amerced except through their peers, and only in accordance with the degree of the offense.

22. A clerk shall not be amerced in respect of his lay holding except after the manner of the others aforesaid; further, he shall not be amerced in accordance with the extent of his ecclesiastical benefice.

23. No village or individual shall be compelled to make bridges at riverbanks, except those who of old were legally bound to do so.

24. No sheriff, constable, coroners, or others of our bailiffs, shall hold pleas of our crown.

25. All counties, hundred, wapentakes, and trithings (except our demesne manors) shall remain at the old rents without any additional payment.

26. If anyone holding of us a lay fief shall die, and our sheriff or bailiff shall exhibit our letters patent of summons for a debt which the deceased owed us, it shall be lawful for our sheriff or bailiff to attach and enroll the chattels of the deceased, found upon the lay fief, to the value of that debt, at the sight of law-worthy men, provided always that nothing whatever be thence removed until the debt which is evident shall be fully paid to us; and the residue shall be left to the executors to fulfill the will of the deceased; and if there be nothing due from him to us, all the chattels shall go to the deceased, saving to his wife and children their reasonable shares.

---

6. [Amerce—To impose a fine. Also to punish by fine or penalty. EDS.]

27. If any freeman shall die intestate,[7] his chattels shall be distributed by the hands of his nearest kinsfolk and friends, under supervision of the church, saving to everyone the debts which the deceased owed to him.

28. No constable or other bailiff of ours shall take corn or other provisions from anyone without immediately tendering money therefor, unless he can have postponement thereof by permission of the seller.

29. No constable shall compel any knight to give money in lieu of castle guard, when he is willing to perform it in his own person, or (if he himself cannot do it from any reasonable cause) then by another responsible man. Further, if we have led or sent him upon military service, he shall be relieved from guard in proportion to the time during which he has been on service because of us.

30. No sheriff or bailiff of ours, or other person, shall take the horses or carts of any freeman for transport duty against the will of the said freeman.

31. Neither we nor our bailiffs shall take for our castles, or for any other work of ours, wood which is not ours against the will of the owner of that wood.

32. We will not retain beyond one year and one day the lands of those who have been convicted of felony, and the lands shall thereafter be handed over to the lords of the fiefs.

33. All fish-weirs for the future shall be removed altogether from Thames and Medway, and throughout all England, except upon the seashore.

34. The writ which is called *praecipe*[8] shall not, for the future, be issued to anyone regarding any tenement whereby a freeman may lose his court.

35. Let there be one measure of wine throughout our whole realm; and one measure of ale; and one measure of corn, to wit, the London quarter; and one width of cloth (whether dyed, or russet, or haberjet),

---

7. [Intestate—To die without a will. EDS.]
8. [Praecipe—An original writ drawn up in the alternative commanding the defendant to do the thing required. EDS.]

to wit, two ells within the selvedges; of weights also let it be as of measures.

36. Nothing in future shall be given or taken for a writ of inquisition of life or limbs, but freely it shall be granted, and never denied.

37. If anyone holds of us by fee-farm, either by socage or by burgage,[9] or of any other land by knight's service, we will not (by reason of that fee-farm, socage, or burgage), have the wardship of the heir, or of such land of his as if of the fief of that other; nor shall we have wardship of that fee-farm, socage, or burgage, unless such fee-farm owes knight's service. We will not by reason of any small sergeanty which anyone may hold of us by the service of rendering to us knives, arrows, or the like, have wardship of his heir or of the land which he holds of another lord by knight's service.

38. No bailiff for the future shall, upon his own unsupported complaint, put anyone to trial, without credible witnesses brought for this purpose.

39. No freemen shall be taken or imprisoned or disseised[10] or exiled or in any way destroyed, nor will we go upon him nor send upon him, except by the lawful judgment of his peers or by the law of the land.

40. To no one will we sell, to no one will we refuse or delay right or justice.

41. All merchants shall have safe and secure exit from England, and entry to England, with the right to tarry there and to move about as well by land as by water, for buying and selling by the ancient and right customs, free from all evil tolls, except (in time of war) such merchants as are of the land at war with us. And if such are found in our land at the beginning of the war, they shall be detained, without injury to their bodies or goods, until information be received by us,

---

9. [Socage—A species of tenure where the tenant held lands in consideration of certain inferior services of husbandry by him to the lord of the fee. Burgage—One of three species of free socage holdings. A tenure where houses and lands formerly the site of houses in an ancient borough are held of some lord by a certain rent. EDS.]

10. [Disseise—To dispossess or to deprive. EDS.]

or by our chief justiciar, how the merchants of our land found in the land at war with us are treated; and if our men are safe there, the others shall be safe in our land.

42. It shall be lawful in future for anyone (excepting always those imprisoned or outlawed in accordance with the law of the kingdom, and natives of any country at war with us, and merchants, who shall be treated as above provided) to leave our kingdom and to return, safe and secure by land and water, except for a short period in time of war, on grounds of public policy—reserving always the allegiance due to us.

43. If anyone holding of some escheat[11] (such as the honor of Wallingford, Nottingham, Boulogne, Lancaster, or of other escheats which are in our hands and are baronies) shall die, his heir shall give no other relief and perform no other service to us than he would have done to the baron if that barony had been in the baron's hand; and we shall hold it in the same manner in which the baron held it.

44. Men who dwell without the forest need not henceforth come before our justiciaries of the forest upon a general summons, unless they are in plea or sureties of one or more, who are attached for the forest.

45. We will appoint as justices, constables, sheriffs, or bailiffs only such as know the law of the realm and mean to observe it well.

46. All barons who have founded abbeys, concerning which they hold charters from the kings of England, or of which they have long continued possession, shall have the wardship of them, when vacant, as they ought to have.

47. All forests that have been made such in our time shall forthwith be disafforested; and a similar course shall be followed with regard to riverbanks that have been enclosed by us in our time.

48. All evil customs connected with forests and warrens, foresters and warreners, sheriffs and their officers, riverbanks and their wardens,

---

11. [Escheat—Right of the lord of a fee to reenter upon the same when it became vacant by the extinction of the blood of the tenant. EDS.]

shall immediately be inquired into in each county by twelve sworn knights of the same county chosen by the honest men of the same county, and shall, within forty days of the said inquest, be utterly abolished, so as never to be restored, provided always that we, or our justiciar if we should not be in England, know of it first.

49. We will immediately restore all hostages and charters delivered to us by Englishmen as sureties of the peace of faithful service.

50. We will entirely remove from their bailiwicks, the relations of Gerard of Athée (so that in future they shall have no bailiwick in England); namely, Engelard of Cigogné, Peter, Guy, and Andrew of Chanceaux, Guy of Cigogné, Geoffrey of Martigny with his brothers, Philip Mark with his brothers and his nephew Geoffrey, and the whole brood of the same.

51. As soon as peace is restored, we will banish from the kingdom all foreign-born knights, crossbowmen, sergeants, and mercenary soldiers who have come with horses and arms to the kingdom's hurt.

52. If anyone has been dispossessed or removed by us, without the legal judgment of his peers, from his lands, castles, franchises, or from his right, we will immediately restore them to him; and if a dispute arises over this, then let it be decided by the five and twenty barons of whom mention is made below in the clause for securing the peace. Moreover, for all those possessions, from which anyone has, without the lawful judgment of his peers, been disseised or removed, by our father, King Henry, or by our brother, King Richard, and which we retain in our hand (or which as possessed by others, to whom we are bound to warrant them) we shall have respite until the usual term of crusaders; excepting those things about which a plea has been raised, or an inquest made by our order, before our taking of the cross; but as soon as we return from the expedition, we will immediately grant full justice therein.

53. We shall have, moreover, the same respite and in the same manner in rendering justice concerning the disafforestation or retention of those forests which Henry our father and Richard our brother afforested, and concerning the wardship of lands which are of the fief of

another (namely, such wardships as we have hitherto had by reason of a fief which anyone held of us by knight's service), and concerning abbeys founded on other fiefs than our own, in which the lord of the fee claims to have right; and when we have returned, or if we desist from our expedition, we will immediately grant full justice to all who complain of such things.

54. No one shall be arrested or imprisoned upon the appeal of a woman, for the death of any other than her husband.

55. All fines made with us unjustly and against the law of the land, and all amercements, imposed unjustly and against the law of the land, shall be entirely remitted, or else it shall be done concerning them according to the decision of the five and twenty barons whom mention is made below in the clause for securing the peace, or according to the judgment of the majority of the same, along with the aforesaid Stephen, Archbishop of Canterbury, if he can be present, and such others as he may wish to bring with him for this purpose. And if he cannot be present, the business shall nevertheless proceed without him, provided always that if any one or more of the aforesaid five and twenty barons are in a similar suit, they shall be removed as far as concerns this particular judgment, others being substituted in their places after having been selected by the rest of the same five and twenty for this purpose only, and after having been sworn.

56. If we have disseised or removed Welshmen from lands, liberties, or other things, without the legal judgment of their peers in England or in Wales, they shall be immediately restored to them; and if a dispute arises over this, then let it be decided in the marches by the judgment of their peers; for the tenements in England according to the law of England, for tenements in Wales according to the law of Wales, and for tenements in the marches according to the law of the marches. Welshmen shall do the same to us and ours.

57. Further, for all those possessions from which any Welshman has, without the lawful judgment of his peers, been disseised or removed by King Henry our father, or King Richard our brother, and which we retain in our hand (or which are possessed by others, and which

we ought to warrant), we will have respite until the usual term of crusaders; excepting those things about which a plea has been raised or an inquest made by our order before we took the cross. But as soon as we return, or if perchance we desist from our expedition, we will immediately grant full justice in accordance with the laws of the Welsh and in relation to the aforesaid regions.

58. We will immediately give up the son of Llywelyn and all the hostages of Wales and the charters delivered to us as security for the peace.

59. We will do toward Alexander, King of the Scots, concerning the return of his sisters and his hostages, and concerning his franchises and his rights, in the same manner as we shall do toward our other barons of England, unless it ought to be otherwise according to the charters which we hold from William his father, formerly King of the Scots; and this shall be according to the judgment of his peers in our court.

60. Moreover, all these aforesaid customs and liberties, the observances of which we have granted in our kingdom as far as pertains to us toward our men, shall be observed by all of our kingdom, clergy as well as laymen, as far as pertains to them toward their men.

61. Since, moreover, for God and the amendment of our kingdom and for the better allaying of the quarrel that has arisen between us and our barons, we have granted all these concessions, desirous that they should enjoy them in complete and firm endurance forever, we give and grant to them the underwritten security, namely, that the barons choose five and twenty barons of the kingdom, whomsoever they will, who shall be bound with all their might to observe and hold and cause to be observed the peace and liberties we have granted and confirmed to them by this our present Charter, so that if we or our justiciar or our bailiffs or any one of our officers shall in anything be at fault toward anyone, or shall have broken any one of the articles of this peace or of this security, and the offense be notified to four barons of the aforesaid five and twenty, the said four barons shall repair to us (or our justiciar, if we are out of the realm) and, laying the transgression before us, petition to have that transgression redressed without delay. And if we shall not have corrected the transgression

(or, in the event of our being out of the realm, if our justiciar shall not have corrected it) within forty days, reckoning from the time it has been intimated to us (or to our justiciar, if we should be out of the realm), the four barons aforesaid shall refer that matter to the rest of the five and twenty barons, and those five and twenty barons shall, together with the community of the whole realm, distrain and distress us in all possible ways, namely, by seizing our castles, lands, possessions, and in any other way they can, until redress has been obtained as they deem fit, saving our own person, and the persons of our queen and children; and when redress has been obtained, they shall resume their old relations toward us. And let whoever in the country desires it, swear to obey the orders of the said five and twenty barons for the execution of all the aforesaid matters, and along with them, to molest us to the utmost of his power; and we publicly and freely grant leave to everyone who wishes to swear, and we shall never forbid anyone to swear. All those, moreover, in the land who of themselves and of their own accord are unwilling to swear to the five and twenty to help them in constraining and molesting us, we shall by our command compel the same to swear to the effect aforesaid. And if any one of the five and twenty barons shall have died or departed from the land or be incapacitated in any other manner which would prevent the aforesaid provisions from being carried out, those of the said five and twenty barons who are left shall choose another in his place according to their own judgment, and he shall be sworn in the same way as the others. Further, in all matters the execution of which is entrusted to these five and twenty barons, if perchance these five and twenty are present and disagree about anything, or if some of them after being summoned are unwilling or unable to be present, that which the majority of those present ordain or command shall be held as fixed and established, exactly as if the whole five and twenty had concurred in this; and the said five and twenty shall swear that they will faithfully observe all that is aforesaid, and cause it to be observed with all their might. And we shall procure nothing from anyone, directly or indirectly, whereby any part of these concessions and liberties might be revoked or diminished; and if any such things has been procured, let it be void and null, and we shall never use it personally or by another.

62. And all the ill will, hatreds, and bitterness that have arisen between us and our men, clergy and lay, from the date of the quarrel, we have completely remitted and pardoned to everyone. Moreover, all trespasses occasioned by the said quarrel, from Easter in the sixteenth year of our reign till the restoration of peace, we have fully remitted to all, both clergy and laymen, and completely forgiven, as far as pertains to us. And on this head, we have caused to be made for them letters testimonial patent of the Lord Stephen, Archbishop of Canterbury, of the Lord Henry, Archbishop of Dublin, of the bishops aforesaid, and of Master Pandulf as touching this security and the concessions aforesaid.

63. Wherefore we will and firmly order that the English Church be free, and that the men in our kingdom have and hold all the aforesaid liberties, rights, and concessions, well and peaceably, freely and quietly, fully and wholly, for themselves and their heirs, of us and our heirs, in all respects and in all places forever, as is aforesaid. An oath, moreover, has been taken, as well on our part as on the part of the barons, that all these conditions aforesaid shall be kept in good faith and without evil intent. Given under our hand—the above named and many others being witnesses—in the meadow which is called Runnymede between Windsor and Staines on the fifteenth day of June in the seventeenth year of our reign.

For Discussion

1. According to Magna Carta, what does the king owe his subjects? Why?
2. Does Magna Carta protect existing rights that the parties involved have ignored or are not aware of, or does it bring these rights into being?

For Further Reflection

1. How does Magna Carta suggest the idea of human rights?
2. Which are the most important rights listed in Magna Carta?

For Further Research

1. Who qualified as "freemen" in England in 1215? What percentage of the population consisted of "freemen"?
2. Research the rights of a specific group (e.g., widows, Jews) that was affected by Magna Carta.

English Bill of Rights

(selection)

England's BILL OF RIGHTS *was signed in 1689, a
year after the Glorious Revolution that removed from
the English throne James II, a Catholic, and replaced
him with his daughter Mary and her husband, William
of Orange, both Protestants. Accepting restrictions on
the monarchy's power, William and Mary approved
the Declaration of Rights (which later became the Bill
of Rights) formulated by Parliament. The bill required
the king or queen to call regular sessions of Parliament and submit to the assembly's control over the
budget, making the monarchy legally and financially
dependent upon Parliament. The bill also reformed the
legal system—it prohibited the sovereign from running
separate courts or acting as a judge and forbade courts
from imposing overly harsh punishments. The king or
queen kept the power to call and dissolve parliamentary sessions, appoint and dismiss ministers, declare
war, and veto legislation, but the Bill of Rights ended
the English monarch's power to act independently. The
sovereign's rule was now contingent upon majority
support in Parliament.*

English Bill of Rights
(selection)

An Act Declaring the Rights and Liberties of the Subject
and Settling the Succession of the Crown

WHEREAS THE LORDS SPIRITUAL and Temporal and Commons assembled at Westminster, lawfully, fully, and freely representing all the estates of the people of this realm, did upon the thirteenth day of February in the year of our Lord one thousand six hundred eighty and eight present unto their Majesties, then called and known by the names and style of William and Mary, Prince and Princess of Orange, being present in their proper persons, a certain declaration in writing made by the said Lords and Commons in the words following, viz.:

Whereas the late King James the Second, by the assistance of divers evil counsellors, judges, and ministers employed by him, did endeavour to subvert and extirpate the Protestant religion and the laws and liberties of this kingdom;

By assuming and exercising a power of dispensing with and suspending of laws and the execution of laws without consent of Parliament;

By committing and prosecuting divers worthy prelates for humbly petitioning to be excused from concurring to the said assumed power;

By issuing and causing to be executed a commission under the great seal for erecting a court called the Court of Commissioners for Ecclesiastical Causes;

By levying money for and to the use of the Crown by pretence of prerogative for other time and in other manner than the same was granted by Parliament;

By raising and keeping a standing army within this kingdom in time of peace without consent of Parliament, and quartering soldiers contrary to law;

By causing several good subjects being Protestants to be disarmed at the same time when papists were both armed and employed contrary to law;

By violating the freedom of election of members to serve in Parliament;

By prosecutions in the Court of King's Bench for matters and causes cognizable only in Parliament, and by divers other arbitrary and illegal courses;

And whereas of late years partial corrupt and unqualified persons have been returned and served on juries in trials, and particularly divers jurors in trials for high treason which were not freeholders;

And excessive bail hath been required of persons committed in criminal cases to elude the benefit of the laws made for the liberty of the subjects;

And excessive fines have been imposed;

And illegal and cruel punishments inflicted;

And several grants and promises made of fines and forfeitures before any conviction or judgment against the persons upon whom the same were to be levied;

All which are utterly and directly contrary to the known laws and statutes and freedom of this realm;

And whereas the said late King James the Second having abdicated the government and the throne being thereby vacant, his Highness the Prince of Orange (whom it hath pleased Almighty God to make the glorious instrument of delivering this kingdom from popery and arbitrary power) did (by the advice of the Lords Spiritual and Temporal and divers principal persons of the Commons) cause letters to be written to the Lords Spiritual and Temporal being Protestants, and other letters to the several counties, cities, universities, boroughs, and cinque ports, for the choosing of such persons to represent them as were of right to be sent to Parliament, to meet and sit at Westminster upon the two and twentieth day of January in this year one thousand six hundred eighty and eight, in order to such an establishment as that their religion, laws, and liberties might not again be in danger of being subverted, upon which letters elections having been accordingly made;

And thereupon the said Lords Spiritual and Temporal and Commons, pursuant to their respective letters and elections, being now assembled in a full and free representative of this nation, taking into their most serious consideration the best means for attaining the ends aforesaid, do in the first place (as their ancestors in like case have usually done) for the vindicating and asserting their ancient rights and liberties declare:

That the pretended power of suspending the laws or the execution of laws by regal authority without consent of Parliament is illegal;

That the pretended power of dispensing with laws or the execution of laws by regal authority, as it hath been assumed and exercised of late, is illegal;

That the commission for erecting the late Court of Commissioners for Ecclesiastical Causes and all other commissions and courts of like nature are illegal and pernicious;

That levying money for or to the use of the Crown by pretence of prerogative, without grant of Parliament, for longer time, or in other manner than the same is or shall be granted, is illegal;

That it is the right of the subjects to petition the king, and all commitments and prosecutions for such petitioning are illegal;

That the raising or keeping a standing army within the kingdom in time of peace, unless it be with consent of Parliament, is against law;

That the subjects which are Protestants may have arms for their defence suitable to their conditions and as allowed by law;

That election of members of Parliament ought to be free;

That the freedom of speech and debates or proceedings in Parliament ought not to be impeached or questioned in any court or place out of Parliament;

That excessive bail ought not to be required, nor excessive fines imposed, nor cruel and unusual punishments inflicted;

That jurors ought to be duly impanelled and returned, and jurors which pass upon men in trials for high treason ought to be freeholders;

That all grants and promises of fines and forfeitures of particular persons before conviction are illegal and void;

And that for redress of all grievances and for the amending, strengthening, and preserving of the laws, Parliaments ought to be held frequently.

And they do claim, demand, and insist upon all and singular the premises as their undoubted rights and liberties, and that no declarations, judgments, doings, or proceedings to the prejudice of the people in any of the said premises ought in any wise to be drawn hereafter into consequence or example; to which demand of their rights they are particularly encouraged by the declaration of his Highness the Prince of Orange as being the only means for obtaining a full redress and remedy therein.

Having therefore an entire confidence that his said Highness the Prince of Orange will perfect the deliverance so far advanced by him, and will still preserve them from the violation of their rights which they have here asserted, and from all other attempts upon their religion, rights, and liberties, the said Lords Spiritual and Temporal and Commons assembled at Westminster do resolve that William and Mary, Prince and Princess of Orange, be and be declared King and Queen of England, France, and Ireland and the dominions thereunto belonging, to hold the crown and royal dignity of the said kingdoms and dominions to them, the said prince and princess, during their lives and the life of the survivor to them, and that the sole and full exercise of the regal power be only in and executed by the said Prince of Orange in the names of the said prince and princess during their joint lives, and after their deceases the said crown and royal dignity of the same kingdoms and dominions to be to the heirs of the body of the said princess, and for default of such issue to the Princess Anne of Denmark and the heirs of her body, and for default of such issue to the heirs of the body of the said Prince of Orange. And the Lords Spiritual and Temporal and Commons do pray the said prince and princess to accept the same accordingly.

And that the oaths hereafter mentioned be taken by all persons of whom the oaths have allegiance and supremacy might be required by law, instead of them; and that the said oaths of allegiance and supremacy be abrogated.

I, A. B., do sincerely promise and swear that I will be faithful and bear true allegiance to their Majesties King William and Queen Mary. So help me God.

I, A. B., do swear that I do from my heart abhor, detest, and abjure as impious and heretical this damnable doctrine and position, that princes excommunicated or deprived by the pope or any authority of the see of Rome may be deposed or murdered by their subjects or any other whatsoever. And I do declare that no foreign prince, person, prelate, state, or potentate hath or ought to have any jurisdiction, power, superiority, preeminence, or authority, ecclesiastical or spiritual, within this realm. So help me God.

Upon which their said Majesties did accept the crown and royal dignity of the kingdoms of England, France, and Ireland, and the dominions thereunto belonging, according to the resolution and desire of the said Lords and Commons contained in the said declaration. And thereupon their Majesties were pleased that the said Lords Spiritual and Temporal and Commons, being the two houses of Parliament, should continue to sit, and with their Majesties' royal concurrence make effectual provision for the settlement of the religion, laws, and liberties of this kingdom, so that the same for the future might not be in danger again of being subverted, to which the said Lords Spiritual and Temporal and Commons did agree, and proceed to act accordingly.

Now in pursuance of the premises the said Lords Spiritual and Temporal and Commons in Parliament assembled, for the ratifying, confirming, and establishing the said declaration and the articles, clauses, matters, and things therein contained by the force of law made in due form by authority of Parliament, do pray that it may be declared and enacted that all and singular the rights and liberties asserted and claimed in the said declaration are the true, ancient, and indubitable rights and liberties of the people of this kingdom, and so shall be esteemed, allowed, adjudged, deemed, and taken to be; and that all and every the particulars aforesaid shall be firmly and strictly holden and observed as they are expressed in the said declaration, and all officers and ministers whatsoever shall serve their Majesties and their successors according to the same in all time to come. . . .

For Discussion

1. What do the lords mean when they claim to "lawfully, fully, and freely" represent the people of England? (47)
2. Why do the lords begin by listing the offenses of James II?
3. How does the Bill of Rights attempt to prevent the exercise of "arbitrary power" by the monarchy? (48)
4. Are the lords more concerned with protecting their authority or protecting the rights of individuals?
5. According to the Bill of Rights, what is the monarch's role in the governance of England?

For Further Reflection

1. Why has religion so often been used to legitimize the special treatment or persecution of individuals?
2. Is it right for the lords to criticize the actions of James II against Protestants while also excluding Catholics from serving in the government?

For Research

1. Research the events of the reign of James II leading up to his removal from the throne and the drafting of the Bill of Rights.
2. When were Catholics again given the right to serve in England's government? What led to this change?
3. Which elements of the Constitution of the United States have their origins in the English Bill of Rights?

Second Treatise of Government

(selection)

JOHN LOCKE (1632–1704)

*John Locke was an early and influential proponent of representative govern-
ment answerable to the people's will. His refutation of the divine right of
kings and his argument that all people are created equal strongly influenced
the Declaration of Independence and the Constitution of the United States.
Locke was educated at Oxford and served as physician and personal adviser
to Lord Ashley (later the first Earl of Shaftesbury), who shared Locke's commitment to civil liberty, religious tolerance, and constitutional monarchy.
During the 1670s and 1680s, Locke spent much of his time in France and
Holland, where he explored a wide range of philosophical and scientific ideas.
In 1688, when the Protestants William and Mary were named successors to
the English throne, Locke returned to England and became the intellectual
leader of the liberal Whig Party. He wrote the parliamentary arguments
used to repeal an act restricting freedom of the press and worked to finish his
books, on which he had been working for many years. His major political
work,* Two Treatises of Government, *appeared in 1690. In the* Second
Treatise, *from which this selection is taken, Locke asserts that government
derives its authority from the trust of the people, who have the right to change
the government if it fails to secure their lives, property, and liberty. Locke's*
Essay Concerning Human Understanding, *published the same year, emphasizes learning about the world through careful observation and reflection—
principles that helped establish the basis of the modern scientific process.*

Second Treatise of Government
(selection)

OF THE STATE OF NATURE

To understand political power right, and derive it from its original, we must consider what state all men are naturally in, and that is, *a state of perfect freedom* to order their actions, and dispose of their possessions and persons, as they think fit, within the bounds of the law of nature, without asking leave, or depending upon the will of any other man.

A *state* also of *equality*, wherein all the power and jurisdiction is reciprocal, no one having more than another; there being nothing more evident, than that creatures of the same species and rank, promiscuously born to all the same advantages of nature, and the use of the same faculties, should also be equal one amongst another without subordination or subjection, unless the lord and master of them all should, by any manifest declaration of his will, set one above another, and confer on him, by an evident and clear appointment an undoubted right to dominion and sovereignty....

But though this be *a state of liberty,* yet *it is not a state of licence*: though man in that state has an uncontrollable liberty to dispose of his person or possessions, yet he has not liberty to destroy himself, or so much as any creature in his possession, but where some nobler use than its bare preservation calls for it. The *state of nature* has a law of nature to govern it, which obliges everyone: and reason, which is that law, teaches all mankind, who will but consult it, that being all *equal and independent*, no one ought to harm another in his life, health, liberty, or possessions: for men being all the workmanship of one omnipotent, and infinitely wise maker; all the servants of one sovereign master, sent into the world by his order, and about his business; they are his property, whose workmanship they are, made to last during his, not one another's pleasure: and being furnished with like faculties, sharing all in one community of nature, there cannot be supposed any such *subordination* among us, that may authorize us to destroy one another, as if we were made for one another's uses, as the inferior ranks of creatures are for ours. Everyone, as he is *bound to preserve himself,* and not to quit his station wilfully, so by the like reason, when his own preservation comes not in competition, ought he, as much as he can, *to preserve the rest of mankind,* and may not, unless it be to do justice to an offender, take away, or impair the life, or what tends to the preservation of the life, the liberty, health, limb, or goods of another.

And that all men may be restrained from invading others' rights, and from doing hurt to one another, and the law of nature be observed, which willeth the peace and *preservation of all mankind,* the *execution* of the law of nature is, in that state, put into every man's hands, whereby everyone has a right to punish the transgressors of that law to such a degree as may hinder its violation: for the *law of nature* would, as all other laws that concern men in this world, be in vain, if there were no body that in the state of nature had a *power to execute* that law, and thereby preserve the innocent and restrain offenders. And if anyone in the state of nature may punish another for any evil he has done, everyone may do so: for in that *state of perfect equality,* where naturally there is no superiority or jurisdiction of one over another, what any may do in prosecution of that law, everyone must needs have a right to do. . . .

OF THE STATE OF WAR

. . . [H]e who attempts to get another man into his absolute power, does thereby *put himself into a state of war* with him; it being to be understood as a declaration of a design upon his life: for I have reason to conclude, that he who would get me into his power without my consent, would use me as he pleased when he had got me there, and destroy me too when he had a fancy to it; for nobody can desire to *have me in his absolute power*, unless it be to compel me by force to that which is against the right of my freedom, i.e., make me a slave. To be free from such force is the only security of my preservation; and reason bids me look on him, as an enemy to my preservation, who would take away that *freedom* which is the fence to it; so that he who makes an *attempt to enslave* me, thereby puts himself into a state of war with me. He that, in the state of nature, *would take away the freedom* that belongs to anyone in that state, must necessarily be supposed to have a design to take away everything else, that *freedom* being the foundation of all the rest; as he that, in the state of society, would take away the *freedom* belonging to those of that society or commonwealth, must be supposed to design to take away from them everything else, and so be looked on as in a *state of war*.

This makes it lawful for a man to *kill a thief*, who has not in the least hurt him, nor declared any design upon his life, any farther than, by the use of force, so to get him in his power, as to take away his money, or what he pleases, from him; because using force, where he has no right, to get me into his power, let his pretence be what it will, I have no reason to suppose, that he, who would *take away my liberty*, would not, when he had me in his power, take away everything else. And therefore it is lawful for me to treat him as one who has *put himself into a state of war* with me, i.e., kill him if I can; for to that hazard does he justly expose himself, whoever introduces a state of war, and is aggressor in it.

And here we have the plain *difference between the state of nature and the state of war*, which however some men have confounded, are as far distant, as a state of peace, good will, mutual assistance, and preservation, and a state of enmity, malice, violence, and mutual destruction, are one from another. Men living together according to reason, without a common superior on earth, with authority to judge between them, is *properly the state of nature*. But force, or a declared design of force, upon the person of another, where there is no common superior on earth to appeal to for relief, *is the state of war*: and it is the want of such an appeal gives a man the right of war even against an *aggressor*, tho' he be in society and a fellow subject. Thus a *thief*, whom I cannot harm, but by appeal to the law, for having stolen all that I am worth, I may kill, when he sets on me to rob me but of my horse or coat; because the law, which was made for my preservation, where it cannot interpose to secure my life from present force, which, if lost, is capable of no reparation, permits me my own defence, and the right of war, a liberty to kill the aggressor, because the aggressor allows not time to appeal to our common judge, nor the decision of the law, for remedy in a case where the mischief may be irreparable. Want of a common judge with authority, puts all men in a state of nature: force without right, upon a man's person, makes a state of war, both where there is, and is not, a common judge.

But when the actual force is over, the *state of war ceases* between those that are in society, and are equally on both sides subjected to the fair determination of the law; because then there lies open the remedy of appeal for the past injury, and to prevent future harm: but where no such appeal is, as in the state of nature, for want of positive laws, and judges with authority to appeal to, the state of war once begun, continues, with a right to the innocent party to destroy the other whenever he can, until the aggressor offers peace, and desires reconciliation on such terms as may repair any wrongs he has already done, and secure the innocent for the future; nay, where an appeal to the law, and constituted judges, lies open, but the remedy is denied by a manifest perverting of justice, and a barefaced wresting of the laws to protect or indemnify the violence or injuries of some men, or party of men, *there* it is hard to imagine anything but *a state of war*: for wherever violence is used, and injury done, though by hands appointed to administer justice, it is still violence and injury, however coloured with the name, pretences, or forms of law, the end whereof being to protect and redress the innocent, by an unbiassed application of it, to all who are under it; wherever that is not bona fide done, *war is made* upon the sufferers, who having no appeal on earth to right them, they are left to the only remedy in such cases, an appeal to heaven.

To avoid this *state of war* (wherein there is no appeal but to heaven, and wherein every the least difference is apt to end, where there is no authority to decide between the contenders) is one great reason of men's putting themselves into society, and quitting the state of nature: for where there is an authority, a power on earth, from which relief can be had by *appeal*, there the continuance of the *state of war* is excluded, and the controversy is decided by that power....

For Discussion

1. On what grounds does Locke believe that in a state of nature everyone would be equal and have equal rights?
2. According to Locke, where does political power come from?
3. How does Locke distinguish between a state of nature and a state of war?
4. Why does Locke believe that having an authority who can judge between people excludes "the continuance of the *state of war*"? (58)
5. Does Locke believe that it is possible for people living in a state of nature to avoid a state of war?

For Further Reflection

1. Is it always desirable to let reason determine our actions?
2. Would you want to live in Locke's state of nature?

For Research

1. Compare Locke's ideas of the state of nature and the state of war to Thomas Hobbes's view of human nature in *Leviathan*.
2. For what audience did Locke intend his work? How did his readers respond?

The Social Contract
(selection)

JEAN-JACQUES ROUSSEAU (1712–1778)

Jean-Jacques Rousseau was the major thinker of the French Revolution, articulating the ideas of liberty and equality that led the citizens of France to overthrow the monarchy and aristocracy. Rousseau argued that legitimate government is based on a "social contract" in which individuals voluntarily give up their liberty to the "general will," but remain sovereign over the government, which they can reconstitute at any time. Rousseau was born in Geneva, Switzerland, the son of a watchmaker. His mother died days after his birth, and Rousseau's relationship with his father was strained. He ran away from home at sixteen and embarked on a series of apprenticeships and tutoring positions. His first publicly distributed writing—a 1750 essay that argued the arts and sciences were corrupt means of keeping the rich in power—led to an intense ongoing debate and established Rousseau as a public figure. His novel Émile: or, On Education *(1762) expressed Rousseau's ideas about proper education, advising parents and tutors to "follow nature" and respect children's independent intelligence.* The Social Contract *was published the same year, and both books were condemned by the Parlement of Paris as contrary to religion and government. Rousseau fled to Switzerland, but his works were banned there as well. He spent his last years in virtual isolation in France, writing the autobiographical* Dialogues *(1780) and* Confessions *(1782–1788), both published after his death.*

The Social Contract
(selection)

SUBJECT OF THE FIRST BOOK

Man is born free, and everywhere he is in chains. One thinks himself the master of others and still remains a greater slave than they. How did this change come about? I do not know. What can make it legitimate? That question I think I can answer.

If I took into account only force and the effects derived from it, I should say: "As long as a people is compelled to obey, and obeys, it does well; as soon as it can shake off the yoke, and shakes it off, it does still better; for regaining its liberty by the same right as took it away, either it is justified in resuming it, or there was no justification for those who took it away." But the social order is a sacred right that is the basis of all rights. Nevertheless, this right does not come from nature and must therefore be founded on conventions. . . .

THE CIVIL STATE

The passage from the state of nature to the civil state produces a very remarkable change in man, by substituting justice for instinct in his conduct and giving his actions the morality they had formerly lacked. Then only, when the voice of duty takes the place of physical impulses and right of appetite, does man, who so far had considered only himself, find that he is forced to act on different principles and to consult his reason before listening to his inclinations. Although, in this state, he deprives himself of some advantages that he got from nature, he gains in return others so great, his faculties are so stimulated and developed, his ideas so extended, his feelings so ennobled, and his whole soul so uplifted, that, did not the abuses of this new condition often degrade him below that which he left, he would be bound to bless continually the happy moment that took him from it forever, and, instead of a stupid and unimaginative animal, made him an intelligent being and a man.

Let us draw up the whole account in terms easily commensurable. What man loses by the social contract is his natural liberty and an unlimited right to everything he tries to get and succeeds in getting; what he gains is civil liberty and the proprietorship of all he possesses. If we are to avoid mistake in weighing one against the other, we must clearly distinguish natural liberty, which is bounded only by the strength of the individual, from civil liberty, which is limited by the general will; and possession, which is merely the effect of force or the right of the first occupier, from property, which can be founded only on a positive title.

We might, over and above all this, add, to what man acquires in the civil state, moral liberty, which alone makes him truly master of himself; for the mere impulse of appetite is slavery, while obedience to a law that we prescribe to ourselves is liberty. But I have already said too much on this head, and the philosophical meaning of the word *liberty* does not now concern us.

For Discussion

1. Why does Rousseau say that a person who "thinks himself the master of others" is "a greater slave than they"? (63)
2. What distinction is Rousseau making between a right based on nature and a right based on conventions?
3. Why does Rousseau believe that "civil liberty" is preferable to "natural liberty"?
4. What does Rousseau mean when he says that "obedience to a law that we prescribe to ourselves is liberty"? (64)
5. According to Rousseau, why do people gain "moral liberty" only in a civil state?

For Further Reflection

1. In your experience, is obedience to the law more beneficial to you, more beneficial to others, or equally beneficial to you and others?
2. If you believe that you have had no part in the making of a law, are you justified in breaking it?

For Research

1. How did Rousseau's ideas influence the leaders of the French Revolution?
2. Research the reception of *The Social Contract*. Why was it condemned and banned? How did Rousseau defend it?

Declaration
of Independence

The Constitutional Congress adopted the DECLARATION OF
INDEPENDENCE *on July 4, 1776. The Declaration is a pivotal
document not only in American history but also in world history.
In proclaiming the freedom of the thirteen colonies from Great
Britain, it marked the first time a group of people had asserted
its right to self-determination and a government of its choosing.
Signed by fifty-six men, the Declaration's primary author was
Thomas Jefferson (1743–1826), who called it "an appeal to the
tribunal of the world." John Adams, Benjamin Franklin, Roger
Sherman, and R. R. Livingston were also on the congressional committee assigned to create the Declaration. Drawing on the ideas of
Locke, Rousseau, and other political thinkers, Jefferson expressed
the ideals of democracy in vivid, memorable prose. The Declaration
lists the grievances of the colonies against King George III, but its
lasting significance lies in its claims of equality and the responsibility of the government to protect the natural rights of the governed. The ideas expressed in the Declaration had a profound effect
on France. The French Revolution of 1789 was in large part an attempt to put these ideas into practice in France, as is evident in the
Declaration of the Rights of Man and of the Citizen (see page 75).
The Declaration of Independence also helped spur the independence
movements of many Latin American countries.*

Declaration
of Independence

In Congress, July 4, 1776
The unanimous Declaration of the
thirteen United States of America

When in the course of human events, it becomes necessary for one people to dissolve the political bands which have connected them with another, and to assume among the powers of the earth, the separate and equal station to which the laws of Nature and of Nature's God entitle them, a decent respect to the opinions of mankind requires that they should declare the causes which impel them to the separation.

We hold these truths to be self-evident, that all men are created equal, that they are endowed by their Creator with certain unalienable rights, that among these are life, liberty, and the pursuit of happiness. That to secure these rights, governments are instituted among men, deriving their just powers from the consent of the governed. That whenever any form of government becomes destructive of these ends, it is the right of the people to alter or to abolish it, and to institute new government, laying its foundation on such principles and organizing its powers in such form, as to them shall seem most likely to effect their safety and happiness. Prudence, indeed, will dictate that governments long established should not be changed for light and transient causes; and accordingly all experience hath shown, that mankind are more disposed to suffer, while evils are sufferable, than to right themselves by abolishing the forms to which they are accustomed. But when a long train of abuses and usurpations, pursuing invariably the same object evinces a design to reduce them under absolute despotism, it is their right, it is their duty, to throw off such government, and to provide new guards for their future security. Such has been the patient sufferance of these colonies; and such is now the necessity which constrains them to alter their former systems of government. The history of the present King of Great Britain is a history of repeated injuries and usurpations, all having in direct object the establishment of an absolute tyranny over these states. To prove this, let facts be submitted to a candid world.

He has refused his assent to laws, the most wholesome and necessary for the public good.

He has forbidden his governors to pass laws of immediate and pressing importance, unless suspended in their operation till his assent should be obtained; and when so suspended, he has utterly neglected to attend to them.

He has refused to pass other laws for the accommodation of large districts of people, unless those people would relinquish the right of representation in the legislature, a right inestimable to them and formidable to tyrants only.

He has called together legislative bodies at places unusual, uncomfortable, and distant from the depository of their public records, for the sole purpose of fatiguing them into compliance with his measures.

He has dissolved representative houses repeatedly, for opposing with manly firmness his invasions on the rights of the people.

He has refused for a long time, after such dissolutions, to cause others to be elected; whereby the legislative powers, incapable of annihilation, have returned to the people at large for their exercise; the state remaining in the meantime exposed to all the danger of invasion from without and convulsions within.

He has endeavored to prevent the population of these states; for that purpose obstructing the laws of naturalization of foreigners; refusing to pass others to encourage their migration hither, and raising the conditions of new appropriations of lands.

He has obstructed the administration of justice, by refusing his assent to laws for establishing judiciary powers.

He has made judges dependent on his will alone, for the tenure of their offices, and the amount and payment of their salaries.

He has erected a multitude of new offices, and sent hither swarms of officers to harass our people, and eat out their substance.

He has kept among us, in times of peace, standing armies without the consent of our legislatures.

He has affected to render the military independent of and superior to the civil power.

He has combined with others to subject us to a jurisdiction foreign to our constitution, and unacknowledged by our laws; giving his assent to their acts of pretended legislation:

For quartering large bodies of armed troops among us:

For protecting them, by a mock trial, from punishment for any murders which they should commit on the inhabitants of these states:

For cutting off our trade with all parts of the world:

For imposing taxes on us without our consent:

For depriving us in many cases, of the benefits of trial by jury:

For transporting us beyond seas to be tried for pretended offenses:

For abolishing the free system of English laws in a neighboring province, establishing therein an arbitrary government, and enlarging its boundaries so as to render it at once an example and fit instrument for introducing the same absolute rule into these colonies:

For taking away our charters, abolishing our most valuable laws, and altering fundamentally the forms of our governments:

For suspending our own legislatures, and declaring themselves invested with power to legislate for us in all cases whatsoever.

He has abdicated government here, by declaring us out of his protection and waging war against us.

He has plundered our seas, ravaged our coasts, burnt our towns, and destroyed the lives of our people.

He is at this time transporting large armies of foreign mercenaries to complete the works of death, desolation, and tyranny, already begun with circumstances of cruelty and perfidy scarcely paralleled in the most barbarous ages, and totally unworthy the head of a civilized nation.

He has constrained our fellow citizens taken captive on the high seas to bear arms against their country, to become the executioners of their friends and brethren, or to fall themselves by their hands.

He has excited domestic insurrections amongst us, and has endeavored to bring on the inhabitants of our frontiers, the merciless Indian savages, whose known rule of warfare is an undistinguished destruction of all ages, sexes, and conditions.

In every stage of these oppressions we have petitioned for redress in the most humble terms: our repeated petitions have been answered only by repeated injury. A prince whose character is thus marked by every act which may define a tyrant is unfit to be the ruler of a free people.

Nor have we been wanting in attention to our British brethren. We have warned them from time to time of attempts by their legislature to extend an unwarrantable jurisdiction over us. We have reminded them of the circumstances of our emigration and settlement here. We have appealed to their native justice and magnanimity, and we have conjured them by the ties of our common kindred to disavow these usurpations, which would inevitably interrupt our connections and correspondence. They too have been deaf to the voice of justice and consanguinity. We must, therefore, acquiesce in the necessity, which denounces our separation, and hold them, as we hold the rest of mankind, enemies in war, in peace friends.

WE, THEREFORE, the Representatives of the UNITED STATES OF AMERICA, in General Congress assembled, appealing to the Supreme Judge of the world for the rectitude of our intentions, do, in the name, and by authority of the good people of these colonies, solemnly publish and declare, That these United Colonies are, and of right ought to be FREE AND INDEPENDENT STATES; that they are absolved from all allegiance to the British Crown, and that all political connection between them and the state of Great Britain, is and ought to be totally dissolved; and that as Free and Independent States, they have full power to levy war, conclude peace, contract alliances, establish commerce, and to do all other acts and things which Independent States may of right do. And for the support of this declaration, with a firm reliance on the protection of divine Providence, we mutually pledge to each other our lives, our fortunes, and our sacred honor.

For Discussion

1. Why do the signers of the Declaration believe it is their duty, as well as their right, to change their system of government?
2. Why do the signers of the Declaration proclaim that the equality of all people is "self-evident" and their rights "unalienable"? Why do they maintain that democracy is ordained by the laws of nature?
3. Are the signers of the Declaration motivated by a sense of moral outrage or by their own self-interest?

For Further Reflection

1. In its historical moment, the Declaration of Independence was a radical and treasonous document. What ideas in it may still be radical today?
2. Under what circumstances is violent revolt justified?
3. Is democracy stronger when Americans think of themselves as "one people," or when they think of themselves as many distinct groups of people?

For Research

1. What did the signers hope the Declaration of Independence would accomplish?
2. What arguments were made against the Declaration of Independence?
3. How did King George III and others in Great Britain respond to the Declaration of Independence?

Declaration of the Rights of Man and of the Citizen

The DECLARATION OF THE RIGHTS OF MAN
AND OF THE CITIZEN *was approved by France's
National Assembly on August 26, 1789. Written to
limit the power of the monarchy and aristocracy and
to codify the rights of the common people, the Declaration lays out the principles of individual freedom and
equality that were the basis of the French Revolution
of 1789. It was inspired in part by the Declaration of
Independence (1776), and was in turn an important
precedent for the Constitution of the United States of
America (1791). The Declaration also served as the
preamble to the French constitutions of 1791, 1793, and
1795. Like the American documents, the French Declaration assumes that all individuals possess a basic set of
rights and that it is the responsibility of any government to recognize and protect those rights. Although its
adoption was quickly followed by the Reign of Terror
and the French revolutionary and Napoleonic wars, the
Declaration has proved to be an influential document
in the history of human rights.*

Declaration of the Rights of Man and of the Citizen

Approved by the National Assembly of France, August 26, 1789

THE REPRESENTATIVES of the French people, organized as a National Assembly, believing that the ignorance, neglect, or contempt of the rights of man are the sole cause of public calamities and of the corruption of governments, have determined to set forth in a solemn declaration the natural, unalienable, and sacred rights of man, in order that this declaration, being constantly before all the members of the social body, shall remind them continually of their rights and duties; in order that the acts of the legislative power, as well as those of the executive power, may be compared at any moment with the objects and purposes of all political institutions and may thus be more respected, and, lastly, in order that the grievances of the citizens, based hereafter upon simple and incontestable principles, shall tend to the maintenance of the constitution and redound to the happiness of all. Therefore the National Assembly recognizes and proclaims, in the presence and under the auspices of the Supreme Being, the following rights of man and of the citizen:

ARTICLE FIRST

Men are born and remain free and equal in rights. Social distinctions may be founded only upon the general good.

ARTICLE 2

The aim of all political association is the preservation of the natural and imprescriptible rights of man. These rights are liberty, property, security, and resistance to oppression.

ARTICLE 3

The principle of all sovereignty resides essentially in the nation. No body, no individual may exercise any authority which does not proceed directly from the nation.

ARTICLE 4

Liberty consists in the freedom to do everything which injures no one else; hence the exercise of the natural rights of each man has no limits except those which assure to the other members of the society the enjoyment of the same rights. These limits can only be determined by law.

ARTICLE 5

Law can only prohibit such actions as are hurtful to society. Nothing may be prevented which is not forbidden by law, and no one may be forced to do anything not provided for by law.

ARTICLE 6

Law is the expression of the general will. Every citizen has a right to participate, personally or through his representative, in its foundation. It must be the same for all, whether it protects or punishes. All citizens, being equal in the eyes of the law, are equally eligible to all dignities and to all public positions and occupations, according to their abilities, and without distinction except that of their virtues and talents.

ARTICLE 7

No person shall be accused, arrested, or imprisoned except in the cases and according to the forms prescribed by law. Anyone soliciting, transmitting, executing, or causing to be executed any arbitrary order shall be punished.

But any citizen summoned or arrested by virtue of the law shall submit without delay, as resistance constitutes an offense.

ARTICLE 8

The law shall provide for such punishments only as are strictly and obviously necessary, and no one shall suffer punishment except it be legally inflicted by virtue of a law passed and promulgated before the commission of the offense.

ARTICLE 9

As all persons are held innocent until they shall have been declared guilty, if arrest shall be deemed indispensable, all harshness not essential to the securing of the prisoner's person shall be severely repressed by law.

ARTICLE 10

No one shall be disquieted on account of his opinions, including his religious views, provided their manifestation does not disturb the public order established by law.

ARTICLE 11

The free communication of ideas and opinions is one of the most precious of the rights of man. Every citizen may accordingly speak, write, and print with freedom, but shall be responsible for such abuses of this freedom as shall be defined by law.

ARTICLE 12

The security of the rights of man and of the citizen requires public military forces. These forces are therefore established for the good of all and not for the personal advantage of those to whom they shall be entrusted.

ARTICLE 13

A common contribution is essential for the maintenance of the public forces and for the cost of administration. This should be equitably distributed among all citizens in proportion to their means.

ARTICLE 14

All citizens have a right to decide, either personally or by their representatives, as to the necessity of the public contribution, to grant this freely, to know to what uses it is put, and to fix the proportion, basis, collection, and duration of the taxes.

ARTICLE 15

Society has the right to require of every public agent an account of his administration.

ARTICLE 16

A society in which the observance of the law is not assured, nor the separation of powers defined, has no constitution at all.

ARTICLE 17

Since property is an inviolable and sacred right, no one shall be deprived thereof except where public necessity, legally determined, shall clearly demand it, and then only on condition that the owner shall have been previously and equitably indemnified.

For Discussion

1. What does it mean that "the ignorance, neglect, or contempt of the rights of man are the sole causes of public calamities and of the corruption of governments"? (77) According to the framers of the Declaration, how will the Declaration remedy this situation?
2. According to the framers, how will the Declaration make the acts of government "more respected"? (77)
3. Does Article 4 of the Declaration mean that laws will ensure or limit the freedom of the individual?
4. According to Article 6 of the Declaration, what is the role of the individual in determining laws?
5. Why do the framers specify that "law is the expression of the general will"? (78)

For Further Reflection

1. Should individuals be allowed to do "everything which injures no one else"?
2. How can you tell if a punishment is "strictly and obviously necessary"?

For Research

1. Why did people throughout Europe and the United States have such high hopes for the French Revolution?
2. Research how prerevolutionary France's three estates were able to unite, despite their competing interests, to overthrow the ancient regime.

Constitution of the United States of America

(Preamble and Bill of Rights)

Having won independence from Great Britain, the former British colonists were soon involved in a heated debate about what form the new American government should take, in particular how much power should be retained by the states and how much vested in a federal government. The proposed Constitution, written in 1787, sought to establish a central government that many Americans saw as too powerful. In response, the Anti-Federalists demanded that the Constitution include a Bill of Rights that would codify the limitations of the government's powers and ensure individual liberties. The final form of the CONSTITUTION OF THE UNITED STATES OF AMERICA, *ratified in 1788, incorporated a Bill of Rights, consisting of the first ten amendments. These ten amendments, along with two others that were not ratified, were proposed by Congress on September 25, 1789. Ratification was completed on December 15, 1791, when the eleventh state (Virginia) approved these amendments, there being then fourteen states in the Union. Together with the Constitution's Preamble, which declares that what follows is an expression of the will of "the people," the Bill of Rights emphasizes that governing authority derives from the citizens and cannot be used to infringe on their freedom.*

Constitution of the
United States of America
(Preamble and Bill of Rights)

PREAMBLE

We the people of the United States, in order to form a more perfect Union, establish justice, insure domestic tranquility, provide for the common defense, promote the general welfare, and secure the blessings of liberty to ourselves and our posterity, do ordain and establish this Constitution for the United States of America.

BILL OF RIGHTS

Articles in addition to, and amendment of, the Constitution of the United States of America, proposed by Congress, and ratified by the several states, pursuant to the fifth article of the original Constitution.

AMENDMENT I

Congress shall make no law respecting an establishment of religion, or prohibiting the free exercise thereof; or abridging the freedom of speech, or of the press; or the right of the people peaceably to assemble, and to petition the government for a redress of grievances.

AMENDMENT II

A well-regulated militia being necessary to the security of a free state, the right of the people to keep and bear arms shall not be infringed.

AMENDMENT III

No soldier shall, in time of peace, be quartered in any house, without the consent of the owner, nor in time of war, but in a manner to be prescribed by law.

AMENDMENT IV

The right of the people to be secure in their persons, houses, papers, and effects, against unreasonable searches and seizures, shall not be violated, and no warrants shall issue, but upon probable cause, supported by oath or affirmation, and particularly describing the place to be searched, and the persons or things to be seized.

AMENDMENT V

No person shall be held to answer for a capital or otherwise infamous crime, unless on a presentment or indictment of a grand jury, except in cases arising in the land or naval forces, or in the militia, when in actual service in time of war or public danger; nor shall any person be subject for the same offense to be twice put in jeopardy of life or limb; nor shall be compelled in any criminal case to be a witness against himself, nor be deprived of life, liberty, or property, without due process of law; nor shall private property be taken for public use, without just compensation.

AMENDMENT VI

In all criminal prosecutions, the accused shall enjoy the right to a speedy and public trial, by an impartial jury of the state and district wherein the crime shall have been committed, which district shall have been previously ascertained by law, and to be informed of the nature and cause of the accusation; to be confronted with the witnesses against him; to have compulsory process for obtaining witnesses in his favor, and to have the assistance of counsel for his defense.

AMENDMENT VII

In suits at common law, where the value in controversy shall exceed twenty dollars, the right of trial by jury shall be preserved, and no fact tried by a jury, shall be otherwise reexamined in any court of the United States, than according to the rules of the common law.

AMENDMENT VIII

Excessive bail shall not be required, nor excessive fines imposed, nor cruel and unusual punishments inflicted.

AMENDMENT IX

The enumeration in the Constitution, of certain rights, shall not be construed to deny or disparage others retained by the people.

AMENDMENT X

The powers not delegated to the United States by the Constitution, nor prohibited by it to the states, are reserved to the states respectively, or to the people.

For Discussion

1. Why are the rights included in the first eight amendments important enough to merit specific mention?
2. What does the opening phrase, "We the people," suggest about the purpose of the Constitution and the basis of the new government?
3. Why does the Bill of Rights not spell out in detail what is meant by such words as *unreasonable* in Amendment IV and *excessive, cruel,* and *unusual* in Amendment VIII?

For Further Reflection

1. Do you consider the federal government to be a threat to individual rights or a protector of them?
2. When the Supreme Court interprets the Constitution and its amendments, should it be guided by what it understands the intent of the framers to have been or by what it perceives as the needs of the nation at the present time?

For Research

1. Choose an amendment from the Bill of Rights and a series of Supreme Court cases related to it, and show how the amendment has been interpreted in different ways throughout American history.
2. Why did the Anti-Federalists demand that a bill of rights be added to the Constitution?
3. How are amendments to the Constitution proposed and ratified?

State of the Union Address
(selection)

ANDREW JACKSON (1767–1845)

Andrew Jackson, the seventh president of the United States, was a celebrated war hero and to many Americans a symbol of the pioneering spirit of the West. During the War of 1812, he won major victories against Great Britain and their allies the Creeks. After their defeat by Jackson, the Creeks surrendered some twenty-three million acres of land to the U.S. government (about a fifth of the state of Georgia and three-fifths of Alabama). Jackson also led an invasion of Spanish-owned Florida, winning a victory against the Seminoles, and helped negotiate many treaties under which Native American tribes gave up their lands to the government. Elected president in 1828, Jackson almost immediately announced a policy of relocating eastern tribes to land west of the Mississippi River in order to make more land available for white settlers. Congress passed the Indian Removal Act in May 1830 to force tribes to move west; while some left quickly, others were compelled to leave by the U.S. Army, some even being taken away in chains. The most infamous government action was the forcible removal, in 1838–1839, of the Cherokees, who were made to walk the eight-hundred-mile-long Trail of Tears from Georgia to what is now Oklahoma. About four thousand Cherokees are estimated to have died on the journey. This selection is taken from Jackson's second State of the Union address (delivered on December 6, 1830), in which he strongly promotes his Indian policy.

State of the
Union Address
(selection)

IT GIVES ME PLEASURE to announce to Congress that the benevolent policy of the government, steadily pursued for nearly thirty years, in relation to the removal of the Indians beyond the white settlements is approaching to a happy consummation. Two important tribes have accepted the provision made for their removal at the last session of Congress, and it is believed that their example will induce the remaining tribes also to seek the same obvious advantages.

The consequence of a speedy removal will be important to the United States, to individual states, and to the Indians themselves. The pecuniary advantages which it promises to the government are the least of its recommendations. It puts an end to all possible danger of collision between the authorities of the general and state governments on account of the Indians. It will place a dense and civilized population in large tracts of country now occupied by a few savage hunters. By opening the whole territory between Tennessee on the north and Louisiana on the south to the settlement of the whites it will incalculably strengthen the southwestern frontier and render the adjacent states strong enough to repel future invasions without remote aid. It will relieve the whole state of Mississippi and the western part of Alabama of Indian occupancy, and enable those states to advance rapidly in population, wealth, and power. It will separate the Indians from immediate contact with settlements of whites; free them from the power of the states;

enable them to pursue happiness in their own way and under the rule of their own rude institutions; will retard the progress of decay, which is lessening their numbers; and perhaps cause them gradually, under the protection of the government and through the influence of good counsels, to cast off their savage habits and become an interesting, civilized, and Christian community. These consequences, some of them so certain and the rest so probable, make the complete execution of the plan sanctioned by Congress at their last session an object of much solicitude.

Toward the aborigines of the country no one can indulge a more friendly feeling than myself, or would go further in attempting to reclaim them from their wandering habits and make them a happy, prosperous people. I have endeavored to impress upon them my own solemn convictions of the duties and powers of the general government in relation to the state authorities. For the justice of the laws passed by the states within the scope of their reserved powers they are not responsible to this government. As individuals we may entertain and express our opinions of their acts, but as a government we have as little right to control them as we have to prescribe laws for other nations.

With a full understanding of the subject, the Choctaw and the Chickasaw tribes have with unanimity determined to avail themselves of the liberal offers presented by the act of Congress, and have agreed to remove beyond the Mississippi River. Treaties have been made with them, which in due season will be submitted for consideration. In negotiating these treaties, they were made to understand their true condition, and they have preferred maintaining their independence in the western forests to submitting to the laws of the states in which they now reside. These treaties, being probably the last which will ever be made with them, are characterized by great liberality on the part of the government. They give the Indians a liberal sum in consideration of their removal and comfortable subsistence on their arrival at their new homes. If it be their real interest to maintain a separate existence, they will there be at liberty to do so without the inconveniences and vexations to which they would unavoidably have been subject in Alabama and Mississippi.

Humanity has often wept over the fate of the aborigines of this country, and philanthropy has been long busily employed in devising means to avert it, but its progress has never for a moment been arrested, and one by one have many powerful tribes disappeared from the earth. To follow to the tomb the last of his race and to tread on the graves of extinct nations excite melancholy reflections. But true philanthropy reconciles the mind to these vicissitudes as it does to the extinction of one generation to make room for another. In the monuments and fortresses of an unknown people, spread over the extensive regions of the West, we behold the memorials of a once powerful race, which was exterminated or has disappeared to make room for the existing savage tribes. Nor is there in this which, upon a comprehensive view of the general interests of the human race, is to be regretted. Philanthropy could not wish to see this continent restored to the condition in which it was found by our forefathers. What good man would prefer a country covered with forests and ranged by a few thousand savages to our extensive republic, studded with cities, towns, and prosperous farms, embellished with all the improvements which art can devise or industry execute, occupied by more than twelve million happy people, and filled with all the blessings of liberty, civilization, and religion?

The present policy of the government is but a continuation of the same progressive change by a milder process. The tribes which occupied the countries now constituting the eastern states were annihilated or have melted away to make room for the whites. The waves of population and civilization are rolling to the westward, and we now propose to acquire the countries occupied by the red men of the South and West by a fair exchange, and, at the expense of the United States, to send them to a land where their existence may be prolonged and perhaps made perpetual. Doubtless it will be painful to leave the graves of their fathers; but what do they more than our ancestors did or than our children are now doing? To better their condition in an unknown land, our forefathers left all that was dear in earthly objects. Our children by thousands yearly leave the land of their birth to seek new homes in distant regions. Does humanity weep at these painful separations from everything, animate and inanimate, with which the young heart has become entwined? Far from it. It is rather a source of joy that our country affords scope where our young population may range unconstrained in body or in mind, developing the power and faculties of man in their highest perfection. These remove hundreds and almost thousands of miles at their own expense, purchase the lands they occupy, and support themselves at their new homes from the moment of their arrival. Can it be cruel in this government when, by events which it cannot control, the Indian is made discontented in his ancient home to purchase his lands, to give him a new and extensive territory, to pay the expense of his removal, and support him a year in his new abode? How many thousands of our own people would gladly embrace the opportunity of removing to the West on such conditions! If the offers made to the Indians were extended to them, they would be hailed with gratitude and joy.

And is it supposed that the wandering savage has a stronger attachment to his home than the settled, civilized Christian? Is it more afflicting to him to leave the graves of his fathers than it is to our brothers and children? Rightly considered, the policy of the general government toward the red man is not only liberal, but generous. He is unwilling to submit to the laws of the states and mingle with their population. To save him from this alternative, or perhaps utter annihilation, the general government kindly offers him a new home, and proposes to pay the whole expense of his removal and settlement.

For Discussion

1. Why does Jackson say that philanthropy tries to avert the extinction of Native Americans while "true philanthropy" accepts its inevitability?

2. Who or what does Jackson think is responsible for the fact that "many powerful tribes" have "disappeared from the earth"? (93)

3. Why does Jackson believe that removing the Cherokees from their land is justified?

4. Based on his speech, what does Jackson think are "the general interests of the human race"? (93)

5. Why does Jackson compare the Native Americans leaving their homes to his forefathers coming to America and young white Americans leaving their hometowns for new homes in faraway regions? (93)

For Further Reflection

1. Do you think that the U.S. government had the right to relocate eastern tribes?

2. Under what circumstances, if any, is a government justified in forcibly removing people from land they occupy?

For Research

1. Research what happened to the Cherokees who were removed from their land.

2. Why did the U.S. government decide that it was justified in forcibly removing the Cherokees from their land? Did anyone oppose their removal within the government?

3. How did Native Americans respond to Jackson's speech?

Emancipation Proclamation

ABRAHAM LINCOLN (1809–1865)

Abraham Lincoln, president of the United States during the Civil War, rose from a log cabin in backwoods Kentucky to the White House. Known for preserving the Union and freeing the slaves, Lincoln was also an eloquent spokesman for the ideals of self-government and liberty. Lincoln worked as a rail splitter and boatman before he began practicing law in 1836. He ran for president in 1860 on a platform of no further expansion of slavery, and upon his election South Carolina seceded from the Union. With the attack on Fort Sumter in April 1861, the Civil War began. On January 1, 1863, Lincoln issued the Emancipation Proclamation, which declared free the slaves living in parts of the country under Confederate control. The Proclamation did not free all slaves (it did not apply to those in loyal slave states or in Confederate areas occupied by the federal government), and it could not by itself guarantee their freedom after the war. But the Emancipation Proclamation was extremely important as a declaration that the Union wanted not only reunion with the Confederate states but also freedom for the slaves. This declaration increased support for the Union abroad and made it possible for the Union to enlist black soldiers. Lincoln was assassinated on April 14, 1865, five days after Confederate military leader General Robert E. Lee surrendered.

Emancipation Proclamation

Whereas, on the twenty-second day of September, in the year of our Lord one thousand eight hundred and sixty-two, a proclamation was issued by the President of the United States, containing, among other things, the following, to wit:

"THAT ON THE FIRST DAY of January, in the year of our Lord one thousand eight hundred and sixty-three, all persons held as slaves within any state or designated part of a state, the people whereof shall then be in rebellion against the United States, shall be then, thenceforward, and forever, free; and the executive government of the United States, including the military and naval authority thereof, will recognize and maintain the freedom of such persons, and will do no act or acts to repress such persons, or any of them, in any efforts they may make for their actual freedom.

"That the executive will, on the first day of January aforesaid, by proclamation, designate the states and parts of states, if any, in which the people thereof, respectively, shall then be in rebellion against the United States; and the fact that any state, or the people thereof, shall on that day be in good faith represented in the Congress of the United States, by members chosen thereto at elections, wherein a majority of the qualified voters of such states shall have participated, shall, in the absence of strong countervailing testimony, be deemed conclusive evidence that such state, and the people thereof, are not then in rebellion against the United States."

Now, therefore, I, Abraham Lincoln, President of the United States, by virtue of the power in me vested as commander in chief of the army and navy of the United States, in time of actual armed rebellion against the authority and government of the United States, and as a fit and necessary war measure for suppressing said rebellion, do, on this first day of January, in the year of our Lord one thousand eight hundred and sixty-three, and in accordance with my purpose so to do, publicly proclaimed for the full period of one hundred days from the day first above mentioned, order and designate as the states and as the parts of states wherein the people thereof, respectively, are this day in rebellion against the United States, the following, to wit:

Arkansas, Texas, Louisiana (except the parishes of St. Bernard, Plaquemines, Jefferson, St. John, St. Charles, St. James, Ascension, Assumption, Terre Bonne, Lafourche, St. Mary, St. Martin, and Orleans, including the city of New Orleans), Mississippi, Alabama, Florida, Georgia, South Carolina, North Carolina, and Virginia (except the forty-eight counties designated as West Virginia, and also the counties of Berkeley, Accomac, Northampton, Elizabeth City, York, Princess Ann, and Norfolk, including the cities of Norfolk and Portsmouth), and which excepted parts are for the present left precisely as if this proclamation were not issued.

And, by virtue of the power and for the purpose aforesaid, I do order and declare that all persons held as slaves within said designated states and parts of states are, and henceforward shall be, free; and that the executive government of the United States, including the military and naval authorities thereof, will recognize and maintain the freedom of said persons.

And I hereby enjoin upon the people so declared to be free to abstain from all violence, unless in necessary self-defense; and I recommend to them that, all cases when allowed, they labor faithfully for reasonable wages.

And I further declare and make known that such persons, of suitable condition, will be received into the armed service of the United States to garrison forts, positions, stations, and other places, and to man vessels of all sorts in said service.

And upon this act, sincerely believed to be an act of justice, warranted by the Constitution upon military necessity, I invoke the considerate judgment of mankind and the gracious favor of almighty God.

In witness whereof, I have hereunto set my hand and caused the seal of the United States to be affixed.

Done at the city of Washington this first day of January, in the year of our Lord one thousand eight hundred and sixty-three, and of the Independence of the United States of America the eighty-seventh.

For Discussion

1. What difference does Lincoln suggest between "actual freedom" and the freedom effected by the Emancipation Proclamation?
2. Why does Lincoln "enjoin upon the people so declared to be free to abstain from all violence, unless in necessary self-defense"? (100)
3. Why does Lincoln say that this act is "sincerely believed to be an act of justice"? (101)

For Further Reflection

1. Is the proclamation politically motivated, morally motivated, or both?
2. Why does Lincoln invoke the powers of the executive government, as well as the favor of God, in making his proclamation?

For Research

1. Research the relationship between the Emancipation Proclamation and the Thirteenth Amendment.
2. What was the practical effect of the Emancipation Proclamation? How did slave owners respond to it?

The United States of America v. Susan B. Anthony

(selection)

SUSAN BROWNELL ANTHONY (1820–1906)

*Susan Brownell Anthony was one of the most important leaders
of the United States woman suffrage movement, which insisted
that women had the same right to vote as men. Her work helped
lay the foundation for the Nineteenth Amendment, ratified in
1920, which recognized and protected women's right to vote.
Born in Rochester, New York, into a Quaker abolitionist household, Anthony was active in the abolitionist movement before
and during the Civil War. In the late 1860s, she collaborated
with fellow suffragist Elizabeth Cady Stanton in publishing the*
Revolution, *a weekly New York newspaper that promoted liberal
causes. With Stanton and Matilda Joslyn Gage, Anthony also
worked on the first four volumes of* History of Woman Suffrage
*(1881–1902). In 1872 Anthony led a group of women to the polls
in Rochester to vote, and she was arrested and charged. This
selection is from the transcript of the resulting trial. She was
convicted but refused to pay the fine. Until her death in 1906,
Anthony continued to campaign full-time for a constitutional
amendment giving women the right to vote. She traveled widely
across the United States and Europe in support of woman suffrage, and she was president of the National American Woman
Suffrage Association from 1892 to 1900.*

The United States of America v. Susan B. Anthony

(selection)

UNITED STATES CIRCUIT COURT, NORTHERN DISTRICT OF NEW YORK,
Hon. Ward Hunt, Presiding. Appearances: For the United
States: Hon. Richard Crowley, U.S. District Attorney; For the
Defendant: Hon. Henry R. Selden, John Van Voorhis, Esq.

1873

Tried at Canandaigua, Tuesday and Wednesday, June 17–18,
1878, before Hon. Ward Hunt, and a jury. Jury impaneled at 2:30 PM.
Mr. Crowley opened the case as follows:

MAY IT PLEASE THE COURT AND GENTLEMEN OF THE JURY:
On November 5, 1872, there was held in this state, as well as in other states
of the Union, a general election for different officers, and among those,
for candidates to represent several districts of this state in the Congress of
the United States. The defendant, Miss Susan B. Anthony, at that time re-
sided in the city of Rochester, in the county of Monroe, Northern District
of New York, and on November 5, 1872, she voted for a representative in the
Congress of the United States, to represent the Twenty-ninth Congressional
District of this state, and also for a representative at large for the state of
New York, to represent the state in the Congress of the United States. At that
time she was a woman. I suppose there will be no question about that. The

question in this case, if there be a question of fact about it at all, will, in my judgment, be rather a question of law than one of fact. I suppose that there will be no question of fact, substantially, in the case when all of the evidence is out, and it will be for you to decide under the charge for his honor, the judge, whether or not the defendant committed the offense of voting for a representative in Congress upon that occasion. We think, on the part of the government, that there is no question about it either one way or the other, neither a question of fact, nor a question of law, and that whatever Miss Anthony's intentions may have been—whether they were good or otherwise—she did not have a right to vote upon that question, and if she did vote without having a lawful right to vote, then there is no question but what she is guilty of violating a law of the United States in that behalf enacted by the Congress of the United States.

We don't claim in this case, gentlemen, that Miss Anthony is of that class of people who go about "repeating." We don't claim that she went from place to place for the purpose of offering her vote. But we do claim that on November 5, 1872, she voted, and whether she believed that she had a right to vote or not, it being a question of law, that she is within the statute. Congress in 1870 passed the following statute: (Reads Nineteenth Section of the Act of 1870, page 144, sixteenth statutes at large.) It is not necessary for me, gentlemen, at this stage of the case, to state all the facts which will be proven on the part of the government. I shall leave that to be shown by the evidence and by the witnesses, and if any question of law shall arise his honor will undoubtedly give you instructions as he shall deem proper. Conceded, that on November 5, 1872, Miss Susan B. Anthony was a woman.

The court, after listening to an argument from the district attorney, denied the motion for a new trial.

The COURT: The prisoner will stand up. Has the prisoner anything to say why sentence shall not be pronounced?

Miss ANTHONY: Yes, your honor. I have many things to say; for in your ordered verdict of guilty, you have trampled underfoot every vital principle of our government. My natural rights, my civil rights, my political rights are all alike ignored. Robbed of the fundamental privilege of citizenship, I am degraded from the status of a citizen to that of a subject; and not only myself individually, but all of my sex, are, by your honor's verdict, doomed to political subjection under this so-called republican government.

Judge HUNT: The court cannot listen to a rehearsal of arguments the prisoner's counsel has already consumed three hours in presenting.

Miss ANTHONY: May it please your honor, I am not arguing the question, but simply stating the reasons why sentence cannot, in justice, be pronounced against me. Your denial of my citizen's right to vote is the denial of my right of consent as one of the governed, the denial of my right of representation as one of the taxed, the denial of my right to a trial by a jury of my peers as an offender against law, therefore, the denial of my sacred rights to life, liberty, property, and—

Judge HUNT: The court cannot allow the prisoner to go on.

Miss ANTHONY: But your honor will not deny me this one and only poor privilege of protest against this high-handed outrage upon my citizen's rights. May it please the court to remember that since the day of my arrest last November, this is the first time that either myself or any person of my disfranchised class has been allowed a word of defense before judge or jury—

Judge HUNT: The prisoner must sit down; the court cannot allow it.

Miss ANTHONY: All my prosecutors, from the Eighth Ward corner grocery politician, who entered the complaint, to the United States marshal, commissioner, district attorney, district judge, your honor on the bench, not one is my peer, but each and all are my political sovereigns; and had your honor submitted my case to the jury, as was clearly your duty, even then I should have had just cause of protest, for not one of those men was my peer; but, native or foreign, white or black, rich or poor, educated or ignorant, awake or asleep, sober or drunk, each and every man of them was my political superior; hence, in no sense, my peer. Even, under such circumstances, a commoner of England, tried before a jury of lords, would have far less cause to complain than should

I, a woman, tried before a jury of men. Even my counsel, the Honorable Henry R. Selden, who has argued my cause so ably, so earnestly, so unanswerably before your honor, is my political sovereign. Precisely as no disfranchised person is entitled to sit upon a jury, and no woman is entitled to the franchise, so, none but a regularly admitted lawyer is allowed to practice in the courts, and no woman can gain admission to the bar—hence, jury, judge, counsel, must all be of the superior class.

Judge HUNT: The court must insist—the prisoner has been tried according to the established forms of law.

Miss ANTHONY: Yes, your honor, but by forms of law all made by men, interpreted by men, administered by men, in favor of men, and against women; and hence, your honor's ordered verdict of guilty, against a United States citizen for the exercise of "that citizen's right to vote," simply because that citizen was a woman and not a man. But, yesterday, the same man-made forms of law declared it a crime punishable with $1,000 fine and six months' imprisonment, for you, or me, or any of us, to give a cup of cold water, a crust of bread, or a night's shelter to a panting fugitive as he was tracking his way to Canada. And every man or woman in whose veins coursed a drop of human sympathy violated that wicked law, reckless of consequences, and was justified in so doing. As then the slaves who got their freedom must take it over, or under, or through the unjust forms of law, precisely so now must women, to get their right to a voice in this government, take it; and I have taken mine, and mean to take it at every possible opportunity.

Judge HUNT: The court orders the prisoner to sit down. It will not allow another word.

Miss ANTHONY: When I was brought before your honor for trial, I hoped for a broad and liberal interpretation of the Constitution and its recent amendments, that should declare all United States citizens under its protecting aegis—that should declare equality of rights the national guarantee to all persons born or naturalized in the United States. But failing to get this justice—failing, even, to get a trial by a jury *not* of my peers—I ask not leniency at your hands—but rather the full rigors of the law.

Judge HUNT: The court must insist—(Here the prisoner sat down.)

Judge HUNT: The prisoner will stand up. (Here Miss Anthony arose again.) The sentence of the court is that you pay a fine of $ 100 and the costs of the prosecution.

Miss ANTHONY: May it please your honor, I shall never pay a dollar of your unjust penalty. All the stock in trade I possess is a $10,000 debt, incurred by publishing my paper—the *Revolution*—four years ago, the sole object of which was to educate all women to do precisely as I have done, rebel against your man-made, unjust, unconstitutional forms of law that tax, fine, imprison, and hang women, while they deny them the right of representation in the government; and I shall work on with might and main to pay every dollar of that honest debt, but not a penny shall go to this unjust claim. And I shall earnestly and persistently continue to urge all women to the practical recognition of the old revolutionary maxim, that "Resistance to tyranny is obedience to God."

Judge HUNT: Madam, the court will not order you committed until the fine is paid.

For Discussion

1. Why does Richard Crowley say, "We think, on the part of the government, that there is no question about it either one way or the other, neither a question of fact nor a question of law"? (106)
2. Why does Judge Ward Hunt say repeatedly that the court cannot allow Anthony to continue to speak, yet continue to allow her to speak?
3. What distinction is Anthony making between a *citizen* and a *subject*?
4. According to Anthony, why would "a broad and liberal interpretation of the Constitution and its recent amendments" support women's right to vote? (108)
5. Why does Anthony ask not for the judge's leniency but rather for "the full rigors of the law"? (108)

For Further Reflection

1. What should a judge or jury member do if he or she believes that a defendant is guilty but also believes that the law in question is unjust?
2. How do you know when disobeying a law is the right thing to do?
3. Is there a current law that you consider unjust? What action would you take to change it?

For Research

1. Research the struggle for women's suffrage, including the links between its advocates and the abolitionists.
2. Research the means used to enforce voting rights for women following ratification of the Nineteenth Amendment in 1920.

Slavery on the Henequen Plantations of Yucatan

CHANNING ARNOLD *and*
FREDERICK J. TABOR FROST

In the mid-nineteenth century, henequen—a form of agave plant, also known as sisal, that could be made into twine and rope—became the biggest cash crop of Mexico's Yucatan peninsula. Harvesting and processing henequen required a huge number of workers, who labored on hundreds of plantations owned by a small class of hacienderos. *These wealthy plantation owners were of Spanish descent, while the laborers were Maya, the indigenous people of the region. When the English archaeologists Channing Arnold and Frederick J. Tabor Frost went to Yucatan in the early 1900s, they discovered that the Maya people, called* indios *by the ruling class, were essentially enslaved. In their 1909 book,* The American Egypt: A Record of Travel in Yucatan, *from which this selection is taken, Arnold and Frost include a detailed description and condemnation of the plantation system.*

This selection is taken from *The American Egypt*, chapter 19, "Slavery on the Haciendas," and chapter 21, "The Green Gold of Yucatan."

Slavery on the Henequen Plantations of Yucatan

THE YUCATECANS HAVE a cruel proverb, *"Los Indios no oigan sino por las nalgas"* ("The Indians can hear only with their backs"). The Spanish half-breeds have taken a race once noble enough and broken them on the wheel of a tyranny so brutal that the heart of them is dead. The relations between the two peoples is ostensibly that of master and servant, but Yucatan is rotten with a foul slavery—the fouler and blacker because of its hypocrisy and pretence.

The peonage system of Spanish America, as specious and treacherous a plan as was ever devised for race-degradation, is that by which a farm labourer is legally bound to work for the landowner, if in debt to him, until that debt is paid. Nothing could sound fairer: nothing could lend itself better to the blackest abuse. In Yucatan, every Indian peon is in debt to his Yucatecan master. Why? Because every Indian is a spendthrift? Not at all; but because the master's interest is to get him and keep him in debt. This is done in two ways. The plantation slave must buy the necessaries of his humble life at the plantation store, where care is taken to charge such prices as are beyond his humble earnings of sixpence a day. Thus he is always in debt to the farm; and if an Indian is discovered to be scraping together the few dollars he owes, the books of the hacienda are "cooked,"—yes, deliberately "cooked,"—and when he presents himself before the magistrate to pay his debt, say, of twenty dollars (£2) the haciendado can show scored against him a debt of fifty dollars. The Indian pleads that he does not owe it. The hacien-dado court smiles. The word of an Indian cannot prevail against the señor's books, it murmurs sweetly, and back to his slave work the miserable peon must go, first to be cruelly flogged to teach him that freedom is not for such as he, and that struggle as he may he will never escape the cruel master who under law as at present administered in Yucatan has as complete a disposal of his body as of one of the pigs which root around in the hacienda yard....

><

If the hardship of the Indians' lot was merely slavery, it might be argued that there were slender grounds for our indictment. Slavery may under cer-tain circumstances be far from an evil, where the backward condition of a race is such as to justify its temporary existence, and where the slave owner can be trusted. But the slave owner can very seldom be trusted, and he cer-tainly cannot be in Yucatan. It is no exaggeration to say that the enslave-ment of the Indians of Yucatan never has had, never can have, justification. Conceived in an unholy alliance between the Church and brute force, it has grown with the centuries into a race degradation which has as its only objects the increasing of the millions of the slave owners and the gratifica-tion of their foul lusts. The social condition of Yucatan today represents as infamous a conspiracy to exploit and prostitute a whole race as the history of the world affords. Yucatan is governed by a group of millionaire mo-nopolists whose interests are identical, banded together to deny all justice to the Indians, who, if need be, are treated in a way an Englishman would blush to treat his dog.

><

Henequen (Spanish *jeniquen* or *geniquen*) is a fibre commercially known as sisal hemp, from the fact that it is obtained from a species of cactus, the *Agave sisalensis,* first cultivated around the tiny port of Sisal in Yucatan. The older Indian name for the plant is *Agave ixtli.* From its fleshy leaves is crushed out a fine fibre which, from the fact that it resists damp better than ordinary hemp, is valuable for making ships' cables, but the real wealth-producing use of which is so bizarre that no one in a hundred guesses would hit on it. It is used in the myriad corn-binding machines of America and Canada. They cannot use wire, and cheap string is too easily broken. Henequen is at once strong enough and cheap enough. Hence the piles of money heaping up to the credit of Yucatecans in the banks of Merida. . . .

For there is money for everyone who touches the magic fibre except the miserable Indian, by whose neverending labours the purse-proud monopolists of the Peninsula are enabled to be ever adding to their ill-gotten gold. There are in Yucantan today some four hundred henequen plantations of from twenty-five to twenty thousand acres, making the total acreage under cultivation some one hundred and forty thousand acres. The cost of production, including shipping expenses, export duties, etc., is now about seven pesos (14 *s*.) per hundred kilogrammes. The average market price of henequen is twenty-eight pesos per hundred kilogrammes, so the planter gets a return of 400 percent. All this is obviously only possible as long as he can get slave labour and the hideous truth about the exploitation of the Mayans is kept dark. The Indian gets a wage of fifty centavos for cutting a thousand leaves, and if he is to earn this in a day he must work ten hours. Near the big towns, seventy-five centavos are paid, but practically, on many haciendas, it is so managed that the labour is paid for by his bare keep.

꒰꒰

And so, after centuries of oppression, the race is dead, a chattel, body and soul, of a corrupt and degraded people. When the task of revivifying these poor Mayans with the elixir of freedom is undertaken, if it ever is (and pray God it be), by the United States of America, it will be as difficult as nursing back to convalescence a patient sick unto death. No beings will at first understand freedom so ill. They are like prisoners who have been for weary years in the darkness of unlighted dungeons. The glare of the sunlight of freedom will be too dazzling for their poor atrophied eyes. They will shade them and cringe back in to the gloom.

For Discussion

1. Why is the system of slavery described by Channing Arnold and Frederick Frost "the fouler and blacker because of its hypocrisy and pretence"? (113)
2. Why do Arnold and Frost explain in detail the way henequen is processed and the economics involved?
3. What makes the system described by Arnold and Frost "slavery," as opposed to a "master and servant" relationship?

For Further Reflection

1. Do Arnold and Frost convince you that the "hypocrisy and pretence" of the system they describe makes it worse than a more explicit form of slavery?
2. Is there an essential difference between slavery and other forms of economic exploitation?

For Research

1. When and how did the system described in this selection change to a more equitable one?
2. Find an example of a sweatshop. What conditions do its workers face? What does it produce? Who buys its products? Have there been any efforts to change it?
3. Research the history of the company store. For specific instances, you might look at coal miners in West Virginia or railroad workers in the Pullman community in Chicago.

Independence
v. Swaraj

Gandhi's Followers
Protest the Salt Tax

MAHATMA GANDHI (1869–1948)

WEBB MILLER (1892–1940)

Mohandas Gandhi, the twentieth century's leading proponent of nonviolent protest,
led India to independence from British rule and powerfully influenced other
human rights activists, most notably Martin Luther King Jr. The title mahatma,
or great soul, was given to him by his followers. Gandhi was born in Porbandar,
India. His father was a government official and his mother was a devout Hindu.
Gandhi grew up in a household that practiced vegetarianism, noninjury to
all living beings, fasting, and religious tolerance. Married at thirteen by the
arrangement of his parents, Gandhi was a mediocre student and athlete. After
studying law in London, he accepted a job in South Africa and was exposed to
overt racism for the first time. His emotional outbursts convinced him that angry
responses only bred more violence, and he adopted a course of nonviolence and
simple living. He gave up material possessions, committed himself to celibacy,
and often dressed only in a loincloth and shawl. Upon his return to India, Gandhi
began a civil disobedience campaign aimed at winning Indian independence.
Frequently jailed, Gandhi continued his protests by fasting. His most famous
campaign of civil disobedience was against the 1930 Salt Tax, which American-
born journalist Webb Miller witnessed and described in his memoir, I Found No
Peace: The Journal of a Foreign Correspondent *(1936). In August 1947, India*
finally achieved independence. The following January, Gandhi was murdered by
a Hindu fanatic angered by Gandhi's acceptance of Muslims.

Independence
v. Swaraj

I SUBMIT THAT SWARAJ IS an all-satisfying goal for all time. . . . It is infinitely greater than and includes independence. It is a vital word. It has been sanctified by the noble sacrifices of thousands of Indians. It is a word which, if it has not penetrated the remotest corner of India, has at least got the largest currency of any similar word. It is a sacrilege to displace that word by a foreign importation of doubtful value. . . .

I long for freedom from the English yoke. I would pay any price for it. I would accept chaos in exchange for it. For the English peace is the peace of the grave. Anything would be better than this living death of a whole people. This satanic rule has well-nigh ruined this fair land materially, morally, and spiritually. I daily see its law courts denying justice and murdering truth. . . . In order to protect its immoral commerce, this rule regards no means too mean, and in order to keep three hundred million under the heels of a hundred thousand, it carries a military expenditure which is keeping millions in a state of semistarvation and polluting thousands of mouths with intoxicating liquor.

But my creed is nonviolence under all circumstances. My method is conversion, not coercion; it is self-suffering, not the suffering of the tyrant. I know that method to be infallible. I know that a whole people can adopt it without accepting it as its creed and without understanding its philosophy. People generally do not understand the philosophy of all their acts.

119

My ambition is much higher than independence. Through the deliverance of India, I seek to deliver the so-called weaker races of the earth from the crushing heels of Western exploitation in which England is the greatest partner. If India converts, as it can convert, Englishmen, it can become the predominant partner in a world commonwealth of which England can have the privilege of becoming a partner if she chooses. India has the right, if she only knew, of becoming the predominant partner by reason of her numbers, geographical position, and culture inherited for ages. This is big talk, I know. For a fallen India to aspire to move the world and protect weaker races is seemingly an impertinence. But in explaining my strong opposition to this cry for independence, I can no longer hide the light under a bushel. Mine is an ambition worth living for and worth dying for. In no case do I want to reconcile myself to a state lower than the best for fear of consequences. It is, therefore, not out of expedience that I oppose independence as my goal. I want India to come to her own and that state cannot be better defined by any single word than *swaraj*. Its content will vary with the action that the nation is able to put forth at a given moment. India's coming to her own will mean every nation doing likewise.

Swaraj does consist in the change of government and its real control by the people, but that would be merely the form. The substance that I am hankering after is a definite acceptance of the means and therefore a real change of heart on the part of the people. I am certain that it does not require ages for Hindus to discard the error of untouchability, for Hindus and Mussulmans to shed enmity and accept heart-friendship as an eternal factor of national life, for all to adopt the charkha [the spinning wheel as a symbol of identification with India's poor] as the only universal means of attaining India's economic salvation, and finally for all to believe that India's freedom lies only through nonviolence and no other method. Definite, intelligent, and free adoption by the nation of this program I hold as the attainment of the substance. The symbol, the transfer of power, is sure to follow, even as the seed truly laid must develop into a tree.

But after all, self-government depends entirely upon our own internal strength, upon our ability to fight against the heaviest odds. Indeed, self-government which does not require that continuous striving to attain it and to sustain it is not worth the name. I have therefore endeavored to show both in word and in deed that political self-government, that is, self-government for a large number of men and women, is no better than individual self-government, and therefore it is to be attained by precisely the same means that are required for individual self-government or self-rule, and so as you know also, I have striven in India to place this ideal before the people, in season and out of season, very often much to the disgust of those who are merely politically minded.

Swaraj is not going to descend on us from the heavens. It will not be received as a gift from the British Empire either. It can only be the reward of our own efforts. The very word *swaraj* means effort by the nation....No one will be able to stand in our way when we have developed the strength to win swaraj. Everyone's freedom is within his own grasp.

There are two alternatives before us. The one is that of violence, the other of nonviolence; the one of physical strength, the other of soul-force; the one of hatred, the other of love; the one of disorder, the other of peace; one that is demoniac, the other that is godly....We shall reap as we sow.

Gandhi's Followers Protest the Salt Tax

AFTER PLODDING ABOUT SIX MILES across country lugging a pack of sandwiches and two quart bottles of water under a sun which was already blazing hot, inquiring from every native I met, I reached the assembling place of the Gandhi followers. Several long, open thatched sheds were surrounded by high cactus thickets. The sheds were literally swarming and buzzed like a beehive with some 2,500 Congress or Gandhi men dressed in the regulation uniform of rough homespun cotton *dhotis* and triangular Gandhi caps, somewhat like American overseas soldiers' hats. They chattered excitely, and when I arrived hundreds surrounded me, with evidences of hostility at first. After they learned my identity, I was warmly welcomed by young college-educated, English-speaking men and escorted to Mme. Naidu. The famous Indian poetess, stocky, swarthy, strong featured, barelegged, dressed in rough, dark homespun robe and sandals, welcomed me. She explained that she was busy martialing her forces for the demonstration against the salt pans and would talk with me more at length later. She was educated in England and spoke English fluently.

Mme. Naidu called for prayer before the march started and the entire assemblage knelt. She exhorted them: "Gandhi's body is in jail but his soul is with you. India's prestige is in your hands. You must not use any violence under any circumstances. You will be beaten but you must not resist; you must not even raise a hand to ward off blows." Wild, shrill cheers terminated her speech.

Slowly and in silence the throng commenced the half-mile march to the salt deposits. A few carried ropes for lassoing the barbed-wire stockade around the salt pans. About a score who were assigned to act as stretcher-bearers wore crude, hand-painted red crosses pinned to their breasts; their stretchers consisted of blankets. Manilal Gandhi, second son of Gandhi, walked among the foremost of the marchers. As the throng drew near the salt pans they commenced chanting the revolutionary slogan, "*Inquilab zindabad*," intoning the two words over and over.

The salt deposits were surrounded by ditches filled with water and guarded by four hundred native Surat police in khaki shorts and brown turbans. Half a dozen British officials commanded them. The police carried *lathis*—five-foot clubs tipped with steel. Inside the stockade twenty-five native riflemen were drawn up.

In complete silence, the Gandhi men drew up and halted a hundred yards from the stockade. A picked column advanced from the crowd, waded the ditches, and approached the barbed-wire stockade, which the Surat police surrounded, holding their clubs at the ready. Police officials ordered the marchers to disperse under a recently imposed regulation which prohibited gatherings of more than five persons in any one place. The column silently ignored the warning and slowly walked forward. I stayed with the main body about a hundred yards from the stockade.

Suddenly, at a word of command, scores of native police rushed upon the advancing marchers and rained blows on their heads with their steel-shod *lathis*. Not one of the marchers even raised an arm to fend off the blows. They went down like tenpins. From where I stood, I heard the sickening whacks of the clubs on unprotected skulls. The waiting crowd of watchers groaned and sucked in their breaths in sympathetic pain at every blow.

Those struck down fell sprawling, unconscious, or writhing in pain with fractured skulls or broken shoulders. In two or three minutes the ground was quilted with bodies. Great patches of blood widened on their white clothes. The survivors, without breaking ranks, silently and doggedly marched on until struck down. When everyone of the first column had been knocked down, stretcher-bearers rushed up unmolested by the police and carried off the injured to a thatched hut, which had been arranged as a temporary hospital.

Then another column formed while the leaders pleaded with them to retain their self-control. They marched slowly toward the police. Although every one knew that within a few minutes he would be beaten down, perhaps killed, I could detect no signs of wavering or fear. They marched steadily with heads up, without the encouragement of music or cheering or any possibility that they might escape serious injury or death. The police rushed out and methodically and mechanically beat down the second column. There was no fight, no struggle; the marchers simply walked forward until struck down. There were no outcries, only groans after they fell. There were not enough stretcher-bearers to carry off the wounded; I saw eighteen injured being carried off simultaneously, while forty-two still lay bleeding on the ground awaiting stretcher-bearers. The blankets used as stretchers were sodden with blood.

At times the spectacle of unresisting men being methodically bashed into a bloody pulp sickened me so much that I had to turn away. The Western mind finds it difficult to grasp the idea of nonresistance. I felt an indefinable sense of helpless rage and loathing, almost as much against the men who were submitting unresistingly to being beaten as against the police wielding the clubs, and this despite the fact that when I came to India I sympathized with the Gandhi cause. . . .

In the middle of the morning V. J. Patel arrived. He had been leading the swaraj movement since Gandhi's arrest, and had just resigned as president of the Indian Legislative Assembly in protest against the British. Scores surrounded him, knelt, and kissed his feet. He was a venerable gentleman of about sixty with white flowing beard and mustache, dressed in the usual undyed, coarse homespun smock. Sitting on the ground under a mango tree, Patel said, "All hope of reconciling India with the British Empire is lost forever. I can understand any government's taking people into custody and punishing them for breaches of the law, but I cannot understand how any government that calls itself civilized could deal as savagely and brutally with nonviolent, unresisting men as the British have this morning."

By eleven, the heat reached 116 in the shade and the activities of the Gandhi volunteers subsided. I went back to the temporary hospital to examine the wounded. They lay in rows on the bare ground in the shade of an open, palm-thatched shed. I counted 320 injured, many still insensible with fractured skulls, others writhing in agony from kicks in the testicles and stomach. The Gandhi men had been able to gather only a few native doctors, who were doing the best they could with the inadequate facilities. Scores of the injured had received no treatment for hours and two had died. The demonstration was finished for the day on account of the heat.

I was the only foreign correspondent who had witnessed the amazing scene—a classic example of *Satyagraha,* or nonviolent civil disobedience.

For Discussion

1. What is swaraj? Why does Gandhi prefer it to independence?
2. What makes Gandhi sure that nonviolence is "infallible"? Why does he believe that "a whole people can adopt it without accepting it as its creed and without understanding its philosophy"? (119)
3. What does Gandhi mean when he says that "the substance that I am hankering after is a definite acceptance of the means" on the part of the Indian people? (120)
4. Why does Gandhi describe the change of government as a "symbol" of the greater change he seeks to promote?
5. Why does Gandhi believe that "self-government which does not require that continuous striving to attain it and to sustain it is not worth the name"? (120–121)

For Further Reflection

1. Do you believe that, with sufficient inner strength, oppressed people can liberate themselves no matter how strong their opposition is?
2. Do you agree that nonviolence is the best and most effective means of producing lasting political change?
3. How do you feel about the resignation with which the protesters face the blows of the Surat police as described by Miller?

For Research

1. Research the significant events that culminated in the departure of the British from India, and the proclamation of Indian independence in 1947.
2. Research the relationship between Hinduism and Islam in India today. Describe a recent incident that illustrates the tension between them.
3. Research the ethical guidelines for journalists posted by the Associated Press or the Society for Professional Journalists.

The Stalin Epigram

The Arrest of
Osip Mandelstam

OSIP MANDELSTAM (1891–1938)

NADEZHDA MANDELSTAM (1899–1980)

*Osip Mandelstam was one of the most important Russian poets of
his generation, part of the Acmeist group—along with poet Anna
Akhmatova—that stressed writing simply and precisely about everyday life. Mandelstam was born in St. Petersburg and was well
educated, attending the University of Heidelberg, the University of
St. Petersburg, and the Sorbonne. He achieved fame with his second
book of poems,* Tristia, *published in 1922. He supported the Russian
Revolution in its early days but despised the repression and political executions that came to characterize Stalin's reign. In 1934,
Mandelstam read "The Stalin Epigram" aloud to a group of friends
and was arrested shortly thereafter, almost certainly because one of
those present gave information to the Soviet secret police. He died in
1938, either at the labor camp he was sentenced to or on his way to it.
His wife, Nadezhda Mandelstam, preserved his poetry by memoriz-
ing it. After her husband's death, Nadezhda went into hiding. She
moved constantly from one small Russian town to the next—as the
widow of an enemy of the state, Nadezha could not safely return to
Moscow until the late 1950s. This account of her husband's arrest is
selected from her memoir* Hope Against Hope *(1970), which had to
be smuggled out of the Soviet Union and published in the West.*

The Stalin Epigram

Our lives no longer feel ground under them.
At ten paces you can't hear our words.

But whenever there's a snatch of talk
it turns to the Kremlin mountaineer,

the ten thick worms his fingers,
his words like measures of weight,

the huge laughing cockroaches on his top lip,
the glitter of his boot-rims.

Ringed with a scum of chicken-necked bosses
he toys with the tributes of half-men.

One whistles, another meows, a third snivels.
He pokes out his finger and he alone goes boom.

He forges decrees in a line like horseshoes,
One for the groin, one the forehead, temple, eye.

He rolls the executions on his tongue like berries.
He wishes he could hug them like big friends from home.

The Arrest of Osip Mandelstam

THE DAY DRAGGED ON with excruciating slowness. In the evening, the translator David Brodski turned up and then just wouldn't leave. There wasn't a bite to eat in the house, and M. went around to the neighbors to try and get something for Akhmatova's supper. We hoped that Brodski might now get bored and leave, but no, he shot after M. and was still with him when he returned with the solitary egg he had managed to scrounge. Sitting down again in his chair, Brodski continued to recite the lines he liked best from his favorite poets, Sluchevski and Polonski (there was nothing he didn't know about both Russian and French poetry). He just went on and on, quoting and reminiscing, and it was only after midnight that we realized why he was being such a nuisance.

Whenever she came to see us, Akhmatova stayed in our small kitchen. The gas had not yet been installed, and I cooked our semblance of a dinner on a kerosene stove in the corridor. In honor of our guest, we covered the gas cooker with oilcloth to disguise it as a table. We called the kitchen "the sanctuary" after Narbut had once looked in there to see Akhmatova and said: "What are you doing here, like a pagan idol in a sanctuary? Why don't you go to some meeting or other where you can sit down properly?" Akhmatova and I had now taken refuge there, leaving M. to the mercy of the poetry-loving Brodski. Suddenly, at about one o'clock in the morning, there was a sharp, unbearably explicit knock on the door. "They've come for Osip," I said, and went to open the door.

Some men in civilian overcoats were standing outside—there seemed to be a lot of them. For a split second, I had a tiny flicker of hope that this still wasn't it—my eye had not made out the uniforms under the covert-cloth topcoats. In fact, topcoats of this kind were also a sort of uniform—though they were intended as a disguise, like the old pea-green coats of the czarist okhrana.[1] But this I did not know then. All hope vanished as soon as the uninvited guests stepped inside.

I had expected them to say "How do you do?" or "Is this Mandelstam's apartment?" or something else of the kind that any visitor says in order to be let in by the person who opens the door. But the night visitors of our times do not stand on such ceremony—like secret police agents the world over, I suppose.

Without a word or a moment's hesitation, but with consummate skill and speed, they came in past me (not pushing, however), and the apartment was suddenly full of people already checking our identity papers, running their hands over our hips with a precise, well-practiced movement, and feeling our pockets to make sure we had no concealed weapons.

M. came out of the large room. "Have you come for me?" he asked. One of the agents, a short man, looked at him with what could have been a faint smile and said, "Your papers." M. took them out of his pocket, and after checking them, the agent handed him a warrant. M. read it and nodded.

In the language of the secret police, this was what was known as a "night operation." As I learned later, they all firmly believed that they were always liable to meet with opposition on such occasions, and to keep their spirits up they regaled each other with romantic tales about the dangers involved in these night raids. I myself once heard the daughter of an important Chekist,[2] who had come to prominence in 1937, telling a story about how Isaac Babel had "seriously wounded one of our men" while resisting arrest. She told such stories as an expression of concern for her kindly, loving father whenever he went out on "night operations." He was fond of children and

1. [Secret police force during the reign of the czars.]
2. [Member of the Soviet secret police organization, later known as the KGB.]

animals—at home he always had the cat on his knee—and he told his daughter never to admit that she had done anything wrong and always to say "no." This homely man with the cat could never forgive the people he interrogated for admitting everything they were accused of. "Why did they do it?" the daughter asked, echoing her father. "Think of the trouble they made for themselves and for us as well!" By *us*, she meant all those who had come at night with warrants, interrogated and passed sentence on the accused, and whiled away their spare time telling stories of the risks they ran. Whenever I hear such tales, I think of the tiny hole in the skull of Isaac Babel, a cautious, clever man with a high forehead, who probably never once in his life held a pistol in his hands.

And so they burst into our poor, hushed apartments as though raiding bandits' lairs or secret laboratories in which masked Carbonari[3] were making dynamite and preparing armed resistance. They visited us on the night of May 13, 1934. After checking our papers, presenting their warrants, and making sure there would be no resistance, they began to search the apartment. Brodski slumped into his chair and sat there motionless, like a huge wooden sculpture of some savage tribe. He puffed and wheezed with an angry, hurt expression on his face. When I chanced at one point to speak to him—asking him, I think, to get some books from the shelves for M. to take with him—he answered rudely: "Let M. get them himself," and again began to wheeze. Toward morning, when we were at last permitted to walk freely around the apartment, and the tired Chekists no longer even looked searchingly at us as we did so, Brodski suddenly roused himself, held up his hand like a schoolboy, and asked permission to go to the toilet. The agent directing the search looked at him with contempt. "You can go home," he said. "What?" Brodski said in astonishment. "Home," the man repeated and turned his back. The secret police despised their civilian helpers. Brodski had no doubt been ordered to sit with us that evening in case we tried to destroy any manuscripts when we heard the knock on the door.

3. [Literally charcoal-burners. A European secret society from the early nineteenth century.]

For Discussion

1. According to the poem, what is the source of Joseph Stalin's power?
2. What does it mean for Stalin's words to be "like measures of weight"?
3. Why are Stalin's bosses described as "chicken-necked" and forming a ring of "scum" around their leader?
4. Why do the men around Stalin only make sounds, rather than speak?
5. Why is Stalin the only one who "goes boom" when he pokes out his finger?
6. Why does Stalin roll "the executions on his tongue like berries"? Why does he wish "he could hug them like big friends from home"?

For Further Reflection

1. Is it possible for poetry to change political reality?
2. Are those who carry out the orders of tyrants equally responsible for the crimes?
3. Are there aspects of this portrayal of Stalin that might describe any dictator?

For Research

1. Research Mandelstam's life from the time he was arrested in 1934. What was his life in exile like? What were the conditions in the labor camp to which he was assigned?
2. Research Stalin's handling of political opposition, especially the assassinations and arrests he ordered.
3. Research the lives and work of other poets who got into trouble with their governments for what they wrote.

I Will Bear Witness

(selection)

VICTOR KLEMPERER (1881–1961)

Victor Klemperer—whose diaries of everyday life in Germany during the Holocaust record the inexorable progress of the Third Reich's campaign to imprison and murder the Jewish population—was one of a handful of Jews in Dresden to survive. (In 1941, the city had 1,265 registered Jews; by the beginning of 1945, the number was 198.) Because he had fought in the German army during World War I and was married to an "Aryan" Christian, Klemperer was allowed to remain in the city after most Jews had been transported.

Klemperer was born in 1881, the son of a rabbi in the most liberal sector of Judaism, which did not observe the traditional Sabbath or dietary restrictions. Klemperer was baptized as a Protestant (not uncommon in Prussia in the nineteenth century), and identified himself primarily as a German, not a Jew. He studied French literature at Munich University and worked as a literary journalist before beginning a career as a professor. He married Eva Schlemmer, a Protestant, in 1906. Klemperer was dismissed from his position at Dresden Technical University in 1935, officially because the government found his post "surplus to requirements." In this selection from his diary, Klemperer recounts the experiences of government harassment that came to characterize daily life for him and Eva, as well as for the other Jews who remained in Germany. The Klemperers survived the war only as result of the Allied fire bombing of Dresden. They were ordered by the Nazis to report for deportation on February 16, 1945, but the confusion that followed the bombing on February 13 allowed them to escape. They returned to their home city, and Klemperer resumed his academic career. He died in Dresden in 1961 at the age of seventy-eight.

I Will Bear Witness
(selection)

FEBRUARY 21, [1933]
AFTERNOON

[. . .] I am not writing a history of the times here. But I shall nevertheless record my embitterment, greater than I would have imagined I was still
capable of feeling. It is a disgrace, which gets worse with every day that passes.
And there's not a sound from anyone and everyone's keeping his head down,
Jewry most of all and their democratic press. One week after Hitler's appointment, we were (on February 5) at the Blumenfelds with Raab. Raab, busybody,
political economist, chairman of the Humboldt Club, made a big speech and
declared it was necessary to vote for the German Nationals, so as to strengthen
the right wing of the coalition. I vehemently took issue with him. More interesting his opinion that Hitler will end in religious madness. . .what is
strangest of all is how one is blind in the face of events, how no one has a clue
to the real balance of power. Who will have the majority on March 5? Will the
terror be tolerated and for how long? It is impossible to make predictions.
Meanwhile the uncertainty of the situation affects every single thing. [. . .]

MARCH 10, [1933]
FRIDAY EVENING

January 30: Hitler Chancellor. What, up to election Sunday on March 5, I
called terror, was a mild prelude. Now the business of 1918 is being exactly

137

repeated, only under a different sign, under the swastika. Again it's astounding how easily everything collapses. What has happened to Bavaria; what has happened to the Reichsbanner etc., etc.? Eight days before the election the clumsy business of the Reichstag fire—I cannot imagine that anyone really believes in Communist perpetrators instead of paid 卐 work. Then the wild prohibitions and acts of violence. And on top of that, the never-ending propaganda in the street, on the radio, etc. On Saturday, the fourth, I heard a part of Hitler's speech from Königsberg. The front of a hotel at the railway station, illuminated, a torchlight procession in front of it, torchbearers and swastika flag bearers on the balconies and loudspeakers. I understood only occasional words. But the tone! The unctuous bawling, truly bawling, of a priest.—On the Sunday I voted for the Democrats, Eva for the Zentrum. In the evening around nine with the Blumenfelds to the Dembers. As a joke, because I entertained hopes of Bavaria, I wore my Bavarian Service Cross. Then the tremendous election victory of the National Socialists. Their vote doubled in Bavaria. The Horst Wessel song between the announcements.— An indignant denial, no harm will come to loyal Jews. Directly afterward the Central Association of Jewish Citizens in Thuringia is banned because it had criticized the government in "Talmudic fashion" and disparaged it. Since then day after day commissioners appointed, provincial governments trampled underfoot, flags raised, buildings taken over, people shot, newspapers banned, etc., etc. Yesterday the dramaturge Karl Wolf dismissed "by order of the Nazi Party"—not even in the name of the government—today the whole Saxon cabinet, etc., etc. A complete revolution and party dictatorship. And all opposing forces as if vanished from the face of the earth. It is this utter collapse of a power only recently present, no, its complete disappearance (just as in 1918) that I find so staggering. [...]

AUGUST 4, [1934]
SATURDAY MORNING

At first, events made us extremely bitter and almost desperate, Eva almost more than myself. Hindenburg dies at nine o'clock on the 2nd of August, one hour later a "law" of the Reich government of August 1 appears: The offices of the president and the chancellor are united in Hitler's person, the army *(Wehrmacht)* will give its oath to him, and at half past six the troops in Dresden swore their oath and everything is completely calm. Our butcher says indifferently, "Why vote first? It just costs a lot of money." The people hardly notice this complete coup d'état; it all takes place in silence, drowned out by hymns to the dead Hindenburg. I would swear that millions upon millions have no idea what a monstrous thing has occurred.—Eva says, "And we belong to this band of slaves." In the evening as a tire bursts, dismissively: "It is not a shot."—We had always placed hopes in the Reichswehr; Johannes Köhler had told us long ago, as a confirmed rumor, that it was only waiting for the imminent death of Hindenburg to act. And now it calmly gives its oath to the new "Commander-in-Chief of the Wehrmacht." [...]

MAY 2, [1935] THURSDAY

[...] On Tuesday morning, without any previous notification—two sheets delivered by mail: (a) On the basis of para 6 of the Law for the Restoration of the Professional Civil Service I have...recommended your dismissal. Notice of dismissal enclosed. The Commissary Director of the Ministry for Popular Education. (b) "In the name of the Reich" the notice itself, signed in a child's hand: Martin Mutschmann. I telephoned the university; no one there had a clue. Göpfert, the commissioner, does not waste time asking the rector's office for advice. At first I felt alternately numb and slightly romantic; now there is only bitterness and wretchedness.

My situation will be very difficult. I shall still receive my salary, the 800M that give me so much trouble, until the end of July, and after that a pension, which will amount to approximately 400M. [...]

MAY 4, [1935]
SATURDAY AFTERNOON

Stepun reports that my chair will be occupied again. So I have not been kicked out to make savings. But as a Jew. Even though I served in the field, etc., etc. [...]

MAY 16, [1936]
SATURDAY AFTERNOON

[...] The mood of the wedding anniversary? I feel old, I have no confidence in my heart, I do not believe that I have much time left to me, I do not believe that I shall live to see the end of the Third Reich, and I let myself drift along fatalistically without especial despair and cannot give up hope. Eva's stubborn attachment to extending the house is a support to me. I cannot imagine how I would bear the pressure, the humiliation, the uncertainty, the loneliness without Eva. Things really are getting worse all the time. Yesterday a farewell greeting from Betty Klemperer from Bremen (and Felix was one of the first doctors to receive the Iron Cross, First Class, he took part in the Hindenburg offensive against the Russians, bound wounds in the trenches); now the women in our family are also leaving Germany, and sometimes my staying here seems dishonorable to me—but what should I, who could not even be a language teacher, do elsewhere? Isakowitz, whom Eva is seeing a lot of again (further financial deterioration), is emigrating to London in a couple of weeks; there is not a word from the Köhlers, *decentes et indecentes*: A civil servant is not allowed to consort "with Jews and disreputable elements." The foreign affairs situation is completely confused, but it undoubtedly presents the Hitler government with the greatest opportunities. The huge German army is feared and used by every party: perhaps Germany will do a deal with England, perhaps with Italy, but a deal will certainly be done and to the advantage of the present government. And I certainly no longer believe that it has enemies inside Germany. The majority of the people is content, a small group accepts Hitler as the lesser evil, no one really wants to be rid of him, all see in him the liberator in foreign affairs, fear Russian conditions, as a child fears the bogeyman, believe, insofar as they are not honestly carried away, that it is inopportune, in terms of realpolitik, to be outraged at such details as the suppression of civil liberties, the persecution of the Jews, the falsification of all scholarly truths, the systematic destruction of all morality. And all are afraid for their livelihood, their life, all are such terrible cowards. (Can I reproach them with it? During my last year in my post, I swore an oath to Hitler; I have remained in the country—I am no better than my Aryan fellow creatures.) [...]

MARCH 27, [1937]
SATURDAY—EASTER TOMORROW,
PROBABLY A WHITE ONE

[...] Week by week we find ourselves in worse straits: my suit is fraying, our home is thick with dirt, neither house nor garden is finished, and I count every penny. We are so proletarianized and constrained, that I often wish not to wake up again. [...]

Nevertheless, what Johanna Krüger wrote to us after her visit in January is right: "You still have so much." In our great loneliness, we are perhaps even closer to one another than in former years. For myself the feeling of How much longer? also no doubt plays a part. [...]

AUGUST 17, [1937] TUESDAY

[...] In the *Stürmer* (which is displayed at every corner) I recently saw a picture: two girls in swimming costumes at a seaside resort. Above it: "Prohibited for Jews," underneath it: "How nice that it's just us now!" Then I remembered a long forgotten incident. September 1900 or 1901 in Landsberg. In the lower sixth, we were 4 Jews among 16, in the upper sixth 3 among 8 pupils. There was little trace of anti-Semitism among either the teachers or the pupils. More precisely none at all. The agitation of Ahlwardt and Stoecker is no more than historical fact to me. I knew only that a Jew could become neither a fraternity member as a student nor an officer. [...] So on the Day of Atonement—Yom Kippur—the Jews did not attend classes. The next day, our comrades told us, laughing and without the least malice (just as the words themselves were also only uttered jokingly by the altogether humane teacher), Kufahl, the mathematician, had said to the reduced class: "Today it's *just us*." In my memory, these words took on a quite horrible significance: to me it confirms the claim of the NSDAP [Nazi Party] to express the true opinion of the German people. And I believe ever more strongly that Hitler really does embody the soul of the German people, that he really stands for "Germany," and that he will consequently maintain himself and justifiably maintain himself. Whereby I have not only outwardly lost my fatherland. And even if the government should change one day: my inner sense of belonging is gone. [...]

NOVEMBER 27, [1938]

On the morning of the eleventh two policemen accompanied by a "resident of Dölzschen." Did I have any weapons?—Certainly my saber, perhaps even my bayonet as a war memento, but I wouldn't know where.—We have to help you find it.—The house was searched for hours. At the beginning Eva made the mistake of quite innocently telling one of the policemen he should not go through the clean linen cupboard without washing his hands. The man, considerably affronted, could hardly be calmed down. A second, younger policeman was more friendly; the civilian was the worst. Pigsty, etc. We said we had been without domestic help for months; many things were dusty and still unpacked. They rummaged through everything; chests and wooden constructions Eva had made were broken open with an ax. The saber was found in a suitcase in the attic; the bayonet was not found. Among the books they found a copy of the *Sozialistische Monatshefte* (Socialist Monthly Magazine—an SPD theoretical journal) [...] this was also confiscated. At one point when Eva wanted to fetch one of her tools, the young policeman ran after her; the older one called out: You are making us suspicious, you are making your situation worse. At about one o'clock, the civilian and the older policeman left the house; the young one remained and took a statement. He was good natured and courteous; I had the feeling he himself found the thing embarrassing. In addition, he complained about an upset stomach, and we offered him a schnapps, which he declined. Then the three of them appeared to hold a conference in the garden. The young policeman returned: You must dress and come to the court building at Münchner Platz with me. There's nothing to fear, you will probably(!) be back by evening. [...] At four o'clock, I was on the street again with the curious feeling, free—but for how long? Since then we have both been unceasingly tormented by the question, go or stay? To go too early, to stay too late? To go where we have nothing, to remain in this corruption? [...]

DECEMBER 3, [1938] SATURDAY

Today is the Day of German Solidarity. Curfew for Jews from 12 noon until eight. When at exactly half-past eleven I went to the mailbox and to the grocer, where I had to wait, I really felt as if I could not breathe. I cannot bear it anymore. Yesterday evening, an order from the Minister of the Interior: local authorities are henceforth at liberty to restrict the movement of Jewish drivers both as to time and place. Yesterday afternoon at the library, Striege or Striegel, who is in charge of the lending section, an old Stahlhelm man of middling position and years [...]: I should come into the back room with him. Just as he had announced the reading room ban a year ago, so he now showed me the complete ban on using the library. The absolute end. But it was different from a year ago. The man was distressed beyond words, I had to calm him. He stroked my hand the whole time, he could not hold back the tears, he stammered: I am boiling over inside...If only something would happen tomorrow...—Why tomorrow?—It's the Day of Solidarity... They're collecting...One could get at them...But not just kill them—torture, torture, torture...They should first of all be made to feel what they've done...Could I not give my manuscripts to one of the consulates for safe-keeping...Could I not get out...And could I write a line for him.—Even before that (I knew nothing about the ban yet) Fräulein Roth, very pale, had gripped my hand in the catalog room: Could I not get away, it was the end here, for us too—St. Mark's was set alight even before the synagogue and the Zion Church was threatened, if it does not change its name...She spoke to me as to a dying man; she took leave of me as if forever. ....But these few, sympathizing and in despair, are isolated, and they too are afraid. [...]

DECEMBER 6, [1938] TUESDAY

[...] Now I note only the ever more frequent phrase: It is in accordance with the healthy sense of justice of the people, which is always printed when some new atrocity is initiated. And that disposes of the contemplative intermezzo.

The healthy sense of justice of every German manifested itself yesterday in a decree from Police Minister Himmler with immediate effect: withdrawal of driving license from all Jews. Justification: Because of the Grünspan murder, Jews are unreliable, are therefore not allowed to sit at the wheel; also their being permitted to drive offends the German traffic community, especially as they have presumptuously made use of the Reich highways built by German workers' hands. This prohibition hits us terribly hard. It is now three years exactly since I learned to drive, my driving license is dated 1/26/36.

DECEMBER 9, [1939] SATURDAY

[...] On Monday I was in the Jewish Community House, 3 Zeughausstrasse, beside the burned-down and leveled synagogue, to pay my tax and Winter Aid. Considerable activity: The coupons for gingerbread and chocolate were being cut from the food ration cards: in favor of those who have family members in the field. The clothing cards had to be surrendered as well: Jews receive clothing only on special application to the Community. Those were the kinds of small unpleasantnesses that no longer count. Then the party official present wanted to talk to me: We would in any case have informed you in the next few days, you must leave your house by April 1; you can sell it, rent it out, leave it empty: that's your business, only you have to be out; you are entitled to a room. Since your wife is Aryan, you will be allocated two rooms if possible. The man was not at all uncivil; he also completely appreciated the difficulties we shall face, without anyone at all benefiting as a result—the sadistic machine simply rolls over us. [...]

MAY 23, [1942]
SATURDAY AFTERNOON

Yesterday morning the news of the death of Ernst Kreidl, in the afternoon the long-expected house search. Essentially I was once again the innocent. I left at quarter to five (very reluctantly) to visit Steinitz once again—the usual conversations, [...] the dreaded wife behaved tolerably—I came back at half-past seven. The raiding squad had appeared here at five and departed shortly before my return. First of all, I saw the chaos on the ground floor through the open front door. Friedheim showed me the side of his neck and chin, black and blue from blows; he complained of a kick to his body that struck a hernia scar. Frau Kreidl and Frau Pick had also been beaten. In our rooms, I found Eva, who was completely calm. Everything had gone according to the familiar pattern. "You're Aryan?—You Jew's whore, why did you marry the Jew? In the Talmud it says: 'To us every non-Jewish woman is a whore'

. . ." She was sent downstairs, where she got a couple of slaps—"stage slaps rather than anything serious," she said, whereas Ida Kreidl, for her part, complained of ringing in her ears. But they repeatedly spat in Eva's face and on her head. In our apartment—and likewise in that of Frau Voss, who like myself arrived after the event, I found exactly the same chaos, the bestial devastation by cruel, drunken apes, which I have often heard described, but the reality of which nevertheless appeared monstrous. Even now we are still sitting in this chaos, which has hardly been cleared at all. Contents of cupboards, drawers, shelves of the desk, all over the floor. Torn playing cards, powder, pieces of sugar, individual pills, contents of a sewing box strewn among them and stamped on: needles, buttons, shards of smashed Christmas decorations, pastilles, tablets, cigarette papers, Eva's clothes, clean linen, hats, shreds of paper—all mixed up. In the bedroom, the space between beds and wardrobes, the beds themselves were strewn with things. It is impossible to ascertain what has been stolen, what destroyed, what arbitrarily hidden, what overlooked. [. . .]

MAY 27, [1942]
WEDNESDAY MIDDAY

[. . .] This afternoon Eva is going to Pirna to fetch some money. I shall give her the diary pages of the last few weeks to take with her. After the house search, I found several books, which had been taken off the shelf, lying on the desk. If one of them had been the Greek dictionary, if the manuscript pages had fallen out and had thus aroused suspicion, it would undoubtedly have meant my death. One is murdered for lesser misdemeanors. [. . .] So these parts will go today. But I shall go on writing. That is *my* heroism. I will bear witness, precise witness!

APRIL 2, [1944]
SUNDAY AFTERNOON

[. . .] Last Saturday, a young woman worker, whose machine had broken down, was assigned to me as assistant. She was immediately friendly, tried to begin a conversation. "Things may take a turn yet." Since I did not react, she repeated it several times. Then: Her husband had fallen at Orel; he had been a good man, a bricklayer; later they had wanted to build their own house, in Dölzschen; she herself had already been inside once for a political offense; our fate "was breaking her heart."...If she goes to the cinema, she avoids the newsreel—"every dead man is my husband." When she left, she pressed my hand, something very unusual among the workers in the factory, and toward us almost a case of race defilement. Since then I see the woman only occasionally at her distant workplace. Then we nod surreptitiously to one another. It was quite similar with Frau Loewe, who works in the printing shop on the first floor. Taken individually, 99 percent of the male and female workers are undoubtedly more or less extremely anti-Nazi, well-disposed to the Jews, opposed to the war, weary of tyranny,... but fear of the 1 percent loyal to the regime, fear of prison, ax, and bullet binds them. [...]

APRIL 8, [1944] SATURDAY
TOWARD EVENING

[...] Conversation with Stühler senior: "I shall bear witness."—"The things you write down, everybody knows, and the big things, Kiev, Minsk, etc., you know nothing about."—"It's not the big things that are important to me, but the everyday life of tyranny, which gets forgotten. A thousand mosquito bites are worse than a blow to the head. I observe, note down the mosquito bites ..." Stühler, a little later: "I once read that fear of something is worse than the event itself. How I dreaded the house search. And when the Gestapo came, I was quite cold and defiant. And how our food tasted afterward! All the good things, which we had hidden and they had not found."—"You see, I'm going to note that down!" [...]

For Discussion

1. What distinction is Klemperer drawing between his diary and history when he says, "I am not writing a history"? (137)

2. Why does remembering the school episode convince Klemperer that the Nazis' claim to express "the true opinion of the German people" is justified? (141)

3. Why does Klemperer say that once he has lost his "inner sense of belonging," it cannot be restored, even if the government were to change? (141)

4. Why does the Nazi government preface each "new atrocity" with the phrase "it is in accordance with the healthy sense of justice of the people"? (143)

5. After having some of his ration coupons taken away, why does Klemperer say that "those were the kinds of small unpleasantnesses that no longer count"? (144)

6. After noting that the party official who tells him that he must leave his house was "not at all uncivil" and "completely appreciated the difficulties we shall face," why does Klemperer then conclude that "the sadistic machine simply rolls over us"? (144)

7. Why does Klemperer believe that giving evidence by continuing to write his diary is worth risking death?

8. Why does Klemperer tell Stühler that it is the "everyday life of tyranny" that "gets forgotten"? Why does he feel that "a thousand mosquito bites are worse than a blow to the head"? (146)

9. What does Klemperer fear most?

For Further Reflection

1. Why do people feel compelled to record their experience of terrible events?

2. How important to your identity is your sense of belonging to your country?

3. By staying in Nazi Germany and practicing only quiet resistance (i.e., keeping his diary), do Klemperer and his wife "belong to this band of slaves," as Eva puts it?

For Research

1. What did the National Socialists promise the German people in order to gain such widespread support?

2. Research the Nuremburg Laws of 1935. How did they affect the daily lives of Jews in Germany?

3. Is it likely Victor and Eva Klemperer would have been able to leave Germany in 1938? How long were the borders open? How many people left, under what circumstances did they leave, and when was it too late to leave?

Universal Declaration
of Human Rights

*In December 1948, the General Assembly of the United Nations
adopted the* UNIVERSAL DECLARATION OF HUMAN
RIGHTS —*the first document intended to set a standard for
basic rights that should be respected by all nations. Following World War II and the realization of the full extent of the
Holocaust, national leaders felt the need to articulate an international understanding of human rights. Eleanor Roosevelt
(1884–1962), widow of U.S. President Franklin D. Roosevelt,
was unanimously elected chair of the UN Commission on Human
Rights and also chaired the committee that drafted the Universal Declaration. Though the Declaration was passed without a
dissenting vote, its provisions are legally binding only for those
countries that have signed covenants covering specific portions
of it. While the Declaration does not have the force of international law, the UN Commission on Human Rights meets each
year to evaluate countries' observance of human rights and to
issue statements against offenders. The Declaration has also
inspired people throughout the world in the struggle for freedom.
The activists who successfully opposed hard-line communist
rule in Eastern Europe and the practice of apartheid in South
Africa used the Universal Declaration of Human Rights as part
of their arguments for change.*

By what authority do the framers of this doc-

Universal Declaration of Human Rights

Adopted without dissent December 10, 1948, by the General Assembly of the United Nations. (Forty-eight countries voted in favor of the resolution. Eight countries abstained: Byelorussian SSR, Czechoslovakia, Poland, Saudi Arabia, Ukrainian SSR, Union of South Africa, USSR, Yugoslavia.)

PREAMBLE

Whereas recognition of the inherent dignity and of the equal and inalienable rights of all members of the human family is the foundation of freedom, justice, and peace in the world,

Whereas disregard and contempt for human rights have resulted in barbarous acts which have outraged the conscience of mankind, and the advent of a world in which human beings shall enjoy freedom of speech and belief and freedom from fear and want has been proclaimed as the highest aspiration of the common people,

Whereas it is essential, if man is not to be compelled to have recourse, as a last resort, to rebellion against tyranny and oppression, that human rights should be protected by the rule of law,

Whereas it is essential to promote the development of friendly relations between nations,

151

Whereas the peoples of the United Nations have in the Charter reaffirmed their faith in fundamental human rights, in the dignity and worth of the human person, and in the equal rights of men and women, and have determined to promote social progress and better standards of life in larger freedom,

Whereas Member States have pledged themselves to achieve, in cooperation with the United Nations, the promotion of universal respect for and observance of human rights and fundamental freedoms,

Whereas a common understanding of these rights and freedoms is of the greatest importance for the full realization of this pledge,

Now, Therefore,

The General Assembly

proclaims This Universal Declaration of Human Rights

as a common standard of achievement for all peoples and all nations, to the end that every individual and every organ of society, keeping this Declaration constantly in mind, shall strive by teaching and education to promote respect for these rights and freedoms and by progressive measures, national and international, to secure their universal and effective recognition and observance, both among the peoples of Member States themselves and among the peoples of territories under their jurisdiction.

ARTICLE 1

All human beings are born free and equal in dignity and rights. They are endowed with reason and conscience and should act toward one another in a spirit of brotherhood.

ARTICLE 2

Everyone is entitled to all the rights and freedoms set forth in this Declaration, without distinction of any kind, such as race, color, sex, language, religion, political or other opinion, national or social origin, property, birth, or other status. Furthermore, no distinction shall be made on the basis of the political, jurisdictional, or international status of the country or territory to which a person belongs, whether it be independent, trust, non-self-governing, or under any other limitation of sovereignty.

ARTICLE 3

Everyone has the right to life, liberty, and security of person.

ARTICLE 4

No one shall be held in slavery or servitude; slavery and the slave trade shall be prohibited in all their forms.

ARTICLE 5

No one shall be subjected to torture or to cruel, inhuman, or degrading, treatment or punishment.

ARTICLE 6

Everyone has the right to recognition everywhere as a person before the law.

ARTICLE 7

All are equal before the law and are entitled without any discrimination to equal protection of the law. All are entitled to equal protection against any discrimination in violation of this Declaration and against any incitement to such discrimination.

ARTICLE 8

Everyone has the right to an effective remedy by the competent national tribunals for acts violating the fundamental rights granted him by the constitution or by law.

ARTICLE 9

No one shall be subjected to arbitrary arrest, detention, or exile.

ARTICLE 10

Everyone is entitled in full equality to a fair and public hearing by an independent and impartial tribunal, in the determination of his rights and obligations and of any criminal charge against him.

ARTICLE 11

1. Everyone charged with a penal offence has the right to be presumed innocent until proved guilty according to law in a public trial at which he has had all the guarantees necessary for his defence.

2. No one shall be held guilty of any penal offence on account of any act or omission which did not constitute a penal offence, under national or international law, at the time when it was committed. Nor shall a heavier penalty be imposed than the one that was applicable at the time the penal offence was committed.

ARTICLE 12

No one shall be subjected to arbitrary interference with his privacy, family, home, or correspondence nor to attacks upon his honor and reputation. Everyone has the right to the protection of the law against such interference or attacks.

ARTICLE 13

1. Everyone has the right to freedom of movement and residence within the borders of each State.

2. Everyone has the right to leave any country, including his own, and to return to his country.

ARTICLE 14

1. Everyone has the right to seek and to enjoy in other countries asylum from persecution.

2. This right may not be invoked in the case of prosecutions genuinely arising from nonpolitical crimes or from acts contrary to the purposes and principles of the United Nations.

ARTICLE 15

1. Everyone has the right to a nationality.

2. No one shall be arbitrarily deprived of his nationality nor denied the right to change his nationality.

ARTICLE 16

1. Men and women of full age, without any limitation due to race, nationality, or religion, have the right to marry and to found a family. They are entitled to equal rights as to marriage, during marriage and at its dissolution.
2. Marriage shall be entered into only with the free and full consent of the intending spouses.
3. The family is the natural and fundamental group unit of society and is entitled to protection by society and the State.

ARTICLE 17

1. Everyone has the right to own property alone as well as in association with others.
2. No one shall be arbitrarily deprived of his property.

ARTICLE 18

Everyone has the right to freedom of thought, conscience, and religion; this right includes freedom to change his religion or belief, and freedom, either alone or in community with others and in public or private, to manifest his religion or belief in teaching, practice, worship, and observance.

ARTICLE 19

Everyone has the right to freedom of opinion and expression; this right includes freedom to hold opinions without interference and to seek, receive, and impart information and ideas through any media and regardless of frontiers.

ARTICLE 20

1. Everyone has the right to freedom of peaceful assembly and association.
2. No one may be compelled to belong to an association.

ARTICLE 21

1. Everyone has the right to take part in the government of his country, directly or through freely chosen representatives.

2. Everyone has the right of equal access to public service in his country.
3. The will of the people shall be the basis of the authority of government; this will shall be expressed in periodic and genuine elections, which shall be by universal and equal suffrage and shall be held by secret vote or by equivalent free voting procedures.

ARTICLE 22

Everyone, as a member of society, has the right to social security and is entitled to realization, through national effort and international cooperation and in accordance with the organization and resources of each State, of the economic, social, and cultural rights indispensable for his dignity and the free development of his personality.

ARTICLE 23

1. Everyone has the right to work, to free choice of employment, to just and favorable conditions of work, and to protection against unemployment.
2. Everyone, without any discrimination, has the right to equal pay for equal work.
3. Everyone who works has the right to just and favorable remuneration ensuring for himself and his family an existence worthy of human dignity, and supplemented, if necessary by other means of social protection.
4. Everyone has the right to form and to join trade unions for the protection of his interests.

ARTICLE 24

Everyone has the right to rest and leisure, including reasonable limitation of working hours and periodic holidays with pay.

ARTICLE 25

1. Everyone has the right to a standard of living adequate for the health and well-being of himself and of his family, including food, clothing, housing, and medical care and necessary social services, and the right to security in the event of unemployment, sickness, disability, widowhood, old age, or other lack of livelihood in circumstances beyond his control.

2. Motherhood and childhood are entitled to special care and assistance. All children, whether born in or out of wedlock, shall enjoy the same social protection.

ARTICLE 26

1. Everyone has the right to education. Education shall be free, at least in the elementary and fundamental stages. Elementary education shall be compulsory. Technical and professional education shall be made generally available, and higher education shall be equally accessible to all on the basis of merit.
2. Education shall be directed to the full development of the human personality and to the strengthening of respect for human rights and fundamental freedoms. It shall promote understanding, tolerance, and friendship among all nations, racial or religious groups, and shall further the activities of the United Nations for the maintenance of peace.
3. Parents have a prior right to choose the kind of education that shall be given to their children.

ARTICLE 27

1. Everyone has the right freely to participate in the cultural life of the community, to enjoy the arts, and to share in scientific advancement and its benefits.
2. Everyone has the right to the protection of the moral and material interests resulting from any scientific, literary, or artistic production of which he is the author.

ARTICLE 28

Everyone is entitled to a social and international order in which the rights and freedoms set forth in this Declaration can be fully realized.

ARTICLE 29

1. Everyone has duties to the community in which alone the free and full development of his personality is possible.

2. In the exercise of his rights and freedoms, everyone shall be subject only to such limitations as are determined by law solely for the purpose of securing due recognition and respect for the rights and freedoms of others and of meeting the just requirements of morality, public order, and the general welfare in a democratic society.
3. These rights and freedoms may in no case be exercised contrary to the purposes and principles of the United Nations.

ARTICLE 30

Nothing in this Declaration may be interpreted as implying for any State, group, or person any right to engage in any activity or to perform any act aimed at the destruction of any of the rights and freedoms set forth herein.

For Discussion

1. On what does the Universal Declaration of Human Rights base its belief in the "inherent dignity and . . . the equal and inalienable rights of all members of the human family"? (151)

2. What is meant by "progressive measures" to secure the recognition and observance of the Declaration's rights and freedoms? (152)

3. What is meant by the "full development of the human personality"? (157)

4. How does the Declaration accommodate the cultural, political, and religious traditions of different groups and nations? (Articles 16, 17, 18, 22, 26) What if a group's religious beliefs conflict with the Declaration?

5. Does Article 28 oblige the international community to participate in the reform or overthrow of governments that do not respect, promote, protect, or recognize these universal human rights?

6. Why does the Declaration put much less emphasis on duties than it does on rights?

7. Why does the Declaration call itself "universal"?

For Further Reflection

1. Is there anything that you would add to or delete from the Declaration?

2. Do you think that every country in the world will eventually agree to recognize and protect a set of basic human rights?

3. At what point, if any, do you think a government's violation of the human rights of its citizens justifies intervention by another country?

For Research

1. Research the process by which the Universal Declaration of Human Rights was written. How was support for the document generated? Who had the most direct hand in its composition?
2. Research opposition in the United States to signing the Declaration. What arguments did the opposition present?
3. Why did eight UN member countries abstain from voting on the resolution to adopt the Declaration?

Harlem [2]

LANGSTON HUGHES (1902–1967)

*Born in Joplin, Missouri, Langston Hughes was raised, following his
parents' divorce, by his mother, stepfather, and grandmother. He published his first poems as a student at a predominantly white high school
in Cleveland, Ohio, where he also had formative encounters with racism.
After spending a year with his father in Mexico City, Hughes went to
New York in 1921 to attend Columbia University. He dropped out after
a year to travel, working odd jobs to support himself and eventually
completing his degree at Lincoln University in 1929. In 1926, Hughes
published his first book of poems,* The Weary Blues, *which placed him at
the forefront of the artistic movement known as the Harlem Renaissance.
The Great Depression and a 1932 visit to the Soviet Union to assist on an
unrealized film project made Hughes sympathetic to socialist and communist ideals, an attitude expressed in the poetry he wrote during the
1930s; but World War II tempered his politics. When he was subpoenaed
in 1953 by the Senate to appear before Joseph McCarthy's subcommittee
investigating "subversive activity," Hughes repudiated his politically
radical writing, damaging his reputation as an activist but enabling his
career to continue. Although he wrote plays, novels, short stories, newspaper columns and essays, Hughes remains best known for his innovative
poetry and its wide-ranging, complex portrayal of black life and culture.
This poem was published in* Montage of a Dream Deferred *in 1951.*

Harlem [2]

What happens to a dream deferred?

Does it dry up
like a raisin in the sun?
Or fester like a sore—
And then run?
Does it stink like rotten meat?
Or crust and sugar over
like a syrupy sweet?

Maybe it just sags
like a heavy load.

Or does it explode?

For Discussion

1. Why doesn't the speaker explain what dream is being deferred?
2. Why does the speaker compare the fate of the dream to different foods?
3. Does the speaker want us to think that all of the answers to the opening question are equally likely to be right?
4. Why does Hughes begin and end the poem with a question? Why is the last line italicized?

For Further Reflection

1. Why do you think this poem spoke so powerfully to people involved in America's black civil rights movement?
2. Do you think this poem could apply to any group of people whose rights have been denied?

For Research

1. Research the Harlem Renaissance. How did it change black America's sense of its political and social prospects?
2. What is the difference between civil rights and human rights?

Survival in Auschwitz

(selection)

PRIMO LEVI (1919–1987)

Born in Turin, Italy, Primo Levi earned a degree in chemistry from the University of Turin in 1941, despite a law passed three years earlier prohibiting higher education for Jews. After working in a pharmaceutical laboratory, Levi joined the anti-Fascist resistance. Arrested by German authorities, he was deported to the concentration camp at Auschwitz in 1944. Levi spent ten months there, working in a rubber factory that was part of the camp. Having fallen ill, he was left behind when the Nazis evacuated the camp ahead of the arrival of Russian forces. After World War II, Levi eventually made his way to Turin and resumed his career as an industrial chemist. Survival in Auschwitz *(or* If This Is a Man*) from which this selection is taken, is Levi's memoir of his experience in the concentration camp; it made him an internationally renowned writer when it was published in 1947. In 1977, he retired from his job managing a chemical factory in Turin to write full-time. In addition to* Survival in Auschwitz, *he wrote several other books in a variety of genres, including* The Periodic Table *(1975),* If Not Now, When? *(1982), and* The Drowned and the Saved *(1986). Though he may have committed suicide, the cause of Levi's death is uncertain. Early one Saturday in 1987, he was found dead at the foot of the staircase in his apartment building. In spite of Levi's serious depression, whether he fell accidentally or deliberately or at all has been much debated.*

Survival in Auschwitz
(selection)

THE GERMAN GOES and we remain silent, although we are a little ashamed of our silence. It is still night and we wonder if the day will ever come. The door opens again, and someone else dressed in stripes comes in. He is different from the others, older, with glasses, a more civilized face, and much less robust. He speaks to us in Italian.

By now we are tired of being amazed. We seem to be watching some mad play, one of those plays in which the witches, the Holy Spirit, and the devil appear. He speaks Italian badly, with a strong foreign accent. He makes a long speech, is very polite, and tries to reply to all our questions. We are at Monowitz, near Auschwitz, in Upper Silesia, a region inhabited by both Poles and Germans. This camp is a work-camp, in German one says *Arbeitslager*; all the prisoners (there are about ten thousand) work in a factory that produces a type of rubber called Buna, so that the camp itself is called Buna.

We will be given shoes and clothes—no, not our own—other shoes, other clothes, like his. We are naked now because we are waiting for the shower and the disinfection, which will take place immediately after the reveille, because one cannot enter the camp without being disinfected.

Certainly there will be work to do, everyone must work here. But there is work, and work: he, for example, acts as doctor. He is a Hungarian doctor who studied in Italy, and he is the dentist of the *Lager*. He has been in the *Lager* for four and a half years (not in this one: Buna has only been open for a year and a half), but we can see that he is still quite well, not very thin. Why is he in the *Lager*? Is he Jewish like us? "No," he says simply, "I am a criminal."

We ask him many questions. He laughs, replies to some and not to others, and it is clear that he avoids certain subjects. He does not speak of the women: he says they are well, that we will see them again soon, but he does not say how or where. Instead he tells us other things, strange and crazy things, perhaps he too is playing with us. Perhaps he is mad—one goes mad in the *Lager*. He says that every Sunday there are concerts and football matches. He says that whoever boxes well can become cook. He says that whoever works well receives prize-coupons with which to buy tobacco and soap. He says that the water is really not drinkable, and that instead a coffee substitute is distributed every day, but generally nobody drinks it as the soup itself is sufficiently watery to quench thirst. We beg him to find us something to drink, but he says he cannot, that he has come to see us secretly, against SS orders, as we still have to be disinfected, and that he must leave at once; he has come because he has a liking for Italians, and because, he says, he "has a little heart." We ask him if there are other Italians in the camp, and he says there are some, a few, he does not know how many, and he at once changes the subject. Meanwhile a bell rang and he immediately hurried off and left us stunned and disconcerted. Some feel refreshed, but I do not. I still think that even this dentist, this incomprehensible person, wanted to amuse himself at our expense, and I do not want to believe a word of what he said.

At the sound of the bell, we can hear the still dark camp waking up. Unexpectedly the water gushes out boiling from the showers—five minutes of bliss; but immediately after, four men (perhaps they are the barbers) burst in yelling and shoving and drive us out, wet and steaming, into the adjoining room, which is freezing; here other shouting people throw at us unrecognizable rags and thrust into our hands a pair of broken-down boots with wooden soles; we have no time to understand, and we already find ourselves in the open, in the blue and icy snow of dawn, barefoot and naked, with all our clothing in our hands, with a hundred yards to run to the next hut. There we are finally allowed to get dressed.

When we finish, everyone remains in his own corner, and we do not dare lift our eyes to look at one another. There is nowhere to look in a mirror, but our appearance stands in front of us, reflected in a hundred livid faces, in a hundred miserable and sordid puppets. We are transformed into the phantoms glimpsed yesterday evening.

Then for the first time, we became aware that our language lacks words to express this offence, the demolition of a man. In a moment, with almost prophetic intuition, the reality was revealed to us: we had reached the bottom. It is not possible to sink lower than this; no human condition is more miserable than this, nor could it conceivably be so. Nothing belongs to us anymore; they have taken away our clothes, our shoes, even our hair; if we speak, they will not listen to us, and if they listen, they will not understand. They will even take away our name: and if we want to keep it, we will have to find ourselves the strength to do so, to manage somehow so that behind the name something of us, of us as we were, still remains.

We know that we will have difficulty in being understood, and this is as it should be. But consider what value, what meaning is enclosed even in the smallest of our daily habits, in the hundred possessions that even the poorest beggar owns: a handkerchief, an old letter, the photo of a cherished person. These things are part of us, almost like limbs of our body; nor is it conceivable that we can be deprived of them in our world, for we immediately find others to substitute the old ones, other objects that are ours in their personification and evocation of our memories.

Imagine now a man who is deprived of everyone he loves, and at the same time of his house, his habits, his clothes, in short, of everything he possesses: he will be a hollow man, reduced to suffering and needs, forgetful of dignity and restraint, for he who loses all often easily loses himself. He will be a man whose life or death can be lightly decided with no sense of human affinity, in the most fortunate of cases, on the basis of a pure judgment of utility. It is in this way that one can understand the double sense of the term *extermination camp*, and it is now clear what we seek to express with the phrase: *to lie on the bottom.*

For Discussion

1. Why does Levi "not want to believe a word" of what the dentist says, thinking that he "wanted to amuse himself at our expense"? (168)
2. After they are dressed, why do the prisoners not want to look at one another?
3. What does Levi mean when he says that the prisoners have been transformed into "phantoms"? (169)
4. Why is the reality of their situation revealed to the prisoners "in a moment, with almost prophetic intuition"? (169)
5. Why does Levi say that the difficulty the prisoners will have in being understood "is as it should be"? (169)
6. What is the double sense that Levi understands in the term *extermination camp*?

For Further Reflection

1. What possessions of yours are particularly meaningful and connected to your identity? What would life be like if you were deprived of them and of the opportunity to choose new ones?

For Research

1. What was the place of Jews in Italian society in the years preceding World War II?
2. Research the routine Levi describes that prisoners had to undergo when they arrived at concentration camps. How did it come to be used? What purposes did it serve?
3. View some video testimony of Holocaust survivors. What does this kind of historical documentation provide that other kinds do not?

Defending Freedom
and Freedom of Speech

LUIS AGUILAR (1926–2008)

In January 1959, Fidel Castro led a revolution that
overthrew Cuba's Batista regime. Castro, who had
trained as a lawyer and who sympathized with the
plight of Cuba's poor, began a guerrilla movement when
other attempts at political change failed. He had been
brought to power by a number of groups, but after the
victory, he forced them all to join the Communist Party
and began systematically silencing dissent. In May
1960, the politically conservative newspaper Diario de
la Marina *was taken over by its workers, abruptly*
ending the paper's criticism of Castro and his govern-
ment. This event led Luis Aguilar, who had attended
law school with Castro and had been named a member
of the Revolutionary Institute of Culture, to publish the
following editorial in the newspaper Prensa Libre. *Two*
days after the editorial appeared, Prensa Libre *was also*
taken over, and a friend in the government encour-
aged Aguilar to leave the country. He immigrated to the
United States and taught Latin American studies
at several universities, including Columbia, Cornell,
and Georgetown where he was professor emeritus.

Defending Freedom
and Freedom of Speech

I thoroughly disagree with what you say,
but I shall defend to the death your right to say it. VOLTAIRE

I want a hundred ideas to germinate in my country and
a hundred buds to sprout. MAO ZEDONG

FREEDOM OF SPEECH, if it is to be real, must be extended to all and not be the prerogative or special gift of anyone. That is the crux of the problem. It is not a question of defending the ideas maintained by the newspaper *Diario de la Marina*. It is a question of defending the *Diario de la Marina*'s right to express its ideas, and the right of thousands of Cuban citizens to read what they think is worth reading. Hard battles have been fought in Cuba on behalf of that freedom of expression and freedom of choice. And it has been said that if one began by persecuting a newspaper for maintaining an idea, he would end up persecuting all ideas. And it has been said that there was a desire for a regime in which there would be room for the newspaper *Hoy*, of the Communists, and the *Diario de la Marina*, of conservative leanings. Despite that, the *Diario de la Marina* has disappeared as a vehicle of thought. And the newspaper *Hoy* remains freer and more firmly established than ever. Evidently the regime has lost its determination to maintain balance.

For those of us who long for full freedom of expression to be crystallized in Cuba once and for all, for those of us who are convinced that in this country of ours union and tolerance among Cubans are essential for carrying forward the purest and most fertile ideals, the ideological death of another newspaper produces a sad and somber echo. For, however it may be presented, the silencing of a public organ of thought or its unconditional enlistment in the government line implies nothing less than the subjugation, by one means or another, of a tenacious critical posture. All the massive propaganda of the government was not enough. There was the voice and there was the argument. And since they did not want or were not able to debate the argument, it was indispensable to choke off the voice. The method is an old one, the results are well known.

Now the time of unanimity is arriving in Cuba, a solid and impenetrable totalitarian unanimity. The same slogan will be repeated by all the organs of news. There will be no disagreeing voices, no possibility of criticism, no public refutations. Control of all the media of expression will facilitate the work of persuasion, collective fear will take charge of the rest. And underneath the sound of the vociferous propaganda, there will remain...the silence. The silence of those who cannot speak. The implicated silence of those who, being able to speak, did not venture to do so.

But it is shouted, the fatherland is in danger. Well then, if it is, let us defend it by making it unattackable both in theory and in practice. Let us wield arms, but also our rights. Let us start by showing the world that here there is a free people, a truly free people, and that here all ideas and attitudes can coexist. Or is it that in order to save our national liberty we must begin by suffocating civil liberties? Or is it that in order to defend our sovereignty we must limit the sovereign rights of the individual? Or is it that in order to demonstrate the justice of our cause we must make common cause with the injustice of totalitarian methods? Would it not be much more beautiful and much more worthy to offer all America the example of a people that makes ready to defend its freedom without impairing the freedom of anyone, without offering even the shade of a pretext to those who suggest that we here are falling into a government of force?

Unfortunately, that does not seem to be the path that has been chosen. Instead of the sane multiplicity of opinions, the formula of a single guide, a single watchword, and common obedience is preferred. This way leads to compulsory unanimity. And then not even those who have remained silent will find shelter in their silence. For unanimity is worse than censorship. Censorship obliges us to hold our own truth silent; unanimity forces us to repeat the truth of others, even though we do not believe it. That is to say, it dissolves our own personalities into a general, monotonous chorus. And there is nothing worse than that for those who do not have the herd instinct.

For Discussion

1. How does Aguilar define "a government of force"? Why does he use the phrase "falling into" to describe how such a government might be established in Cuba? (174)
2. Why does Aguilar believe that freedom of expression is essential for "union and tolerance among Cubans"? (174)
3. Why does Aguilar say that allowing freedom of expression will make Cuba "unattackable both in theory and in practice"? (174)
4. Why does Aguilar use a series of questions to attack the idea that the government must limit freedom of speech in order to protect the country from its enemies?
5. What does Aguilar mean by "the sane multiplicity of opinions"? (175)
6. According to Aguilar, why is unanimity worse than censorship?

For Further Reflection

1. Are there times when freedom of speech for individuals must be limited for the common good?
2. What is the price for expressing unpopular opinions in your community? Are there issues on which you feel pressured to express a particular opinion? If so, what is the source of that pressure?

For Research

1. Research the efforts of Fidel Castro's government to consolidate its power after the overthrow of the Batista government in 1959. How much freedom of expression is allowed in Cuba today?
2. Research the context of the quotations from Mao Zedong and Voltaire with which Aguilar prefaces his essay.
3. Research the facts pertaining to the decline in the number of daily newspapers in the United States between 1900 and 2000. Balancing this trend against other factors, such as the rise of the Internet, do you think freedom of speech increased, decreased, or stayed the same in the United States over the course of the twentieth century?

Letter from Birmingham Jail

MARTIN LUTHER KING JR. (1929–1968)

The leader of the first mass civil rights movement in the United States, Martin Luther King Jr. was born in Atlanta, Georgia. The son and grandson of Baptist preachers, King attended Morehouse College and Crozer Theological Seminary before earning a PhD from Boston University, where he first learned about Gandhi's philosophy of non-violent protest. As a pastor in Montgomery, Alabama, King led a boycott of the city's transit system after Rosa Parks was arrested for refusing to give up her bus seat to a white passenger in 1955. King gained national recognition when Montgomery officials capitulated and desegregated their buses. King formed and led the Southern Christian Leadership Conference, which organized civil rights activities in the South and later throughout the nation. In 1963, King and many of his supporters were jailed for demonstrating against segregated lunch counters and discriminatory hiring practices in Birmingham, Alabama. While in jail, King wrote this letter—addressed to members of the clergy who were critical of him—to explain his actions and his philosophy of non-violence. Later that year, as part of the March on Washington, he delivered his most famous speech, "I have a dream," to over two hundred thousand civil rights demonstrators at the Lincoln Memorial. The attention King brought to the injustices faced by black Americans was instrumental in the passage of the Civil Rights Act of 1964 and the Voting Rights Act of 1965. King was awarded the Nobel Prize for Peace in 1964. Although support for his practices and projects waned in the last years of his life, he had established himself as an inspiring figure in the history of the struggle for equal rights for all. King was assassinated on April 4, 1968, in Memphis, Tennessee.

Letter from
Birmingham Jail

AUTHOR'S NOTE: This response to a published statement by eight fellow clergymen from Alabama (Bishop C. C. J. Carpenter, Bishop Joseph A. Durick, Rabbi Hilton L. Grafman, Bishop Paul Hardin, Bishop Holan B. Harmon, the Reverend George M. Murray, the Reverend Edward V. Rampage, and the Reverend Earl Stallings) was composed under somewhat constricting circumstances. Begun on the margins of the newspaper in which the statement appeared while I was in jail, the letter was continued on scraps of writing paper supplied by a friendly Negro trusty, and concluded on a pad my attorneys were eventually permitted to leave me. Although the text remains in substance unaltered, I have indulged in the author's prerogative of polishing it for publication.

APRIL 16, 1963

My Dear Fellow Clergymen:

While confined here in the Birmingham city jail, I came across your recent statement calling my present activities "unwise and untimely." Seldom do I pause to answer criticism of my work and ideas. If I sought to answer all the criticisms that cross my desk, my secretaries would have little time for anything other than such correspondence in the course of the day, and I would have no time for constructive work. But since I feel that you are men of genuine good will and that your criticisms are sincerely set forth, I want to try to answer your statement in what I hope will be patient and reasonable terms.

I think I should indicate why I am here in Birmingham, since you have been influenced by the view which argues against "outsiders coming in." I have the honor of serving as president of the Southern Christian Leadership Conference, an organization operating in every southern state, with headquarters in Atlanta, Georgia. We have some eighty-five affiliated organizations across the South, and one of them is the Alabama Christian Movement for Human Rights. Frequently we share staff, educational, and financial resources with our affiliates. Several months ago the affiliate here in Birmingham asked us to be on call to engage in a nonviolent direct-action program if such were deemed necessary. We readily consented, and when the hour came we lived up to our promise. So I, along with several members of my staff, am here because I was invited here. I am here because I have organizational ties here.

But more basically, I am in Birmingham because injustice is here. Just as the prophets of the eighth century BC left their villages and carried their "thus saith the Lord" far beyond the boundaries of their home towns, and, just as the Apostle Paul left his village of Tarsus and carried the gospel of Jesus Christ to the far corners of the Greco-Roman world, so am I compelled to carry the gospel of freedom beyond my own hometown. Like Paul, I must constantly respond to the Macedonian call for aid.

Moreover, I am cognizant of the interrelatedness of all communities and states. I cannot sit idly by in Atlanta and not be concerned about what happens in Birmingham. Injustice anywhere is a threat to justice everywhere. We are caught in an inescapable network of mutuality, tied in a single garment of destiny. Whatever affects one directly, affects all indirectly. Never again can we afford to live with the narrow, provincial "outside agitator" idea. Anyone who lives inside the United States can never be considered an outsider anywhere within its bounds.

You deplore the demonstrations taking place in Birmingham. But your statement, I am sorry to say, fails to express a similar concern for the conditions that brought about the demonstrations. I am sure that none of you would want to rest content with the superficial kind of social analysis that deals merely with effects and does not grapple with underlying causes. It is unfortunate that demonstrations are taking place in Birmingham, but it is even more unfortunate that the city's white power structure left the Negro community with no alternative.

In any nonviolent campaign there are four basic steps: collection of the facts to determine whether injustices exist; negotiation; self-purification; and direct action. We have gone through all these steps in Birmingham. There can be no gainsaying the fact that racial injustice engulfs this community. Birmingham is probably the most thoroughly segregated city in the United States. An ugly record of brutality is widely known. Negroes have experienced grossly unjust treatment in the courts. There have been more unsolved bombings of Negro homes and churches in Birmingham than in any other city in the nation. These are the hard brutal facts of the case. On the basis of these conditions, Negro leaders sought to negotiate with the city fathers. But the latter consistently refused to engage in good-faith negotiation.

Then, last September, came the opportunity to talk with leaders of Birmingham's economic community. In the course of the negotiations, certain promises were made by the merchants—for example, to remove the stores' humiliating racial signs. On the basis of these promises, the Reverend Fred Shuttlesworth and the leaders of the Alabama Christian Movement for Human Rights agreed to a moratorium on all demonstrations. As the weeks and months went by, we realized that we were the victims of a broken promise. A few signs, briefly removed, returned; the others remained.

As in so many past experiences, our hopes had been blasted, and the shadow of deep disappointment settled upon us. We had no alternative except to prepare for direct action, whereby we would present our very bodies as a means of laying our case before the conscience of the local and the national community. Mindful of the difficulties involved, we decided to undertake a process of self-purification. We began a series of workshops on nonviolence, and we repeatedly asked ourselves: "Are you able to accept blows without retaliating?" "Are you able to endure the ordeal of jail?" We decided to schedule our direct-action program for the Easter season, realizing that except for Christmas, this is the main shopping period of the year. Knowing that a strong economic-withdrawal program would be the by-product of direct action, we felt that this would be the best time to bring pressure to bear on the merchants for the needed change.

Then it occurred to us that Birmingham's mayoralty election was coming up in March, and we speedily decided to postpone action until after election day. When we discovered that the Commissioner of Public Safety, Eugene "Bull" Connor, had piled up enough votes to be in the runoff, we decided again to postpone action until the day after the runoff so that the demonstrations could not be used to cloud the issues. Like many others, we waited to see Mr. Connor defeated, and to this end we endured postponement after postponement. Having aided in this community need, we felt that our direct-action program could be delayed no longer.

You may well ask "Why direct action? Why sit-ins, marches, and so forth? Isn't negotiation a better path?" You are quite right in calling for negotiation. Indeed, this is the very purpose of direct action. Nonviolent direct action seeks to create such a crisis and foster such a tension that a community which has constantly refused to negotiate is forced to confront the issue. It seeks to so dramatize the issue that it can no longer be ignored. My citing the creation of tension as part of the work of the nonviolent-resister may sound rather shocking. But I must confess that I am not afraid of the word *tension*. I have earnestly opposed violent tension, but there is a type of constructive nonviolent tension which is necessary for growth. Just as Socrates felt that it was necessary to create a tension in the mind so that individuals could rise from the bondage of myths and half-truths to the unfettered realm of creative analysis and objective appraisal, so must we see the need for nonviolent gadflies to create the kind of tension in society that will help men rise from the dark depths of prejudice and racism to the majestic heights of understanding and brotherhood.

The purpose of our direct-action program is to create a situation so crisis-packed that it will inevitably open the door to negotiation. I therefore concur with you in your call for negotiation. Too long has our beloved Southland been bogged down in a tragic effort to live in monologue rather than dialogue.

One of the basic points in your statement is that the action that I and my associates have taken in Birmingham is untimely. Some have asked: "Why didn't you give the new city administration time to act?" The only answer that I can give to this query is that the new Birmingham administration must be prodded about as much as the outgoing one, before it will act. We are sadly mistaken if we feel that the election of Albert Boutwell as mayor will bring the millennium to Birmingham. While Mr. Boutwell is a much more gentle person than Mr. Connor, they are both segregationists, dedicated to maintenance of the status quo. I have hope that Mr. Boutwell will be reasonable enough to see the futility of massive resistance to desegregation. But he will not see this without pressure from devotees of civil rights. My friends, I must say to you that we have not made a single gain in civil rights without determined legal and nonviolent pressure. Lamentably, it is a historical fact that privileged groups seldom give up their privileges voluntarily. Individuals may see the moral light and voluntarily give up their unjust posture; but, as Reinhold Niebuhr has reminded us, groups tend to be more immoral than individuals.

We know through painful experience that freedom is never voluntarily given by the oppressor; it must be demanded by the oppressed. Frankly, I have yet to engage in a direct-action campaign that was "well-timed" in the view of those who have not suffered unduly from the disease of segregation. For years now I have heard the word "Wait!" It rings in the ear of every Negro with piercing familiarity. This "Wait" has almost always meant "Never." We must come to see, with one of our distinguished jurists, that "justice too long delayed is justice denied."

We have waited for more than 340 years for our constitutional and God-given rights. The nations of Asia and Africa are moving with jetlike speed toward gaining political independence, but we still creep at horse-and-buggy pace toward gaining a cup of coffee at a lunch counter. Perhaps it is easy for those who have never felt the stinging darts of segregation to say, "Wait." But when you have seen vicious mobs lynch your mothers and fathers at will and drown your sisters and brothers at whim; when you have seen hate-filled policemen curse, kick, and even kill your black brothers and sisters; when you see the vast majority of your twenty million Negro brothers smothering in an airtight cage of poverty in the midst of an affluent society; when you suddenly find your tongue twisted and your speech stammering as you seek to explain to your six-year-old daughter why she can't go to the public amusement park that has just been advertised on television, and see tears welling up in her eyes when she is told that Funtown is closed to colored children, and see ominous clouds of inferiority beginning to form in her little mental sky, and see her beginning to distort her personality by developing an unconscious bitterness toward white people; when you have to concoct an answer for a five-year-old son who is asking: "Daddy, why do white people treat colored people so mean?"; when you take a cross-county drive and find it necessary to sleep night after night in the uncomfortable corners of your automobile because no motel will accept you; when you are humiliated day in and day out by nagging signs reading "white" and "colored"; when your first name becomes "nigger," your middle name becomes "boy" (however old you are), and your last name becomes "John," and your wife and mother are never given the respected title "Mrs."; when you are harried by day and haunted by night by the fact that you are a Negro, living constantly at tiptoe stance, never quite knowing what to expect next, and are plagued with inner fears and outer resentments; when you are forever fighting a degenerating sense of "nobodiness"—then you will understand why we find it difficult to wait. There comes a time when the cup of endurance runs over, and men are no longer willing to be plunged into the abyss of despair. I hope, sirs, you can understand our legitimate and unavoidable impatience.

You express a great deal of anxiety over our willingness to break laws. This is certainly a legitimate concern. Since we so diligently urge people to obey the Supreme Court's decision of 1954 outlawing segregation in the public schools, at first glance it may seem rather paradoxical for us consciously to break laws. One may well ask: "How can you advocate breaking some laws and obeying others?" The answer lies in the fact that there are two types of laws: just and unjust. I would be the first to advocate obeying just laws. One has not only a legal but a moral responsibility to obey just laws. Conversely, one has a moral responsibility to disobey unjust laws. I would agree with St. Augustine that "an unjust law is no law at all."

Now, what is the difference between the two? How does one determine whether a law is just or unjust? A just law is a man-made code that squares with the moral law or the law of God. An unjust law is a code that is out of harmony with the moral law. To put it in the terms of St. Thomas Aquinas: An unjust law is a human law that is not rooted in eternal law and natural law. Any law that uplifts human personality is just. Any law that degrades human personality is unjust. All segregation statutes are unjust because segregation distorts the soul and damages the personality. It gives the segregator a false sense of superiority and the segregated a false sense of inferiority. Segregation, to use the terminology of the Jewish philosopher Martin Buber, substitutes an "I-it" relationship for an "I-thou" relationship and ends up relegating persons to the status of things. Hence segregation is not only politically, economically, and sociologically unsound, it is morally wrong and sinful. Paul Tillich has said that sin is separation. Is not segregation an existential expression of man's tragic separation, his awful estrangement, his terrible sinfulness? Thus it is that I can urge men to obey the 1954 decision of the Supreme Court, for it is morally right; and I can urge them to disobey segregation ordinances, for they are morally wrong.

Let us consider a more concrete example of just and unjust laws. An unjust law is a code that a numerical or power majority group compels a minority group to obey but does not make binding on itself. This is *difference* made legal. By the same token, a just law is a code that a majority compels a minority to follow and that it is willing to follow itself. This is *sameness* made legal.

Let me give another explanation. A law is unjust if it is inflicted on a minority that, as a result of being denied the right to vote, had no part in enacting or devising the law. Who can say that the legislature of Alabama which set up that state's segregation laws was democratically elected? Throughout Alabama all sorts of devious methods are used to prevent Negroes from becoming registered voters, and there are some counties in which even though Negroes constitute a majority of the population, not a single Negro is registered. Can any law enacted under such circumstances be considered democratically structured?

Sometimes a law is just on its face and unjust in its application. For instance, I have been arrested on a charge of parading without a permit. Now, there is nothing wrong in having an ordinance which requires a permit for a parade. But such an ordinance becomes unjust when it is used to maintain segregation and to deny citizens the First-Amendment privilege of peaceful assembly and protest.

I hope you are able to see the distinction I am trying to point out. In no sense do I advocate evading or defying the law, as would the rabid segregationist. That would lead to anarchy. One who breaks an unjust law must do so openly, lovingly, and with a willingness to accept the penalty. I submit that an individual who breaks a law that conscience tells him is unjust, and who willingly accepts the penalty of imprisonment in order to arouse the conscience of the community over its injustice, is in reality expressing the highest respect for law.

Of course, there is nothing new about this kind of civil disobedience. It was evidenced sublimely in the refusal of Shadrach, Meshach, and Abednego to obey the laws of Nebuchadnezzar, on the ground that a higher moral law was at stake. It was practiced superbly by the early Christians, who were willing to face hungry lions and the excruciating pain of chopping blocks rather than submit to certain unjust laws of the Roman Empire. To a degree, academic freedom is a reality today because Socrates practiced civil disobedience. In our own nation, the Boston Tea Party represented a massive act of civil disobedience.

We should never forget that everything Adolf Hitler did in Germany was "legal" and everything the Hungarian freedom fighters did in Hungary was "illegal." It was "illegal" to aid and comfort a Jew in Hitler's Germany. Even so, I am sure that, had I lived in Germany at the time, I would have aided and comforted my Jewish brothers. If today I lived in a Communist country where certain principles dear to the Christian faith are suppressed, I would openly advocate disobeying that country's antireligious laws.

I must make two honest confessions to you, my Christian and Jewish brothers. First, I must confess that over the past few years I have been gravely disappointed with the white moderate. I have almost reached the regrettable conclusion that the Negro's great stumbling block in his stride toward freedom is not the White Citizen's Counciler or the Ku Klux Klanner, but the white moderate, who is more devoted to "order" than to justice; who prefers a negative peace which is the absence of tension to a positive peace which is the presence of justice; who constantly says: "I agree with you in the goal you seek, but I cannot agree with your methods of direct action"; who paternalistically believes he can set the timetable for another man's freedom; who lives by a mythical concept of time and who constantly advises the Negro to wait for a "more convenient season." Shallow understanding from people of good will is more frustrating than absolute misunderstanding from people of ill will. Lukewarm acceptance is much more bewildering than outright rejection.

I had hoped that the white moderate would understand that law and order exist for the purpose of establishing justice and that when they fail in this purpose they become the dangerously structured dams that block the flow of social progress. I had hoped that the white moderate would understand that the present tension in the South is a necessary phase of the transition from an obnoxious negative peace, in which the Negro passively accepted his unjust plight, to a substantive and positive peace, in which all men will respect the dignity and worth of human personality. Actually, we who engage in nonviolent direct action are not the creators of tension. We merely bring to the surface the hidden tension that is already alive. We bring it out in the open, where it can be seen and dealt with. Like a boil that can never be cured so long as it is covered up but must be opened with all its ugliness to the natural medicines of air and light, injustice must be exposed, with all the tension its exposure creates, to the light of human conscience and the air of national opinion before it can be cured.

In your statement you assert that our actions, even though peaceful, must be condemned because they precipitate violence. But is this a logical assertion? Isn't this like condemning a robbed man because his possession of money precipitated the evil act of robbery? Isn't this like condemning Socrates because his unswerving commitment to truth and his philosophical inquiries precipitated the act by the misguided populace in which they made him drink hemlock? Isn't this like condemning Jesus because his unique God-consciousness and never-ceasing devotion to God's will precipitated the evil act of crucifixion? We must come to see that, as the federal courts have consistently affirmed, it is wrong to urge an individual to cease his efforts to gain his basic constitutional rights because the quest may precipitate violence. Society must protect the robbed and punish the robber.

I had also hoped that the white moderate would reject the myth concerning time in relation to the struggle for freedom. I have just received a letter from a white brother in Texas. He writes: "All Christians know that the colored people will receive equal rights eventually, but it is possible that you are in too great a religious hurry. It has taken Christianity almost two thousand years to accomplish what it has. The teachings of Christ take time to come to earth." Such an attitude stems from a tragic misconception of time, from the strangely irrational notion that there is something in the very flow of time that will inevitably cure all ills. Actually, time itself is neutral; it can be used either destructively or constructively. More and more I feel that the people of ill will have used time much more effectively than have the people of good will. We will have to repent in this generation not merely for the hateful words and actions of the bad people but for the appalling silence of the good people. Human progress never rolls in on wheels of inevitability; it comes through the tireless efforts of men willing to be coworkers with God, and without this hard work, time itself becomes an ally of the forces of social stagnation. We must use time creatively, in the knowledge that the time is always ripe to do right. Now is the time to make real the promise of democracy and transform our pending national elegy into a creative psalm of brotherhood. Now is the time to lift our national policy from the quicksand of racial injustice to the solid rock of human dignity.

You speak of our activity in Birmingham as extreme. At first I was rather disappointed that fellow clergymen would see my nonviolent efforts as those of an extremist. I began thinking about the fact that I stand in the middle of two opposing forces in the Negro community. One is a force of complacency, made up in part of Negroes who, as a result of long years of oppression, are so drained of self-respect and a sense of "somebodiness" that they have adjusted to segregation; and in part of a few middle-class Negroes who, because of a degree of academic and economic security and because in some ways they profit by segregation, have become insensitive to the problems of the masses. The other force is one of bitterness and hatred, and it comes perilously close to advocating violence. It is expressed in the various black nationalist groups that are springing up across the nation, the largest and best-known being Elijah Muhammad's Muslim movement. Nourished by the Negro's frustration over the continued existence of racial discrimination, this movement is made up of people who have lost faith in America, who have absolutely repudiated Christianity, and who have concluded that the white man is an incorrigible "devil."

I have tried to stand between these two forces, saying that we need emulate neither the "do-nothingism" of the complacent nor the hatred and despair of the black nationalist. For there is the more excellent way of love and non-violent protest. I am grateful to God that, through the influence of the Negro church, the way of nonviolence became an integral part of our struggle.

If this philosophy had not emerged, by now many streets of the South would, I am convinced, be flowing with blood. And I am further convinced that if our white brothers dismiss as "rabble-rousers" and "outside agitators" those of us who employ nonviolent direct action, and if they refuse to support our nonviolent efforts, millions of Negroes will, out of frustration and despair, seek solace and security in black-nationalist ideologies—a development that would inevitably lead to a frightening racial nightmare.

Oppressed people cannot remain oppressed forever. The yearning for freedom eventually manifests itself, and that is what has happened to the American Negro. Something within has reminded him of his birthright of freedom, and something without has reminded him that it can be gained. Consciously or unconsciously, he has been caught up by the Zeitgeist, and with his black brothers of Africa and his brown and yellow brothers of Asia, South America, and the Caribbean, the United States Negro is moving with a sense of great urgency toward the promised land of racial justice. If one recognizes this vital urge that has engulfed the Negro community, one should readily understand why public demonstrations are taking place. The Negro has many pent-up resentments and latent frustrations, and he must release them. So let him march; let him make prayer pilgrimages to the city hall; let him go on freedom rides—and try to understand why he must do so. If his repressed emotions are not released in nonviolent ways, they will seek expression through violence; this is not a threat but a fact of history.

So I have not said to my people: "Get rid of your discontent." Rather, I have tried to say that this normal and healthy discontent can be channeled into the creative outlet of nonviolent direct action. And now this approach is being termed extremist.

But though I was initially disappointed at being categorized as an extremist, as I continued to think about the matter I gradually gained a measure of satisfaction from the label. Was not Jesus an extremist for love: "Love your enemies, bless them that curse you, do good to them that hate you, and pray for them which despitefully use you, and persecute you." Was not Amos an extremist for justice: "Let justice roll down like waters and righteousness like an ever-flowing stream." Was not Paul an extremist for the Christian gospel: "I bear in my body the marks of the Lord Jesus." Was not Martin Luther an extremist: "Here I stand; I cannot do otherwise, so help me God." And John Bunyan: "I will stay in jail to the end of my days before I make a butchery of my conscience." And Abraham Lincoln: "This nation cannot survive half slave and half free." And Thomas Jefferson: "We hold these truths to be self-evident, that all men are created equal. . . ." So the question is not whether we will be extremists, but what kind of extremists we will be. Will we be extremists for hate or for love? Will we be extremists for the preservation of injustice or for the extension of justice? In that dramatic scene on Calvary's hill three men were crucified. We must never forget that all three were crucified for the same crime—the crime of extremism. Two were extremists for immorality, and thus fell below their environment. The other, Jesus Christ, was an extremist for love, truth, and goodness, and thereby rose above his environment. Perhaps the South, the nation, and the world are in dire need of creative extremists.

I had hoped that the white moderate would see this need. Perhaps I was too optimistic; perhaps I expected too much. I suppose I should have realized that few members of the oppressor race can understand the deep groans and passionate yearnings of the oppressed race, and still fewer have the vision to see that injustice must be rooted out by strong, persistent, and determined action. I am thankful, however, that some of our white brothers in the South have grasped the meaning of this social revolution and committed themselves to it. They are still too few in quantity, but they are big in quality. Some—such as Ralph McGill, Lillian Smith, Harry Golden, James McBride Dabbs, Ann Braden, and Sarah Patton Boyle—have written about our struggle in eloquent and prophetic terms. Others have marched with us down nameless streets of the South. They have languished in filthy, roach-infested jails, suffering the abuse and brutality of policemen who view them as "dirty nigger-lovers." Unlike so many of their moderate brothers and sisters, they have recognized the urgency of the moment and sensed the need for powerful "action" antidotes to combat the disease of segregation.

Let me take note of my other major disappointment. I have been so greatly disappointed with the white church and its leadership. Of course, there are some notable exceptions. I am not unmindful of the fact that each of you has taken some significant stands on this issue. I commend you, Reverend Stallings, for your Christian stand on this past Sunday, in welcoming Negroes to your worship service on a nonsegregated basis. I commend the Catholic leaders of this state for integrating Spring Hill College several years ago.

But despite these notable exceptions, I must honestly reiterate that I have been disappointed with the church. I do not say this as one of those negative critics who can always find something wrong with the church. I say this as a minister of the gospel, who loves the church; who was nurtured in its bosom; who has been sustained by its spiritual blessings and who will remain true to it as long as the cord of life shall lengthen.

When I was suddenly catapulted into the leadership of the bus protest in Montgomery, Alabama, a few years ago, I felt we would be supported by the white church. I felt that the white ministers, priests, and rabbis of the South would be among our strongest allies. Instead, some have been outright opponents, refusing to understand the freedom movement and misrepresenting its leaders; all too many others have been more cautious than courageous and have remained silent behind the anesthetizing security of stained-glass windows.

In spite of my shattered dreams, I came to Birmingham with the hope that the white religious leadership of this community would see the justice of our cause and, with deep moral concern, would serve as the channel through which our just grievances could reach the power structure. I had hoped that each of you would understand. But again I have been disappointed.

I have heard numerous southern religious leaders admonish their worshipers to comply with a desegregation decision because it is the law, but I have longed to hear white ministers declare: "Follow this decree because integration is morally right and because the Negro is your brother." In the midst of blatant injustices inflicted upon the Negro, I have watched white churchmen stand on the sideline and mouth pious irrelevancies and sanctimonious trivialities. In the midst of a mighty struggle to rid our nation of racial and economic injustice, I have heard many ministers say: "Those are social issues, with which the gospel has no real concern." And I have watched many churches commit themselves to a completely other-worldly religion which makes a strange, un-Biblical distinction between body and soul, between the sacred and the secular.

I have traveled the length and breadth of Alabama, Mississippi, and all the other southern states. On sweltering summer days and crisp autumn mornings I have looked at the South's beautiful churches with their lofty spires pointing heavenward. I have beheld the impressive outlines of her massive religious-education buildings. Over and over I have found myself asking: "What kind of people worship here? Who is their God? Where were their voices when the lips of Governor Barnett dripped with words of interposition and nullification? Where were they when Governor Wallace gave a clarion call for defiance and hatred? Where were their voices of support when bruised and weary Negro men and women decided to rise from the dark dungeons of complacency to the bright hills of creative protest?"

Yes, these questions are still in my mind. In deep disappointment I have wept over the laxity of the church. But be assured that my tears have been tears of love. There can be no deep disappointment where there is not deep love. Yes, I love the church. How could I do otherwise? I am in the rather unique position of being the son, the grandson, and the great-grandson of preachers. Yes, I see the church as the body of Christ. But, oh! How we have blemished and scarred that body through social neglect and through fear of being nonconformists.

There was a time when the church was very powerful—in the time when the early Christians rejoiced at being deemed worthy to suffer for what they believed. In those days the church was not merely a thermometer that recorded the ideas and principles of popular opinion; it was a thermostat that transformed the mores of society. Whenever the early Christians entered a town, the people in power became disturbed and immediately sought to convict the Christians for being "disturbers of the peace" and "outside agitators." But the Christians pressed on, in the conviction that they were "a colony of heaven," called to obey God rather than man. Small in number, they were big in commitment. They were too God-intoxicated to be "astronomically intimidated." By their effort and example they brought an end to such ancient evils as infanticide and gladiatorial contests.

Things are different now. So often the contemporary church is a weak, ineffectual voice with an uncertain sound. So often it is an archdefender of the status quo. Far from being disturbed by the presence of the church, the power structure of the average community is consoled by the church's silent—and often even vocal—sanction of things as they are.

But the judgment of God is upon the church as never before. If today's church does not recapture the sacrificial spirit of the early church, it will lose its authenticity, forfeit the loyalty of millions, and be dismissed as an irrelevant social club with no meaning for the twentieth century. Every day I meet young people whose disappointment with the church has turned into outright disgust.

Perhaps I have once again been too optimistic. Is organized religion too inextricably bound to the status quo to save our nation and the world? Perhaps I must turn my faith to the inner spiritual church, the church within the church, as the true *ekklesia* and the hope of the world. But again I am thankful to God that some noble souls from the ranks of organized religion have broken loose from the paralyzing chains of conformity and joined us as active partners in the struggle for freedom. They have left their secure congregations and walked the streets of Albany, Georgia, with us. They have gone down the highways of the South on tortuous rides for freedom. Yes, they have gone to jail with us. Some have been dismissed from their churches, have lost the support of their bishops and fellow ministers. But they have acted in the faith that right defeated is stronger than evil triumphant. Their witness has been the spiritual salt that has preserved the true meaning of the gospel in these troubled times. They have carved a tunnel of hope through the dark mountain of disappointment.

I hope the church as a whole will meet the challenge of this decisive hour. But even if the church does not come to the aid of justice, I have no despair about the future. I have no fear about the outcome of our struggle in Birmingham, even if our motives are at present misunderstood. We will reach the goal of freedom in Birmingham and all over the nation, because the goal of America is freedom. Abused and scorned though we may be, our destiny is tied up with America's destiny. Before the pilgrims landed at Plymouth, we were here. Before the pen of Jefferson etched the majestic words of the Declaration of Independence across the pages of history, we were here. For more than two centuries our forebears labored in this country without wages; they made cotton king; they built the homes of their masters while suffering gross injustice and shameful humiliation—and yet out of a bottomless vitality they continued to thrive and develop. If the inexpressible cruelties of slavery could not stop us, the opposition we now face will surely fail. We will win our freedom because the sacred heritage of our nation and the eternal will of God are embodied in our echoing demands.

Before closing I feel impelled to mention one other point in your statement that has troubled me profoundly. You warmly commended the Birmingham police force for keeping "order" and "preventing violence." I doubt that you would have so warmly commended the police force if you had seen its dogs sinking their teeth into unarmed, nonviolent Negroes. I doubt that you would so quickly commend the policemen if you were to observe their ugly and inhumane treatment of Negroes here in the city jail; if you were to watch them push and curse old Negro women and young Negro girls; if you were to see them slap and kick old Negro men and young boys; if you were to observe them as they did on two occasions, refuse to give us food because we wanted to sing our grace together. I cannot join you in your praise of the Birmingham police department.

It is true that the police have exercised a degree of discipline in handling the demonstrators. In this sense they have conducted themselves rather "nonviolently" in public. But for what purpose? To preserve the evil system of segregation. Over the past few years I have consistently preached that nonviolence demands that the means we use must be as pure as the ends we seek. I have tried to make clear that it is wrong to use immoral means to attain moral ends. But now I must affirm that it is just as wrong, or perhaps even more so, to use moral means to preserve immoral ends. Perhaps Mr. Connor and his policemen have been rather nonviolent in public, as was Chief Pritchett in Albany, Georgia, but they have used the moral means of nonviolence to maintain the immoral end of racial injustice. As T. S. Eliot has said: "The last temptation is the greatest treason: To do the right deed for the wrong reason."

I wish you had commended the Negro sit-inners and demonstrators of Birmingham for their sublime courage, their willingness to suffer, and their amazing discipline in the midst of great provocation. One day the South will recognize its real heroes. They will be the James Merediths, with the noble sense of purpose that enables them to face jeering and hostile mobs, and with the agonizing loneliness that characterizes the life of the pioneer. They will be old, oppressed, battered Negro women, symbolized in a seventy-two-year-old woman in Montgomery, Alabama, who rose up with a sense of dignity and with her people decided not to ride segregated buses, and who responded with ungrammatical profundity to one who inquired about her weariness: "My feet is tired, but my soul is at rest." They will be the young high school and college students, the young ministers of the gospel and a host of their elders, courageously and nonviolently sitting in at lunch counters and willingly going to jail for conscience' sake. One day the South will know that when these disinherited children of God sat down at lunch counters, they were in reality standing up for what is best in the American dream and for the most sacred values in our Judaeo-Christian heritage, thereby bringing our nation back to those great wells of democracy which were dug deep by the founding fathers in their formulation of the Constitution and the Declaration of Independence.

Never before have I written so long a letter. I'm afraid it is much too long to take your precious time. I can assure you that it would have been much shorter if I had been writing from a comfortable desk, but what else can one do when he is alone in a narrow jail cell, other than write long letters, think long thoughts, and pray long prayers?

If I have said anything in this letter that overstates the truth and indicates an unreasonable impatience, I beg you to forgive me. If I have said anything that understates the truth and indicates my having a patience that allows me to settle for anything less than brotherhood, I beg God to forgive me.

I hope this letter finds you strong in the faith. I also hope that circumstances will soon make it possible for me to meet each of you, not as an integrationist or a civil-rights leader but as a fellow clergyman and a Christian brother. Let us all hope that the dark clouds of racial prejudice will soon pass away and the deep fog of misunderstanding will be lifted from our fear-drenched communities, and in some not too distant tomorrow the radiant stars of love and brotherhood will shine over our great nation with all their scintillating beauty.

Yours for the cause of Peace and Brotherhood,
Martin Luther King Jr.

For Discussion

1. Why is most of the white community, including the clergy, blind to the justice of King's protest? What does King hope to accomplish by writing his letter?

2. Why does King believe that "injustice anywhere is a threat to justice everywhere"? (180)

3. Why does King find it especially difficult to explain racism to children?

4. Why is King committed to nonviolent direct action?

5. Why does King declare that "one who breaks an unjust law must do so openly, lovingly, and with a willingness to accept the penalty"? (186)

6. Why is King confident that exposing the injustice faced by blacks to "national opinion" will have a positive effect? (187)

7. Why does King compare the actions of the protesters to those of religious leaders and Biblical figures?

For Further Reflection

1. Since 1963, when King wrote his letter, have Americans come to recognize the "real heroes" of the fight for racial equality, as he suggested they would?

2. Is King right that an oppressed people must demand their rights because "freedom is never voluntarily given by the oppressor"?

3. Do you agree with the distinction King draws between just and unjust laws?

4. How prevalent is racism in the United States today?

For Research

1. Research the Montgomery bus boycott and its effect on the civil rights movement.

2. Research the events in Birmingham, Alabama, in 1963 that helped to raise awareness of the struggle for civil rights and galvanize the movement.

3. Research the Civil Rights Act of 1964 and the Voting Rights Act of 1965. To what extent were they initiated by King's activities?

4. Research *Plessy v. Ferguson* and *Brown v. Board of Education of Topeka Kansas*, two important civil rights Supreme Court cases. What were their roles in the history of equal rights for black Americans?

The Rivonia Trial:
Second Court Statement

(selection)

NELSON MANDELA (1918–)

Nelson Mandela was born in a village near Umata in Transkei, South Africa, where his father was councilor to a chief of the Tembu tribe. Mandela attended a local mission school, University College of Fort Hare, and University of Witwatersrand, where he earned a law degree. He joined the African National Congress (ANC) in 1944, helped found the ANC Youth League, and became engaged in resistance against the South African government's policies of apartheid. In 1952, Mandela started the first black law practice with Oliver Tambo. Throughout the 1950s, Mandela was banned, arrested, and imprisoned. After the Sharpeville Massacre in 1960—when police fired submachine guns at black protesters, killing about seventy people and wounding many more—the ANC itself was banned. In 1963, Mandela was charged with sabotage. Instead of mounting a legal defense, Mandela chose to simply make a statement—from which this selection is taken—at what became known as the Rivonia Trial (for the town where the arrests were made that led to the charges). He made this statement at the opening of the case for the defense in April 1964. Mandela was convicted, sentenced to life in prison, and confined at first to a maximum security prison on a small island off the South African coast near Cape Town. In prison, Mandela educated the other prisoners and upheld his principles, becoming the symbolic leader of the worldwide antiapartheid movement. Mandela was released on February 11, 1990. The next year, he was elected president of the African National Congress. He was awarded the 1993 Nobel Prize for Peace (along with then-president F. W. de Klerk), and served as the first democratically elected president of South Africa from 1994 to 1999.

The Rivonia Trial:
Second Court Statement[1]
(selection)

I AM THE FIRST ACCUSED.

I hold a bachelor's degree in arts and practised as an attorney in Johannesburg for a number of years in partnership with Oliver Tambo. I am a convicted prisoner serving five years for leaving the country without a permit and for inciting people to go on strike at the end of May 1961.

At the outset, I want to say that the suggestion made by the State in its opening that the struggle in South Africa is under the influence of foreigners or communists is wholly incorrect. I have done whatever I did, both as an individual and as a leader of my people, because of my experience in South Africa and my own proudly felt African background, and not because of what any outsider might have said.

In my youth in the Transkei, I listened to the elders of my tribe telling stories of the old days. Amongst the tales they related to me were those of wars fought by our ancestors in defence of the fatherland. The names of Dingane and Bambata, Hintsa and Makana, Squngthi and Dalasile, Moshoeshoe and Sekhukhuni, were praised as the glory of the entire African

---

1. [It is customary to omit sections of this statement which deal in detail with points of evidence made by some witnesses. These were clearly important at the time in the trial, but have little meaning for readers today, and only serve to lessen the impact of the statement as a whole. EDS.]

nation. I hoped then that life might offer me the opportunity to serve my people and make my own humble contribution to their freedom struggle. This is what has motivated me in all that I have done in relation to the charges made against me in this case.

Having said this, I must deal immediately and at some length with the question of violence. Some of the things so far told to the court are true, and some are untrue. I do not, however, deny that I planned sabotage. I did not plan it in a spirit of recklessness, nor because I have any love of violence. I planned it as a result of a calm and sober assessment of the political situation that had arisen after many years of tyranny, exploitation, and oppression of my people by the whites.

I admit immediately that I was one of the persons who helped to form Umkhonto we Sizwe, and that I played a prominent role in its affairs until I was arrested in August 1962....

I deny that Umkhonto was responsible for a number of acts which clearly fell outside the policy of the organisation, and which have been charged in the indictment against us. I do not know what justification there was for these acts, but to demonstrate that they could not have been authorised by Umkhonto, I want to refer briefly to the roots and policy of the organisation.

I have already mentioned that I was one of the persons who helped to form Umkhonto. I, and the others who started the organisation, did so for two reasons. Firstly, we believed that as a result of government policy, violence by the African people had become inevitable, and that unless responsible leadership was given to canalise and control the feelings of our people, there would be outbreaks of terrorism which would produce an intensity of bitterness and hostility between the various races of this country which is not produced even by war. Secondly, we felt that without violence there would be no way open to the African people to succeed in their struggle against the principle of white supremacy. All lawful modes of expressing opposition to this principle had been closed by legislation, and we were placed in a position in which we had either to accept a permanent state of inferiority or to defy the government. We chose to defy the law. We first broke the law in a way which avoided any recourse to violence; when this form was legislated against, and then the government resorted to a show of force to crush opposition to its policies, only then did we decide to answer violence with violence.

But the violence which we chose to adopt was not terrorism. We who formed Umkhonto were all members of the African National Congress and had behind us the ANC tradition of nonviolence and negotiation as a means of solving political disputes. We believe that South Africa belongs to all the people who live in it, and not to one group, be it black or white. We did not want an interracial war, and tried to avoid it to the last minute. If the court is in doubt about this, it will be seen that the whole history of our organisation bears out what I have said, and what I will subsequently say, when I describe the tactics which Umkhonto decided to adopt. I want, therefore, to say something about the African National Congress.

The African National Congress was formed in 1912 to defend the rights of the African people which had been seriously curtailed by the South Africa Act, and which were then being threatened by the Native Land Act. For thirty-seven years—that is, until 1949—it adhered strictly to a constitutional struggle. It put forward demands and resolutions; it sent delegations to the government in the belief that African grievances could be settled through peaceful discussion and that Africans could advance gradually to full political rights. But white governments remained unmoved, and the rights of Africans became less instead of becoming greater. In the words of my leader, Chief Lutuli, who became president of the ANC in 1952, and who was later awarded the Nobel Peace Prize: "Who will deny that thirty years of my life have been spent knocking in vain, patiently, moderately, and modestly at a closed and barred door? What have been the fruits of moderation? The past thirty years have seen the greatest number of laws restricting our rights and progress, until today we have reached a stage where we have almost no rights at all."

Even after 1949, the ANC remained determined to avoid violence. At this time, however, there was a change from the strictly constitutional means of protest which had been employed in the past. The change was embodied in a decision which was taken to protest against apartheid legislation by peaceful, but unlawful, demonstrations against certain laws. Pursuant to this policy, the ANC launched the Defiance Campaign, in which I was placed in charge of volunteers. This campaign was based on the principles of passive resistance. More than 8,500 people defied apartheid laws and went to jail. Yet there was not a single instance of violence in the course of this campaign on the part of any defier. I and nineteen colleagues were convicted for the role which we played in organising the campaign, but our sentences were suspended mainly because the judge found that discipline and nonviolence had been stressed throughout. This was the time when the volunteer section of the ANC was established, and when the word *Amadelakufa*[1] was first used: this was the time when the volunteers were asked to take a pledge to uphold certain principles. Evidence dealing with volunteers and their pledges has been introduced into this case, but completely out of context. The volunteers were not, and are not, the soldiers of a black army pledged to fight a civil war against the whites. They were, and are, dedicated workers who are prepared to lead campaigns initiated by the ANC to distribute leaflets, to organise strikes, or do whatever the particular campaign required. They are called volunteers because they volunteer to face the penalties of imprisonment and whipping which are now prescribed by the legislature for such acts.

During the Defiance Campaign, the Public Safety Act and the Criminal Law Amendment Act were passed. These statutes provided harsher penalties for offences committed by way of protests against laws. Despite this, the protests continued and the ANC adhered to its policy of nonviolence. In 1956, 156 leading members of the Congress Alliance, including myself, were arrested on a charge of high treason and charges under the Suppression of Communism Act. The nonviolent policy of the ANC was put in issue by the State, but when the court gave judgement some five years later, it found that the ANC did not have a policy of violence. We were acquitted on all counts, which included a count that the ANC sought to set up a communist state in place of the existing regime. The government has always sought to label all its opponents as communists. This allegation has been repeated in the present case but, as I will show, the ANC is not and never has been a communist organisation.

In 1960, there was the shooting at Sharpeville, which resulted in the proclamation of a state of emergency and the declaration of the ANC as an unlawful organisation. My colleagues and I, after careful consideration, de-

1. [Amadelakufa: those who are prepared to make sacrifices. EDS.]

cided that we would not obey this decree. The African people were not part of the government and did not make the laws by which they were governed. We believed in the words of the Universal Declaration of Human Rights, that "the will of the people shall be the basis of authority of government," and for us to accept the banning was equivalent to accepting the silencing of the Africans for all time. The ANC refused to dissolve, but instead went underground. We believed it was our duty to preserve this organisation, which had been built up with almost fifty years of unremitting toil. I have no doubt that no self-respecting white political organisation would disband itself if declared illegal by a government in which it had no say.

In 1960, the government held a referendum which led to the establishment of the republic. Africans, who constituted approximately 70 percent of the population of South Africa, were not entitled to vote, and were not even consulted about the proposed constitutional change. All of us were apprehensive of our future under the proposed white republic, and a resolution was taken to hold an All-in African Conference to call for a national convention, and to organise mass demonstrations on the eve of the unwanted republic, if the government failed to call the convention. The conference was attended by Africans of various political persuasions. I was the secretary of the conference and undertook to be responsible for organising the national stay-at-home which was subsequently called to coincide with the declaration of the republic. As all strikes by Africans are illegal, the person organising such a strike must avoid arrest. I was chosen to be this person, and consequently I had to leave my home and family and my practise and go into hiding to avoid arrest.

The stay-at-home, in accordance with ANC policy, was to be a peaceful demonstration. Careful instructions were given to organisers and members to avoid any recourse to violence. The government's answer was to introduce newer and harsher laws, to mobilise its armed forces, and to send Saracens,[2] armed vehicles, and soldiers into the townships in a massive show of force designed to intimidate the people. This was an indication that the govern-

---

2. [Saracen armoured vehicles: British-made military troop carriers. EDS.]

ment had decided to rule by force alone, and this decision was a milestone on the road to Umkhonto....

We had no doubt that we had to continue the fight. Anything else would have been abject surrender. Our problem was not whether to fight, but was how to continue the fight. We of the ANC had always stood for a nonracial democracy, and we shrank from any action which might drive the races further apart than they already were. But the hard facts were that fifty years of nonviolence had brought the African people nothing but more and more repressive legislation and fewer and fewer rights. It may not be easy for this court to understand, but it is a fact that for a long time the people had been talking of violence—of the day when they would fight the white man and win back their country—and we, the leaders of the ANC, had nevertheless always prevailed upon them to avoid violence and to pursue peaceful methods. When some of us discussed this in May and June of 1961, it could not be denied that our policy to achieve a nonracial State by nonviolence had achieved nothing, and that our followers were beginning to lose confidence in this policy and were developing disturbing ideas of terrorism.

It must not be forgotten that by this time violence had, in fact, become a feature of the South African political scene. There had been violence in 1957 when the women of Zeerust were ordered to carry passes; there was violence in 1958 with the enforcement of cattle culling in Sekhukhuneland; there was violence in 1959 when the people of Cato Manor protested against pass raids; there was violence in 1960 when the government attempted to impose Bantu Authorities in Pondoland. Thirty-nine Africans died in these disturbances. In 1961, there had been riots in Warmbaths, and all this time the Transkei had been a seething mass of unrest. Each disturbance pointed clearly to the inevitable growth among Africans of the belief that violence was the only way out—it showed that a government which uses force to maintain its rule teaches the oppressed to use force to oppose it. Already small groups had arisen in the urban areas and were spontaneously making plans for violent forms of political struggle. There now arose a danger that these groups would adopt terrorism against Africans, as well as whites, if not properly directed. Particularly disturbing was the type of violence engendered in places such as Zeerust, Sekhukhuneland, and Pondoland amongst

Africans. It was increasingly taking the form, not of struggle against the government—though this is what prompted it—but of civil strife amongst themselves, conducted in such a way that it could not hope to achieve anything other than a loss of life and bitterness.

At the beginning of June 1961, after a long and anxious assessment of the South African situation, I and some colleagues came to the conclusion that, as violence in this country was inevitable, it would be unrealistic and wrong for African leaders to continue preaching peace and nonviolence at a time when the government met our peaceful demands with force.

This conclusion was not easily arrived at. It was only when all else had failed, when all channels of peaceful protest had been barred to us, that the decision was made to embark on violent forms of political struggle, and to form Umkhonto we Sizwe. We did so not because we desired such a course, but solely because the government had left us with no other choice. In the manifesto of Umkhonto, published on 16 December 1961, which is Exhibit AD, we said: "The time comes in the life of any nation when there remain only two choices—submit or fight. That time has now come to South Africa. We shall not submit and we have no choice but to hit back by all means in our power in defence of our people, our future, and our freedom."

This was our feeling in June of 1961 when we decided to press for a change in the policy of the national liberation movement. I can only say that I felt morally obliged to do what I did. . . .

Four forms of violence were possible. There is sabotage, there is guerrilla warfare, there is terrorism, and there is open revolution. We chose to adopt the first method and to exhaust it before taking any other decision.

In the light of our political background, the choice was a logical one. Sabotage did not involve loss of life, and it offered the best hope for future race relations. Bitterness would be kept to a minimum and, if the policy bore fruit, democratic government could become a reality. This is what we felt at the time, and this is what we said in our manifesto (Exhibit AD):

We of Umkhonto we Sizwe have always sought to achieve liberation without bloodshed and civil clash. We hope, even at this late hour, that our first actions will awaken everyone to a realisation of the disastrous situation to which the

Nationalist policy is leading. We hope that we will bring the government and its supporters to their senses before it is too late, so that both the government and its policies can be changed before matters reach the desperate stage of civil war....

Africans want to be paid a living wage. Africans want to perform work which they are capable of doing, and not work which the government declares them to be capable of. Africans want to be allowed to live where they obtain work, and not be endorsed out of an area because they were not born there. Africans want to be allowed to own land in places where they work, and not to be obliged to live in rented houses which they can never call their own. Africans want to be part of the general population, and not confined to living in their own ghettoes. African men want to have their wives and children to live with them where they work, and not be forced into an unnatural existence in men's hostels. African women want to be with their menfolk and not be left permanently widowed in the Reserves. Africans want to be allowed out after eleven o'clock at night and not to be confined to their rooms like little children. Africans want to be allowed to travel in their own country and to seek work where they want to and not where the Labour Bureau tells them to. Africans want a just share in the whole of South Africa; they want security and a stake in society.

Above all, we want equal political rights, because without them our disabilities will be permanent. I know this sounds revolutionary to the whites in this country because the majority of voters will be Africans. This makes the white man fear democracy.

But this fear cannot be allowed to stand in the way of the only solution which will guarantee racial harmony and freedom for all. It is not true that the enfranchisement of all will result in racial domination. Political division, based on colour, is entirely artificial and, when it disappears, so will the domination of one colour group by another. The ANC has spent half a century fighting against racialism. When it triumphs it will not change that policy.

This then is what the ANC is fighting. Their struggle is a truly national one. It is a struggle of the African people, inspired by their own suffering and their own experience. It is a struggle for the right to live.

During my lifetime I have dedicated myself to this struggle of the African people. I have fought against white domination, and I have fought against black domination. I have cherished the ideal of a democratic and free society in which all persons live together in harmony and with equal opportunities. It is an ideal which I hope to live for and to achieve. But if needs be, it is an ideal for which I am prepared to die.

For Discussion

1. Why does Mandela begin by emphasizing the African roots of his belief in human rights?
2. How does Mandela distinguish the violence that Umkhonto adopted from terrorism?
3. According to Mandela, why were the members of the ANC driven to adopt violence?
4. Why does Mandela consider the ANC's struggle "a truly national one"? (208)
5. Is Mandela's statement an admission of guilt or a plea for understanding? Why does he simply make a statement, instead of present evidence in his defense?
6. Why does Mandela conclude his statement with words that speak of racial harmony and freedom for all people? Why does he say that this is an ideal for which he is prepared to die?

For Further Reflection

1. How do you define the term *terrorism*? What makes a violent act an act of terrorism?
2. If a government uses force to oppress some or all of its citizens, are the oppressed justified in using force to resist?

For Research

1. Read the Constitution of the Republic of South Africa, adopted in 1996. How does it address the issues discussed by Mandela in his statement?
2. Research the system of apartheid in South Africa. How were people classified? What rights did different groups have?
3. How did pressure from other countries contribute to the end of apartheid in South Africa?

Letter to
Deng Xiaoping

WEI JINGSHENG (1950–)

Deng Xiaoping, who dominated the Chinese government and Communist Party in the 1980s, at first seemed to support some of the growing demands for democratic reform. Once in power, however, he began arresting and imprisoning activists.

Wei Jingsheng has been called the "father of Chinese democracy." Born in Beijing to committed revolutionary parents a year after the founding of the People's Republic of China, Wei was a loyal Communist until the oppression and injustice he saw during the Cultural Revolution disillusioned him. He began his public career as a dissident in 1978, when he posted an essay demanding democratic change on Democracy Wall, near Tiananmen Square in Beijing. In 1979, he was arrested after posting a second essay and was sentenced to fifteen years in prison. He was first kept on death row and then in solitary confinement for five years; while in prison, several of his teeth fell out, and he developed a weak heart, high blood pressure, and arthritis. Despite the difficulty of getting pen and paper, he wrote many letters to government leaders and his family; when necessary, he wrote on toilet paper. Wei's fame as a political prisoner began to embarrass the Chinese government, and he was released on parole in 1993. He was arrested again six months later for resuming his prodemocracy work. On November 16, 1997, strong international pressure finally brought about Wei's release, but he was not allowed to remain in China. He immediately immigrated to the United States and has continued to write and speak about human rights abuses in China. The Courage to Stand Alone, *a collection of his prison letters from which this letter is taken, was published in 1997.*

Letter to Deng Xiaoping

JULY 6, 1987

Dear Deng Xiaoping:

You might not be able to remember a person you wronged, but it isn't easy for me to forget the one who wronged me. Our situations are very different—you are at the top of a billion people and I am at the very bottom—but life isn't easy for either of us. It's just that I am not the one making your life difficult, while you're the one making it hard for me. Therefore, when things start looking up for you, you might still on occasion remember a person you once wronged. But if my days get better, then perhaps I won't have time to remember all of the people who once wronged me. For the number of people you have wronged and who have wronged me are many.

Even if this letter does manage to make it into your hands, it will most likely have passed through many inspections along the way. All these readers probably had to cover their mouths and stifle their laughter: What a madman! An emperor and a prisoner—how can the two even speak to one another! But that's not actually the case.

Your Excellency Deng, you hold supreme powers, but after eight years of "reform" the results are inflation and an upsurge in popular dissatisfaction; you're cut off from the people and deserted by your followers; you have troubles at home and abroad; and you're so confused and unsure that you're "groping for stones to cross the river." Moreover, there are signs that you haven't made it to the other side yet and are still pacing back and forth along your old path. "Emperor of emperors" and "chairman of the Central Advisory Committee"—such titles do you little good, and the honey-laden words of flattery from abroad don't give you much comfort either! I don't think that your weak points include being taken in by flattery anyway, otherwise you would have an easier conscience by now. Your weakness is that you have great ambition, but you're untalented and small-minded. You certainly wouldn't be happy to hear me say that you're like Yuan Shao in *The Three Kingdoms*, and perhaps your attendants will see to it that you never have to read these words at all. But such a person doesn't really cause much harm to others either, and few people would aspire to be ambitious, untalented, as well as small-minded. Being small-minded but without ambition, like a farmer or a craftsperson, presents no great obstacle either; at worst people might just look down on you. To have ambition but little talent is also not that harmful. The first and last emperors of the Han dynasty and the founding emperors of the Tang and Song dynasties were all ambitious and lacked talent, yet they managed to accomplish great things nevertheless.

It is the people who possess all three of these qualities (one positive, two negative), however, who have never come to any good. Not only is this bad for the individual himself, but it's even worse for the people and society, especially for those who possess little power. On this basis, I no longer place any great hope in the future of China before your death. This isn't because your plans for reform don't have their reason, and it isn't because China is without the social and material conditions for rapid development, but it's because you, a man well into his eighties, are unable to overcome your greatest weaknesses and continue to persecute those who try to put a check on you. It's already too late and, from the look of things, this situation is irreversible. If you feel happy living your days this way, then you're not wise enough to go down in history as either a great sage leader or an infamous despot, but you'll probably end up as one or the other anyway. You couldn't end up mediocre even if you wanted to, I know you're at least up to that level. But which one to choose? Of course you would like to go down in glory, not infamy. But things often depend on your actions, not your choice. Even having good intentions or putting on a good show won't guarantee that your future will turn out as you like!

But Wei What's-His-Name's days are not easy either. I've passed eight years in this prison-within-a-prison. As a result, I've managed to contract a nervous condition, coronary heart disease, stomach problems, and chronic arthritis; I don't know what's going on in the outside world or how my family is. I'm confused and unsure too, but I don't know what stones to grope or even what river to cross, and besides, from all indications there isn't even hope of there being a riverbank on the other side or an old road for me to pace back and forth on. "Human rights pioneer" and "champion of democracy"—such titles do me little good, and the attacks and smears being flung by those "antidemocracy, antireform heroes" don't give me much comfort either. My weak points don't include the self-comforting spirit of an Ah Q, nor do they include the self-condemning spirit of a "capitalist-roader" like yourself, otherwise I'd be able to set my mind at ease a bit more.

My weakness is that I lack great ambitions, but I am not entirely without talent, and I may in fact not be as small-minded as I should be. I don't have just one positive point, nor only two negative ones—but then again, nobody aspires to be this way either. With no ambition, but a few talents, I'm not one of those who can learn to shamelessly flatter others, jockey for position, or undertake other such trivial maneuvers. I often incur the jealousy of others, and yet I'm unable to perform the tricks that might improve my situation. Whether in prison or out, I will always face endless troubles. If back in 1979 I had been a bit more small-minded and not waited at home for your police to come, but had hidden away instead in a place where you couldn't find me or even run away abroad, I don't think it would have been particularly good for you or, indirectly, for the country, but it wouldn't necessarily have been bad for me! Why should I act on behalf of others and the country? It seems that this too is an incurable weakness that is extremely easy for people like yourself to exploit. Just as Mao Zedong was able to take advantage of your "capitalist-roader spirit."

Of course, my optimism had something to do with it as well. It made me believe that you were actually moving toward reform and democracy and that you would show at least a bit of conscience, since I thought you would remember how you yourself suffered when you were once persecuted! But this was my biggest mistake. Admittedly, you Party elders have fought for democracy and freedom ever since your youth, but it has been for yourselves alone; once power came into your hands, you didn't plan to give the people the right to freedom and democracy. Your perspective is not much different from that of an emperor or king, of a Duvalier or Marcos. When others suffer even worse persecution than you ever did, you feel confident that you are justified in taking actions that are "proper and necessary."

During the fascist dictatorship under Mao Zedong, many of you were accused of unwarranted charges. How did you feel then? Did not Mao Zedong and Jiang Qing consider their actions to be "proper and necessary" as well? This is no different from when you feel you have "proper and necessary" grounds to use unwarranted charges to blatantly slander and persecute others. Must we wait until after Deng Xiaoping's death to clear away another "Gang of X" and for another Hu So-and-So to redress mishandled and mistaken cases? Sometimes history too is ambitious but lacking in talent and must pace back and forth along the old road before crossing to the other side of the river.

Of course, just as you yourselves boast, things are no longer the same as they once were. As political prisoners in the past, you generally enjoyed special treatment in prison. If I had been treated in such a way from the beginning, I wouldn't be in my present condition. In passing, please let me remind you: the medical checkup carried out in your prison hospital in late 1979 proves that my health was excellent at the time—there's a record of it in your files. But my current state of health is much worse than most of yours when you were released from prison. If I remember correctly, most of you were either rehabilitated or released on "medical parole." This includes Peng Zhen, Bo Yibo, Wang Guangmei, the late Ding Ling, and many others. Why, then, when I am so ill, is it only appropriate for me to receive "treatment" in prison? I guess this is just another example of how things are different today from the time of the Gang of Four!

Is it possible for one to "recuperate" in prison? What a joke! A few of you probably heard this illogical sort of reasoning before as well! How did you feel then? But now you seem to think it is very reasonable. Not only am I denied the special treatment that you once had, but even if I received it, there would be no way for me to "recuperate" in prison. My health is so poor that I need a great deal of sleep. Actually, all outsiders who come to the Qinghai highlands need more sleep—this is medical fact, not something I made up. I've been saying this for years, but it's ignored, and I still can't sleep well. It's extremely cold here in this region, and people in poor health have even greater trouble bearing it. I've been wasting ink writing about the lack of coal every year since I've been in Qinghai, but the problem still persists. I won't even bother raising any other matters again. My health continues to deteriorate at almost the same rate that the inflation caused by your reforms grows.

I'm complaining and being somewhat disrespectful and you're probably grumbling about how this Wei-What's-His-Name is always criticizing the reforms, and so on and so on. But this is just a habit of mine; I don't pose any real threat. For a long time now I've been learning to be more small-minded and to keep my mouth shut and stay out of national affairs or other people's business. After all, what I do to help others might be bad for me! Why should I harm myself for the sake of others? If you really change, or just pretend to, for better or for worse, it's no concern of mine, I'll stay out of it. I ask only that you actually keep the promises you have made many times and show more respect for human rights. Now that my condition is serious, I should be permitted to recuperate in more suitable conditions in accordance with the law—that is, I should be released on medical parole. As for a review of my case and a dismissal of the mistaken verdict against me, I'm still asking for this, but I've given up hope!

Wei Jingsheng

For Discussion

1. Why does Wei Jingsheng write to Deng Xiaoping?
2. Why does Wei begin his letter by suggesting that his situation is similar to Deng Xiaoping's, saying "life isn't easy for either of us"? (213)
3. Why does Wei refer to himself as "Wei What's-His-Name"?
4. Why does Wei call his inclination to act on behalf of others and the country "an incurable weakness"? (215)
5. Why does Wei admit that he "no longer place[s] any great hope in the future of China" before Deng's death? How much control over China's fate does Wei believe Deng has? (214)
6. What does Wei mean when he says that "sometimes history too is ambitious but lacking in talent"? (216)
7. Why does Wei take such a personal, "disrespectful" tone? (217)
8. Why does Wei assure Deng that his complaints are "just a habit"; and he doesn't "pose any real threat"? (217)
9. At the end of his letter, why does Wei say that he's given up hope that the verdict against him will be dismissed?

For Further Reflection

1. Wei asks, "Why should I harm myself for the sake of others?" In your opinion, under what circumstances should one do so?
2. Are acts of resistance to oppression always heroic, no matter how unlikely they are to have an effect?

For Research

1. Research Deng Xiaoping and his rule. How did his statements and actions change over time? How many people were arrested and imprisoned for their political beliefs during his rule, and how were they treated?
2. Research the life of Wei Jingsheng, including the other letters collected in *The Courage to Stand Alone*. What effect did he have on the struggle for democracy?
3. Research how the Chinese government currently deals with political dissidents.

The Censors

LUISA VALENZUELA (1938–)

Luisa Valenzuela was born in Buenos Aires, Argentina. Her mother was a writer, and Valenzuela grew up in a literary circle that included writers like Jorge Luis Borges. As a journalist, Valenzuela wrote political articles for Argentine newspapers before publishing her first novel, Hay que Sonreír, (translated as Clara: Thirteen Stories and a Novel), in 1966. When Jorge Videla and his military junta overthrew the Argentine government in 1976, Valenzuela left Argentina for the United States, where she taught at Columbia and New York universities. Upon seizing power, Videla began a seven-year reign of terror, dissolving Congress and suspending the constitution in the name of defending the country against communism. Under Videla's direction, thousands of suspected guerrillas and dissidents were "disappeared"—secretly captured, imprisoned, tortured, and usually killed, with their families unable to learn what had happened to them. Estimates by human rights groups have placed the number of los desaparecidos, or "disappeared" persons, as high as thirty thousand. During this time, Valenzuela's fiction explored the violence and corruption at the heart of what became known as the Guerra Sucia, or Dirty War. In 1983, civilian government was restored to Argentina, and many of the military leaders were tried and convicted for human rights violations; however, they were later pardoned by the government. Valenzuela moved back to Buenos Aires in 1989.

The Censors

POOR JUAN! One day they caught him with his guard down before he could even realize that what he had taken to be a stroke of luck was really one of fate's dirty tricks. These things happen the minute you're careless, as one often is. Juancito let happiness—a feeling you can't trust—get the better of him when he received from a confidential source Mariana's new address in Paris and knew that she hadn't forgotten him. Without thinking twice, he sat down at his table and wrote her a letter. The letter. The same one that now keeps his mind off his job during the day and won't let him sleep at night (what had he scrawled, what had he put on that sheet of paper he sent to Mariana?).

Juan knows there won't be a problem with the letter's contents, that it's irreproachable, harmless. But what about the rest? He knows that they examine, sniff, feel, and read between the lines of each and every letter, and check its tiniest comma and most accidental stain. He knows that all letters pass from hand to hand and go through all sorts of tests in the huge censorship offices and that, in the end, very few continue on their way. Usually it takes months, even years, if there aren't any snags; all this time the freedom, maybe even the life, of both sender and receiver is in jeopardy. And that's why Juan's so troubled, thinking that something might happen to Mariana because of his letter. Of all people, Mariana, who must finally feel safe there where she always dreamt about living. But he knows that the *Censor's Secret*

Command operates all over the world and cashes in on the discount in air-fares; there's nothing to stop them from going as far as that obscure Paris neighborhood, kidnapping Mariana, and returning to their cozy homes, certain of having fulfilled their noble mission.

Well, you've got to beat them to the punch, do what everyone tries to do: sabotage the machinery, throw sand in its gears, that is to say get to the bottom of the problem to try to stop it.

This was Juan's sound plan when he, along with many others, applied for a censor's job—not because he had a calling like others or needed a job: no, he applied simply to intercept his own letter, an idea none too original but comforting. He was hired immediately, for each day more and more censors are needed, and no one would bother to check on his references.

Ulterior motives couldn't be overlooked by the *Censorship Division*, but they needn't be too strict with those who applied. They knew how hard it would be for the poor guys to find the letter they wanted and even if they did, what's a letter or two compared to all the others that the new censor would snap up? That's how Juan managed to join the *Post Office's Censorship Division*, with a certain goal in mind.

The building had a festive air on the outside that contrasted with its inner staidness. Little by little, Juan was absorbed by his job, and he felt at peace since he was doing everything he could to retrieve his letter to Mariana. He didn't even worry when, in his first month, he was sent to *Section K*, where envelopes are very carefully screened for explosives.

It's true that on the third day a fellow worker had his right hand blown off by a letter, but the division chief claimed it was sheer negligence on the victim's part. Juan and the other employees were allowed to go back to their work, though feeling less secure. After work, one of them tried to organize a strike to demand higher wages for unhealthy work, but Juan didn't join in; after thinking it over, he reported the man to his superiors and thus he got promoted.

You don't form a habit by doing something once, he told himself as he left his boss's office. And when he was transferred to *Section J*, where letters are carefully checked for poison dust, he felt he had climbed a rung in the ladder.

By working hard, he quickly reached *Section E*, where the job became more interesting, for he could now read and analyze the letters' contents. Here he could even hope to get hold of his letter to Mariana, which, judging by the time that had elapsed, would have gone through the other sections and was probably floating around in this one.

Soon his work became so absorbing that his noble mission blurred in his mind. Day after day he crossed out whole paragraphs in red ink, pitilessly chucking many letters into the censored basket. These were horrible days when he was shocked by the subtle and conniving ways employed by people to pass on subversive messages; his instincts were so sharp that he found behind a simple "the weather's unsettled" or "prices continue to soar" the wavering hand of someone secretly scheming to overthrow the government.

His zeal brought him swift promotion. We don't know if this made him happy. Very few letters reached him in *Section B*—only a handful passed the other hurdles—so he read them over and over again, passed them under a magnifying glass, searched for microdots with an electron microscope, and tuned his sense of smell so that he was beat by the time he made it home. He'd barely manage to warm up his soup, eat some fruit, and fall into bed, satisfied with having done his duty. Only his darling mother worried, but she couldn't get him back on the right track. She'd say, though it wasn't always true: Lola called, she's at the bar with the girls, they miss you, they're waiting for you. Or else she'd leave a bottle of red wine on the table. But Juan wouldn't indulge: any distraction could make him lose his edge, and the perfect censor had to be alert, keen, attentive, and sharp to nab cheats. He had a truly patriotic task, both self-sacrificing and uplifting.

His basket for censored letters became the best fed as well as the most cunning in the whole *Censorship Division*. He was about to congratulate himself for having finally discovered his true mission, when his letter to Mariana reached his hands. Naturally, he censored it without regret. And just as naturally, he couldn't stop them from executing him the following morning, one more victim of his devotion to his work.

For Discussion

1. Why is happiness "a feeling you can't trust"? (223)
2. Why does Juan begin worrying about his letter to Mariana?
3. What is the narrator's attitude toward "Juan's sound plan" of joining the censors? (224)
4. Why do those who run the censorship department not worry about one or two letters compared to "all the others that the new censor would snap up"? (224)
5. Why does Juan become so absorbed in his work that "his noble mission blurred in his mind"? (225)
6. After Juan's swift promotion, why does the narrator say, "We don't know if this made him happy"? (225)
7. Why does Juan come to believe that "he had a truly patriotic task, both self-sacrificing and uplifting"? (225)
8. When his letter to Mariana reaches him, why does Juan "naturally" censor it "without regret"? (225)

For Further Reflection

1. Why do even the most oppressive governments pretend that they act in the people's best interest?
2. Is it possible to reform a corrupt system from within, or will one inevitably be corrupted by the system?
3. Why might a censor enjoy his or her job?

For Research

1. Research the military dictatorships that ruled Argentina in the 1970s and 1980s. Why were their campaigns against dissidents referred to as the Dirty War?

2. Research current efforts to gather information about the fate of "the disappeared"—civilians killed by the military junta that seized power in Argentina in 1976.

3. Research current efforts to prosecute Leopoldo Galtieri, one of Argentina's military leaders during the Dirty War and president of Argentina.

We Say No

EDUARDO GALEANO (1940–)

*Forced into exile by two politically repressive governments, Eduardo
Galeano has become a forceful critic of the exploitation of Latin American people and resources. He was born in Montevideo, Uruguay, and
sold his first political cartoons to a newspaper when he was fourteen
years old. He went on to a career as a journalist, becoming the editor of
the daily paper* Épocha *and the editor-in-chief of the University Press
of Montevideo. When the military overthrew the Uruguayan government in 1973 and forced him to leave the country, Galeano went to
Argentina, where he started the cultural magazine* Crisis. *Three years
later, the Videla military junta took over the Argentine government,
and Galeano was listed as one of those to be killed. He moved to Spain
for several years before returning to Montevideo in 1985 after the res-
torations of civilian rule. Galeano's writing combines the techniques
of fiction, history, and political argument. His best-known work is the
trilogy* Memory of Fire, *a history, in fictional form, of the coloniza-
tion of the Americas. This selection is a speech that Galeano delivered,
in July 1988, at Chile Creates, an international meeting of artists,
scientists, and others who supported democracy in Chile and opposed the
brutal government of dictator Augusto Pinochet. Three months after
the meeting, Pinochet lost a public vote intended to affirm his rule,
beginning his fall from power.*

We Say No

WE HAVE COME from different countries, and we are here—reunited under the generous shade of Pablo Neruda—to join the people of Chile, who say no.

We also say no.

We say no to the praise of money and of death. We say no to a system that assigns prices to people and things, within which he who has the most is hence he who is most worthy, and we say no to a world that spends two million dollars each minute on arms for war, while each minute it kills thirty children with hunger or curable illnesses. The neutron bomb, which saves things and annihilates people, is a perfect symbol of our times. To the murderous system that converts the stars of the night sky into military objectives, the human being is no more than a factor of production and of consumption and an object of use; time, no more than an economic resource; and the entire planet a source of income that must yield up to the last drop of its juice. Poverty is multiplied in order to multiply wealth, and the arms that guard this wealth—the wealth of very few—are multiplied and keep all others on the brink of poverty. Meanwhile, solitude is also multiplied: we say no to a system that neither feeds its people nor loves them, that condemns many to a hunger for food and many more to a hunger for the embrace.

We say no to the lie. The dominant culture, which the mass media irradiates on a universal scale, invites us to confuse the world with a supermarket or a racetrack, where one's fellow man can be merchandise or competition, but never a brother. This culture of lies, which vulgarly speculates with human love in order to extract its appreciation, is in reality a culture of broken bonds: its gods are its winners, the successful masters of money and of power, and its heroes are uniformed "Rambos" who use their influence while applying the Doctrine of National Security. By what it says and what it fails to say, the dominant culture lies when it claims that the poverty of the poor is not a result of the wealth of the wealthy, but rather the daughter of no one, originating in a goat's ear or in the will of God, who created the lazy poor and the donkey. In the same way, the humiliation of some men by others does not necessarily have to motivate shared indignance or scandal, because it belongs to the natural order of things: let us suppose that Latin American dictatorships form part of our exuberant nature and not part of the imperialist system of power.

Disdain betrays history and mutilates the world. The powerful opinion-makers treat us as though we do not exist, or as though we are silly shadows. The colonial inheritance obliges the so-called Third World—populated by third-class people—to accept as its own the memory of the victors who conquered it and to take on the lies of others and use them as its own reality. They reward our obedience, punish our intelligence, and discourage our creative energy. We are opinionated, yet we cannot offer our opinions. We have a right to the echo, not to the voice, and those who rule praise our talent to repeat parrot fashion. We say no: we refuse to accept this mediocrity as our destiny.

We say no to fear. No to the fear of speaking, of doing, of being. Visible colonialism forbids us to speak, to do, to be. Invisible colonialism, more efficient, convinces us that one cannot speak, cannot do, cannot be. Fear disguises itself as realism: to prevent realism from becoming unreal, or so claim the ideologists of impotence, morals must be immoral. Confronted with indignity, misery, lies, and deceit, we have no alternative other than that of resignation. Marked by fatality, we are born irresponsible, violent, stupid, picturesque, and condemned to military bondage. At best, we can aspire to convert ourselves into model prisoners, to be able to conscientiously pay our share of a colossal foreign debt contracted to finance the luxury that humiliates us and the club that beats us.

And within this framework, we say no to the neutrality of the human word. We say no to those who invite us to wash our hands of the crucifixions we witness daily. To the bored fascination of an art that is cold, indifferent, contemplative of its mirrored reflection, we prefer a warm art, one that celebrates the human adventure in the world and participates in this adventure, an art that is incurably enamored and pugnacious. Would beauty be beautiful if it were not just? Would justice be just if it were not beautiful? We say no to the divorce of beauty and justice, because we say yes to the powerful and fertile embrace they share.

As it happens, we are saying no, and by saying no we are saying yes.

By saying no to dictatorships, and no to dictatorships disguised as democracies, we are saying yes to the struggle for true democracy, one that will deny no one bread or the power of speech, and one that will be as beautiful and dangerous as a poem by Neruda or a song by Violeta.

By saying no to the devastating empire of greed, whose center lies in North America, we are saying yes to another possible America, which will be born of the most ancient of American traditions, the communitarian tradition that the Chilean Indians have defended, desperately, defeat after defeat, during the last five centuries.

In saying no to a peace without dignity, we are saying yes to the sacred right of rebellion against injustice and its long history, as long as the history of popular resistance on the long map of Chile. By saying no to the freedom of money, we are saying yes to the freedom of people: a mistreated and wounded freedom, a thousand times defeated as in Chile and, as in Chile, a thousand times arisen.

To say no to the suicidal egotism of the powerful, who have converted the world into a vast barracks, we are saying yes to human solidarity, which gives us a universal sense and confirms the power of a brotherhood that is stronger than all borders and their guardians: the force that invades us, like the music of Chile, and like the wine of Chile, embraces us.

And by saying no to the sad charm of disenchantment, we are saying yes to hope, the famished and crazy and loving and loved hope of Chile, the obstinate hope, like the sons of Chile shattering the night.

For Discussion

1. According to Galeano, why is it that, in addition to poverty and arms, "solitude is also multiplied" by the current world economic system? (231)
2. According to Galeano, what motivates the dominant culture to lie?
3. How does Galeano define "invisible colonialism"? What makes it "more efficient" than "visible colonialism"? (232)
4. Why does Galeano say, "at best, we can aspire to convert ourselves into model prisoners"? (232)
5. Why does Galeano include his views on art with his positions on political and economic issues?
6. Why does Galeano say that "true democracy" will be "beautiful and dangerous"? (233)

For Further Reflection

1. What strengths and weaknesses do you think artists bring to the struggle for human rights?
2. Do you agree with Galeano that the contemporary world places more value on things than people?
3. Do you agree with Galeano that North America is the center of a "devastating empire of greed"?

For Research

1. Research the military coup in Chile led by Augusto Pinochet against the government of President Salvador Allende in 1973.
2. Research the activities of the Chilean National Commission on Truth and Reconciliation, established to investigate Pinochet's regime.
3. Research the protests against globalization during the 1999 meeting of the World Trade Organization in Seattle, Washington.

A Few Remarks

VÁCLAV HAVEL (1936–)

Václav Havel was a key figure in the wave of peaceful revolutions that swept through Eastern Europe beginning in 1989. Born in Prague, Havel was forced to finish high school by taking night courses and working as a laboratory technician because his wealthy family was declared an enemy of Czechoslovakia's Communist government and was stripped of their property. After two years at the Czech University of Technology, he joined the military, where he became interested in drama. Havel took a job as a stagehand in 1959 and began writing plays during a period of increasing liberalization, which culminated in the Prague Spring of 1968 and was crushed by Soviet tanks that August. Subsequently, Havel's plays were banned, and he could only find work in a brewery. His plays include The Garden Party *(1963),* The Memorandum *(1965), and* Largo Desolato *(1985). He wrote an open letter to President Gustav Husák in 1975, for which he was arrested, complaining of the process by which the government instilled just enough fear in its citizens to keep them silent and complacent. In 1977, he and other Czech intellectuals signed a manifesto called Charter 77 that appealed to the government to respect basic human rights. Havel was arrested, tried, and sentenced to four years of hard labor. Havel was one of four primary authors of this selection, "A Few Remarks," which was written in 1989 and signed by an estimated twenty thousand people. Havel and the other three authors—*STANISLAV DEVDRY, JIRI KRIZAN, *and* SASA VONDRA—*were charged with incitement. When the communist regime collapsed later that year in what is known as the Velvet Revolution, Havel was elected president of Czechoslovakia. He then served two five-year terms as president of the Czech Republic after it split from Slovakia in 1992.*

A Few Remarks

THE EVENTS OF EARLY 1989 clearly demonstrate again that the Czecho-slovak leadership, for all its talk of *perestroika* and democratization, is desperately resisting anything that promotes, or even faintly resembles, democracy. The leadership has rejected citizens' petitions and independent initiatives as "acts of coercion." It condemns divergent political opinions as "antisocialist" and "hostile." It breaks up peaceful public assemblies. And it allows the public no say whatsoever in the creation of new laws.

The early months of 1989 also demonstrate, however, that the citizenry is stirring from its lethargy. More and more people now have the courage to express their longing for social change publicly.

The growth of social activity is thus increasingly on a collision course with the inflexibility of the authorities. Social tensions are on the rise, and there is the danger of an open crisis.

None of us wants such a crisis.

We are therefore calling upon the leadership of our country to realize that the time has come for genuine and comprehensive systemic change and, moreover, that such change is possible and can succeed only if preceded by truly free and democratic discussion. A first step toward effecting meaningful change—from rewriting the constitution to reforming the economy—must be a fundamental change in the social climate of our country: it must recover its spirit of freedom, confidence, tolerance, and pluralism.

In our view, this requires:

- the immediate release of all political prisoners;
- ending restrictions on freedom of assembly;
- ending the persecution of independent initiatives and the treatment of such groups as criminal organizations: the government must understand that these initiatives are a natural part of public life and a legitimate expression of its diversity, as indeed the public has perceived them to be. Similarly, no obstacles should be placed in the way of the formation of new civic movements, including independent trade unions, clubs, and associations;
- freeing the media and all cultural activity from all forms of political manipulation and from all censorship. They must be open to a free exchange of ideas, and the existing independent media should be legalized;
- respect for the justified demands of all citizens who are religious;
- the presentation to both experts and the general public, without delay, of all proposed and completed projects that might have permanent effects on the environment of our country and thus affect future generations;
- the initiation of free discussion on not only the events of the 1950s, but also of the Prague Spring, the Warsaw Pact invasion, and the subsequent period of "normalization." It is sad to see that whereas serious discussion of these topics is now possible in the countries that participated in the invasion, this part of our history remains taboo here—because those responsible for Czechoslovakia's decline over the past two decades don't want to relinquish their party and government posts.

Anyone who is in agreement with us is welcome to express their support by adding his or her signature.

We call upon the government not to respond to this appeal in the manner it usually responds to inconvenient opinions; that would be a fatal blow to the hopes that guide us, namely the hope for a genuine dialogue within our society. Such dialogue is the only feasible way out of the blind alley in which Czechoslovakia finds itself today.

For Discussion

1. What do the authors of "A Few Remarks" mean when they refer to "an open crisis"? Who is included in "us" when the authors say that "none of us wants such a crisis"? (237)

2. According to the authors, why is "truly free and democratic discussion" essential before meaningful change can take place? (237)

3. As part of their list of conditions to be met in order to change the future of Czechoslovakia, why do the authors include the discussion of events from the country's past?

4. Why do the authors describe Czechoslovakia's current position as a "blind alley"? (238)

For Further Reflection

1. Faced with a repressive government, is it reasonable to appeal for openness? Is there a value to such an appeal even if it seems hopeless?

2. What do you think inspired so many people (twenty thousand) to sign this statement?

3. Would the United States today meet the conditions demanded by the authors of this statement?

For Research

1. Research the historical events that the authors mention—the Prague Spring, the Warsaw Pact invasion, and the period of "normalization." What happened to Czechoslovakia and its people during these events?

2. Research *perestroika* as the term was used by communist governments in Eastern Europe and the Soviet Union in the 1980s. What led governments to embrace this policy? What did it mean in practice, and what effects did it have?

3. Research the other peaceful revolutions that occurred in Eastern Europe in 1989. Why did they happen over such a short period of time?

Comrades

NADINE GORDIMER (1923–)

Nadine Gordimer is one of the best-known and most cele-brated South African writers, the author of numerous novels and short story collections, and the winner of the 1991 Nobel Prize in Literature. She was born in Springs, a small mining town, and has lived in South Africa all her life. Gordimer published her first story when she was fifteen and her first book of short stories, The Soft Voice of the Serpent *(1952), about fifteen years later. A member of the white middle class, her outspoken criticism of apartheid—the legally enforced system of racial discrimination that kept white South Africans in power—led the government to ban three of her books. "Comrades" was first published in* Harper's *magazine in 1991, two years after South African President F. W. de Klerk publicly admitted apartheid's failure and began moving the country toward open elections. Gordimer is an executive member of the Congress of South African Writers and the vice president of International PEN, a worldwide association of writers that promotes cooperation among writers of all nations and defends free speech.*

Comrades

AS MRS. HATTIE TELFORD pressed the electronic gadget that deactivates the alarm device in her car a group of youngsters came up behind her. Black. But no need to be afraid; this was not a city street. This was a nonracial enclave of learning, a place where tended flowerbeds and trees bearing botanical identification plates civilized the wild reminder of campus guards and dogs. The youngsters, like her, were part of the crowd loosening into dispersion after a university conference on People's Education. They were the people to be educated; she was one of the committee of white and black activists (convenient generic for revolutionaries, leftists, secular and Christian, fellow-travellers and liberals) up on the platform.

—Comrade . . .—She was settling in the driver's seat when one so slight and slim he seemed a figure in profile came up to her window. He drew courage from the friendly lift of the woman's eyebrows above blue eyes, the tilt of her freckled white face:—Comrade, are you going to town?—

No, she was going in the opposite direction, home . . . but quickly, in the spirit of the hall where these young people had been somewhere, somehow present with her (ah no, she with them) stamping and singing Freedom songs, she would take them to the bus station their spokesman named.—Climb aboard!—

The others got in the back, the spokesman beside her. She saw the nervous white of his eyes as he glanced at and away from her. She searched for

243

talk to set them at ease. Questions, of course. Older people always start with questioning young ones. Did they come from Soweto?

They came from Harrismith, Phoneng Location.

She made the calculation: about two hundred kilometres distant. How did they get here? Who told them about the conference?

—We are Youth Congress in Phoneng.—

A delegation. They had come by bus; one of the groups and stragglers who kept arriving long after the conference had started. They had missed, then, the free lunch?

At the back, no one seemed even to be breathing. The spokesman must have had some silent communication with them, some obligation to speak for them created by the journey or by other shared experience in the mysterious bonds of the young—these young.—We are hungry.—And from the back seats was drawn an assent like the suction of air in a compressing silence.

She was silent in response, for the beat of a breath or two. These large gatherings both excited and left her overexposed, open and vulnerable to the rub and twitch of the mass shuffling across rows of seats and loping up the aisles, babies' fudge-brown soft legs waving as their napkins are changed on mothers' laps, little girls with plaited loops on their heads listening like old crones, heavy women swaying to chants, men with fierce, unreadably black faces breaking into harmony tender and deep as they sing to God for his protection of Umkhonto we Sizwe, as people on both sides have always, everywhere, claimed divine protection for their soldiers, their wars. At the end of a day like this she wanted a drink, she wanted the depraved luxury of solitude and quiet in which she would be restored (enriched, oh yes! by the day) to the familiar limits of her own being.

Hungry. Not for iced whisky and feet up. It seemed she had scarcely hesitated: —Look, I live nearby, come back to my house and have something to eat. Then I'll run you into town.—

—That will be very nice. We can be glad for that.—And at the back the tight vacuum relaxed.

They followed her in through the gate, shrinking away from the dog— she assured them he was harmless but he was large, with a fancy collar by which she held him. She trooped them in through the kitchen because that was the way she always entered her house, something she would not have done if they had been adult, her black friends whose sophistication might lead them to believe the choice of entrance was an unthinking historical slight. As she was going to feed them, she took them not into her living room with its sofas and flowers but into her dining room, so that they could sit at table right away. It was a room in confident taste that could afford to be spare: bare floorboards, matching golden wooden ceiling, antique brass chandelier, reed blinds instead of stuffy curtains. An African wooden sculpture represented a lion marvellously released from its matrix in the grain of a Mukwa tree trunk. She pulled up the chairs and left the four young men while she went back to the kitchen to make coffee and see what there was in the refrigerator for sandwiches. They had greeted the maid, in the language she and they shared, on their way through the kitchen, but when the maid and the lady of the house had finished preparing cold meat and bread, and the coffee was ready, she suddenly did not want them to see that the maid waited on her. She herself carried the heavy tray into the dining room.

They are sitting round the table, silent, and there is no impression that they stopped an undertone exchange when they heard her approaching. She doles out plates, cups. They stare at the food but their eyes seem focused on something she can't see; something that overwhelms. She urges them—Just cold meat, I'm afraid, but there's chutney if you like it. . .Milk everybody? . . .Is the coffee too strong? I have a heavy hand, I know. Would anyone like to add some hot water?—

They eat. When she tries to talk to one of the others, he says *Ekskuus?* And she realizes he doesn't understand English, of the white man's languages knows perhaps only a little of that of the Afrikaners in the rural town he comes from. Another gives his name, as if in some delicate acknowledgement of the food.—I'm Shadrack Nsutsha.—She repeats the surname to get it right. But he does not speak again. There is an urgent exchange of eye-language, and the spokesman holds out the emptied sugar bowl to her.—Please.—She hurries to the kitchen and brings it back refilled. They need carbohydrate, they are hungry, they are young, they need it, they burn it up. She is distressed at the inadequacy of the meal and then notices the fruit bowl, her big copper fruit bowl, filled with apples and bananas and perhaps there is a peach or two under the grape leaves with which she likes to complete an edible still life.—Have some fruit. Help yourselves.—

They are stacking their plates and cups, not knowing what they are expected to do with them in this room which is a room where apparently people only eat, do not cook, do not sleep. While they finish the bananas and apples (Shadrack Nsutsha had seen the single peach and quickly got there first) she talks to the spokesman, whose name she has asked for: Dumile. —Are you still at school, Dumile? —Of course he is not at school—*they* are not at school; youngsters their age have not been at school for several years, they are the children growing into young men and women for whom school is a battleground, a place of boycotts and demonstrations, the literacy of political rhetoric, the education of revolt against having to live the life their parents live. They have pompous titles of responsibility beyond child-hood: he is chairman of his branch of the Youth Congress, he was expelled two years ago—for leading a boycott? Throwing stones at the police? Maybe burning the school down? He calls it all—quietly, abstractly, doesn't know many ordinary, concrete words but knows these euphemisms—"political activity." No school for two years? No.—So what have you been able to do with yourself, all that time?—

She isn't giving him a chance to eat his apple. He swallows a large bite, shaking his head on its thin, little-boy neck.—I was inside. Detained from this June for six months.—

She looks round the others.—And you?—

Shadrack seems to nod slightly. The other two look at her. She should know, she should have known, it's a common enough answer from youths like them, their colour. They're not going to be saying they've been selected for the 1st Eleven at cricket or that they're off on a student tour to Europe in the school holidays.

The spokesman, Dumile, tells her he wants to study by correspondence, "get his matric" that he was preparing for two years ago; two years ago when he was still a child, when he didn't have the hair that is now appearing on his face, making him a man, taking away the childhood. In the hesitations, the silences of the table, where there is nervously spilt coffee among plates of banana skins, there grows the certainty that he will never get the papers filled in for the correspondence college, he will never get the two years back. She looks at them all and cannot believe what she knows: that they, suddenly here in her house, will carry the AK-47s they only sing about, now, miming death as they sing. They will have a career of wiring explosives to the undersides of vehicles, they will go away and come back through the bush to dig holes not to plant trees to shade home, but to plant land mines. She can see they have been terribly harmed but cannot believe they could harm. They are wiping their fruit-sticky hands furtively palm against palm.

She breaks the silence; says something, anything.

—How d'you like my lion? Isn't he beautiful? He's made by a Zimbabwean artist, I think the name's Dube.—

But the foolish interruption becomes revelation. Dumile, in his gaze—distant, lingering, speechless this time—reveals what has overwhelmed them. In this room, the space, the expensive antique chandelier, the consciously simple choice of reed blinds, the carved lion: all are on the same level of impact, phenomena undifferentiated, undecipherable. Only the food that fed their hunger was real.

For Discussion

1. Why does the boy who speaks to Hattie address her as "comrade"? (243)

2. Why does Hattie invite the boys to come home with her to have something to eat, even though she would rather be alone?

3. We are told that the boys, when they are about to eat, "seem focused on something she can't see; something that overwhelms" (245). What is it that the boys seem focused on?

4. Why does Hattie ask Dumile if he is in school even though she knows he is not? Why does it start to seem certain that "he will never get the papers filled in for the correspondence college, he will never get the two years back"? (247)

5. Although Hattie knows that the boys "will carry the AK-47s they only sing about," why is it that she "cannot believe what she knows"? Why can she see that "they have been terribly harmed but cannot believe they could harm"? (247)

6. Why does asking Dumile if he likes her carved lion become a revelation to Hattie? What is the revelation?

7. Are Hattie and her guests comrades?

For Further Reflection

1. Is Hattie a good person?

2. If you support the liberation of oppressed peoples, is your support compromised if you do not suffer what they do?

For Research

1. Research the antiapartheid organizations created for South African youth.

2. How were the lives of black South African children shaped by apartheid? How did their educational opportunities compare to those of white South African children? What did they typically do once their formal education ended?

The War
and the Law

MAX FRANKEL (1930–)

Max Frankel was born in Gera, Germany. His father was separated from the family when World War II began, but in 1940 his mother was able to secure last-minute visas to New York for herself and Frankel. After ending up in a Soviet gulag, his father joined them in 1946. Though Frankel couldn't speak English when he arrived in the United States, he developed an interest in journalism when he enrolled at Columbia University, where he edited the student newspaper and became the campus stringer for the New York Times. *He took a job at the* Times *in 1952, first doing night rewrites, then working as a foreign correspondent in Moscow and Cuba. As the paper's Washington bureau chief, he won a Pulitzer Prize in 1973 for his coverage of Richard Nixon's historic trip to China. He edited the* Times *editorial page before serving as executive editor from 1986 to 1994. In 1999, he published a memoir,* The Times of My Life and My Life with the *Times. This selection is an essay Frankel wrote for the* New York Times Magazine *in 1995, not long after the United Nations had established international criminal tribunals to address war atrocities in the former Yugoslavia and Rwanda.*

The War and the Law

WHEN IT STARTED, I was standing on a ticket line, behind my mother, in the giant rib cage that was Leipzig's main railroad station. Suddenly, from a hundred speakers atop the station's girders, Adolf Hitler was screaming blood and thunder: Germany is on the march! It must avenge this dastardly attack!—by Poland's pathetic infantry. Although that speech made me an "enemy alien," in a place where being Jewish was bad enough, I don't remember much else about September 1, 1939, except the satisfaction my mother took whenever in later years she recalled the mumbled comment of the stunned German man in line behind us. "I knew when I saw the synagogues burn," he said, "I knew then that we would some day pay for it."

What I remember all too well is my simultaneous pleasure and despair when they did finally pay for it. I was among the lucky few who escaped from Europe's cauldron. When the war ended, I could celebrate the ruin of Germany and relish the execution of the top Nazis. But having now been thoroughly steeped in American jurisprudence, I could never endorse the pretense that by starting a war, like men in every generation, and murdering civilians, as even the ancient Greeks had done, the Nazis had violated some kind of "law" and were now subject to trial and sentence by a hurriedly conjured court.

There in a Nuremberg dock sat the porcine Hermann Göring and twenty-one other German warlords before four Allied "judges" pretending to weigh the defenses that a pickup team of German lawyers could muster against the massive evidence of Nazi barbarities and aggressions. There was no doubt about that gang's guilt before God and the victors' duty to avenge the Nazis' victims. But the winners were producing a false image of justice, a theater of the absurd, as if the peoples of the world had created a government and passed laws against war and wartime acts of cruelty.

Now I realize that a half century of history has failed to relieve my adolescent concerns. There has been no end of war and barbarism; Nuremberg deterred nothing. And in their frustration, good people continue to pretend that the crimes of war can be punished judicially. New tribunals are being summoned to invoke a nonexistent law against the few barbarians of Bosnia and Rwanda that might be captured by a society lacking a police.

Don't misunderstand: the sins of the Nazis and their contemporary successors are unforgivable and deserve to be avenged. But in an anarchic world where there is no authority to define the crimes of nations or individuals who lead them, those deeds are not *unlawful.* No one has been authorized to write such laws or to appoint judges and prosecutors and to raise the taxes to pay jailers and executioners. In the evolution of human institutions, these are major missing links.

The leading Nazis were tried in Nuremberg for "crimes against peace"—waging a war of aggression; for "war crimes"—abusing prisoners and enemy civilians, and for "crimes against humanity"—inflicting genocidal horrors upon millions of Jews and other undesirables. The indictments were grounded in a postwar agreement among Allied diplomats who realized that they were invoking a retroactive jurisprudence that would surely be unconstitutional in an American court. They justified their creativity by invoking international conventions and protocols. But since none of these prescribed any enforcement mechanisms, there was much straining to cite the "common law" of war and to buttress it with literary and religious allusions. Didn't the Old Testament recognize "war crimes" by forbidding the destruction of fruit-bearing trees in enemy territory? Didn't Homer imply "rules of war" governing the enslavement of conquered peoples and the burial of enemy dead?

Indeed, the fastidious framers of the Nuremberg rules claimed no right to punish nonwar crimes—those committed either *before* September 1939 or *after* V-E Day. Though they proclaimed all nations subject to the same rules in the future, they never addressed the problem of who could punish atrocities committed in peacetime or in undeclared wars. They could thus escape the paradox that one of the Nuremberg judges was hanging Nazis for conduct that both before and after the war was rewarded in his own country with Orders of Stalin.

The extermination, deportation, and torture of entire classes of people has not, even in this century, been a uniquely German or Japanese policy. Only the total defeat of those two peoples rendered their leaders indictable for the "supreme international crime" of aggression. The evidence of their guilt was overwhelming. But the legality of their prosecution struck even their prosecutors as shaky.

As we can see in the case of Bosnia or Rwanda, not even outraged nations elsewhere are disposed to go to war in the service of justice. So the chances are slim that anyone will ever catch up with the major perpetrators of crimes against humanity in those countries. The tribunals that have been convened for them trace their authority to resolutions of the United Nations—a league of nations formed to protect, not to penetrate, the "sovereignty" of its members. If it were otherwise, many of the members, from Argentina to Zaire, would be haled into courts for their crimes against humanity.

It is deplorable that a great many such crimes go unpunished. But even more regrettable is the pretense, over these past fifty years, that the world's nations and their leaders are moving to subject themselves to a regime of supranational law. The ugly truth is that international crime pays. Aggressors walk free if they win the wars they start. Atrocities are customarily cited only against losers. The civilized world cannot prosecute the most heinous crimes without first defeating the perpetrators. It can't defeat them without an army. It can't raise an army without levying taxes. And it can't collect taxes without a parliament or international revenue service.

We are no closer to such a regime than we were at the end of World War II, when E. B. White offered this prescient warning in the *New Yorker*: "These so-called war trials...will be extremely valuable as precedents if they are presented as a preview of the justice that may some day exist, not as an example of the justice that we have on hand....Nobody, not even victors, should forget that when a man hangs from a tree, it doesn't spell justice unless he helped write the law that hanged him."

For Discussion

1. Why does Frankel's mother take such satisfaction in remembering what the man at the station said after Hitler's announcement? What attitude does the man's remark display?
2. What does Frankel mean when he says that massive atrocities committed by nations and their leaders should be "avenged"? (252)
3. According to Frankel, why couldn't the Nuremberg trials render true justice?
4. Why does Frankel consider the "pretense" of international justice "more regrettable" than the fact that many atrocities go unpunished? (253)
5. According to Frankel, why does true justice require that if a man is hanged, he must have helped write the law that hanged him?

For Further Reflection

1. Is a legal system to which the entire world is subject a desirable or reasonable goal?
2. Can a legal system be devised to encompass acts of war?
3. How should crimes like those committed by the Nazis be avenged?
4. Do you agree that "Nuremberg deterred nothing"? Did the trials have any lasting effects, for good or ill?

For Research

1. Research how the Nuremberg Code was written and how the trials were conducted. What effect did they have at the time? How have they influenced later efforts to prosecute human rights violations?
2. Research the International Criminal Court established in 1998. What kinds of authority does it have? What kinds of penalties can it impose?
3. Research another attempt to bring justice to those who have violated human rights on a large scale—for example, in Rwanda, Chile, or the former Yugoslavia.

Safeguard Your Lives

JAN WONG (1952–)

*The death on April 15, 1989 of Hu Yaobang, a high-ranking
member of the Chinese Communist Party who advocated reform,
prompted a mass gathering of students in Beijing's Tiananmen
Square to mourn him. The gathering evolved into a demonstration
advocating a more democratic China. When government officials
refused to meet with students and respond to their demands for
change, the protestors began a hunger strike in the square. They
held the strike during Soviet leader Mikhail Gorbachev's visit to
Beijing, deeply embarrassing the Chinese government. On June
4, 1989, the government used military force to rid Tiananmen
Square of prodemocracy protestors. At least several hundred people
were killed as tanks rolled into the square, firing on or running
over the unarmed protestors, many of whom were university students. The Tiananmen Square protests were the most serious recent
challenge to the Chinese communist state. Journalist Jan Wong
covered these events for the Toronto's* Globe and Mail. *A Canadian
of Chinese descent, she originally went to China in 1972, fully
committed to communism and the Cultural Revolution. After six
years, disillusionment led her to return to the West. This selection
is taken from* Red China Blues, *a memoir about her time in China,
first as a dedicated follower of Mao and later as a journalist.*

Safeguard Your Lives

ON FRIDAY NIGHT, June 2, I stayed up all night to chronicle a ridiculous invasion of six thousand unarmed foot soldiers. Some thought the government was trying to position troops near the square. Others believed it was a last attempt to retake the square without violence. Still others thought the soldiers were under orders to topple the Goddess of Democracy. In any case, the mission failed miserably. I watched as irate citizens upbraided the soldiers who cowered in bushes across from the Beijing Hotel while radioing frantically for instructions.

After sleeping three hours, I gulped down some yogurt and ran out to see what was happening on Saturday. At noon, soldiers fired tear gas on demonstrators who had waylaid an ammunition truck. That afternoon five thousand troops confronted even more demonstrators outside the Great Hall of the People. But except for a beating, or two, the showdown was uneventful. At one point, the two sides—soldiers and protesters—even competed to see who best sang *Without the Communist Party There Would Be No New China*.

The government had lost all credibility. It buzzed the square with military helicopters—and people laughed. It had tried to send in armored personnel carriers—and old ladies lay down in their path. The night before, it had dispatched foot soldiers—and civilians trapped them in the bushes. Many thought the battle of Beijing was over and the people had won. Most expected the army to go home and stop bothering them. Everyone, myself included, forgot one of Mao's most famous quotations: "Political power grows out of the barrel of a gun."

That night around six, on the northeast edge of the city, I spied another military convoy stopped on a road littered with broken glass. The *Globe* didn't publish on Sunday, but by force of habit, I got out of my car and counted eighteen truckloads of soldiers toting AK-47 assault rifles. I noticed their faces. They weren't green recruits but grim-faced, seasoned troops. I also noticed they were no longer wearing canvas running shoes.

"They're wearing boots," I told Jim Abrams, the AP bureau chief, when I called to swap information.

"I know," he said. "The army is coming in from every direction."

It was clear something would happen tonight. Had the government any finesse, it would have aired a trio of James Bond movies, and everyone would have stayed glued to their television sets. Instead, it broadcast this warning: "Do not come into the streets. Do not go to Tiananmen Square. Stay at home to safeguard your lives." The government might as well have issued engraved invitations.

"History will be made tonight," I said melodramatically to [husband] Norman. He was tired of allnighters.

"That's what you said last time," he reminded me. I had said the same thing a week earlier when the AP's John Pomfret put out an urgent bulletin, which turned out to be false, that troops were marching down the Avenue of Eternal Peace clubbing anyone in their path. But Norman grudgingly came along for the second time. On the way, we stopped by the Reuters office, where they were frantically trying to confirm the first death, reportedly at Muxidi, a neighborhood on the far west side of the city. I volunteered to call the Fuxing Hospital in the area. The phone rang and rang, but no one answered, an ominous sign.

I did not know that the massacre had already begun. That Saturday evening, Deng Xiaoping had ordered the army to take the square by using "all necessary measures." At Muxidi, the troops found their way completely blocked by enormous crowds. As they tried to press forward, some in the crowd began stoning the soldiers in the front lines, People's Armed Police troops armed only with truncheons. The People's Armed Police, a huge para-military force that Deng had split off from the PLA in the 1980s, specialized in quelling domestic dissent. Yet their fiberglass helmets cracked under the torrent of stones. Some soldiers were injured. Behind them, their officers, armed with pistols, panicked and began shooting. Behind the People's Armed Police was the 38th Army, toting AK-47s. As all hell broke loose, they also began firing into the dense crowds. Soon soldiers were chasing civilians down alleyways and killing them in cold blood.

Residents screamed curses and hurled dishes and tea cups from their windows. The army units, from the provinces, probably had no idea those buildings housed the Communist Party elite, and raked the apartments with gunfire. Several people died in their homes that night. The nephew of the chief justice of the Supreme Court of China was shot in his own kitchen.

In the confusion, the army even shot some of its own soldiers. Behind the 38th Army was an armored personnel carrier unit belonging to the 27th Army. Driving in the darkness with their hatches down in an unfamiliar city, they inadvertently crushed to death soldiers from the 38th Army.

Norman and I got to the Beijing Hotel around 11 PM, just as several armored personnel carriers whizzed by. So as not to advertise my presence, I parked the *Globe*'s car on Wangfujing, a busy shopping street adjacent to the hotel. Catherine Sampson, a reporter for the Times of London, offered to share her fourteenth-floor room. Simon Long, a BBC reporter, was also there filing a story. I needed quotes, and persuaded Norman to go with me to the square. Before I went out, I ditched my notebook so I wouldn't attract the attention of plainclothes police and, as a precaution against tear gas, stuffed a hankie in my pocket.

The square felt like a cross between a New York street festival and a British soccer riot. All the floodlights had been switched on, presumably for the benefit of the videocameras. Several hundred thousand people milled around, students in T-shirts, women in flowered dresses, roughly dressed peasants with unkempt hair. Parents snapped photos for the memory book of their children posing in front of the Goddess of Democracy. Western tourists in pedicabs filmed the raucous scene with videocameras. Since mid-April, Tiananmen Square had been a bigger tourist draw than the Great Wall.

The night before, the invasion of the foot soldiers had been harmless fun. With the radio and television warnings on Saturday evening, people were quivering like excited rabbits waiting to see what would happen next. Every ten minutes or so, a panic rippled through the crowd, sparking a mass stampede. After regrouping, another wave of hysteria hit the crowd, and they fled in a different direction. You had to run with them or risk being trampled to death. Once, I tried to take refuge behind a skinny lamppost, but a dozen others had the same idea.

No one had any idea how bad the situation was. Some had heard that the troops had begun to shoot, but the true magnitude of casualties wasn't yet known. People were indignant, not afraid. "It's unspeakable," said one young woman, her hands on her hips. "Worse than fascists." A young man stood on a traffic kiosk with a bullhorn, a small supply of bricks at his feet, shouting, "Down with fascists!" Others like me clutched their hankies. A couple of young men readied Molotov cocktails.

Norman and I walked toward the north end of the square, where an armored personnel carrier was burning. "Are there any soldiers inside?" I asked a student in a red headband. "We pulled them out first," he said. In the distance, I saw another armored personnel carrier in flames just in front of the Communist Party headquarters at Zhongnanhai. I had to pinch myself to make sure I wasn't dreaming. I looked at my watch. It was just past midnight on Sunday, June 4, 1989.

Some people claimed to hear gunfire. I strained to listen, but the din of stampeding humans was too loud. Someone whispered that the soldiers were holed up inside the Great Hall of the People. An Italian journalist grabbed my arm and told me the troops were inside the Forbidden City and would come pouring out any minute. By 12:50 AM, I was frightened and tired. I had my quotes. "I'm not a cameraman," I said to Norman. "I've got what I need. Let's go."

We made our way back to the Beijing Hotel. Someone had fastened the wrought-iron gates shut with steel wire. We clambered over them and scurried across the parking lot. Plainclothes agents were frisking foreign reporters on the main steps. I walked around them and into the lobby, where a reporter for *USA Today* was filing a story on a pay phone. An agent armed with a pair of heavy shears cut the cord in midsentence. The reporter was so astonished his jaw dropped. Without a word, the policeman methodically chopped the wires on the rest of the lobby phones. Norman and I took the elevator up, still unnoticed.

That night, many reporters like myself used the Beijing Hotel as a base of operations. This was not the proverbial wartime-reporting-from-the-hotel-bar-stool-by-jaded-hacks syndrome. The Beijing Hotel had direct-dial telephones, bathrooms, and an unparalleled view of the north end of Tiananmen Square. It was so close, in fact, that we were within range of the guns. A small number of reporters, like Andrew Higgins of the *Independent*, stayed among the crowds on the street. And an even smaller number, including UPI's Dave Schweisberg, remained in the center of the square all night with the students. Still other reporters never left their offices in the diplomatic compounds, relying on reports from their news assistants and wire service copy to write their first stories.

Back in Cathy Sampson's fourteenth-floor room, I moved a chair onto the balcony and began taking notes. Norman and I had left the square in the nick of time. Ten minutes later, the troops tolled in from the west side, the armored personnel carriers roaring easily over makeshift barricades. Protesters hurled stones. A cyclist gave impotent chase. I could hear the crackle of gunfire clearly now. I watched in horror as the army shot directly into the crowds, who stampeded screaming and cursing down the Avenue of Eternal Peace. At first, some protesters held blankets and jackets in front of them, apparently believing the army was using rubber bullets. Only after the first people fell, with gaping wounds, did people comprehend that the soldiers were using live ammunition.

I could not believe what was happening. I swore and cursed in Chinese and English, every epithet I knew. Then I realized I was ruining Simon's tape of the gunfire for his BBC broadcasts. I decided the only useful thing I could do was to stay calm and take the best notes of my life. A crowd below frantically tried to rip down a metal fence to erect another barricade. When it wouldn't budge, they smashed a window of a parked bus, put the gears in neutral, and rolled it onto the street. They did that with a second and then a third bus. The rest of the crowd shouted, "Hao!" ("Good!").

The troops and tanks began closing in from all directions. At 1:20, I heard bursts of gunfire front the south, then another burst five minutes later. At 2:10, several thousand troops marched across the north side of the square. At 2:15, they raised their guns and fired into the dense crowd. I timed the murderous volley on my watch. It lasted more than a minute. Although the square was brightly lit, the streets surrounding it were dark. I couldn't see clearly if anyone had been hit. I assumed they must have been because of the angle of the guns, the length of the volley, and the density of the crowds. A few minutes later I knew I was right as five ambulances raced by the hotel through the crowds. Cyclists and pedicab drivers helped evacuate the wounded and dying. I hadn't even noticed that a man had been shot in the back below my balcony until an ambulance stopped to pick him up.

At 2:23, ranks from the east fired their mounted machine guns at the crowds. At 2:28, I counted five more ambulances racing back to the square as people frantically cheered them on. In the distance, I saw red dots trace perfect arcs through the sky. "Fireworks?" I asked, turning to Cathy. Neither of us knew they were tracer bullets, and even if I did, I had no idea they were real bullets, coated with phosphorus to glow in the dark. In my first story, I called them "flares."

Cathy heard a bullet lilt our balcony and pointed it out to me at the time. I have no memory of it. I should have realized the lead was flying, but I was so completely absorbed in taking notes. Nor did it occur to me that, as soldiers advanced across the north side of the square, pushing back protesters toward the hotel and beyond, our balcony was in the line of fire. The next day, when I examined the bullet hole, I felt nothing. It was insignificant compared to all the death and destruction going on around me. Besides, the hotel felt so normal, with its twin beds, blond-wood furniture, and lace curtains. I learned only later that a tourist in the hotel had been grazed in the neck and the neon sign on the roof had been blasted to smithereens.

As the soldiers massacred people, the loudspeakers broadcast the earlier government message warning everyone to stay home. I leaned over the balcony to watch some people cowering in the parking lot. The crowd ran away after each heavy volley, then to my amazement crept back slowly, screaming curses and weeping with rage. Perhaps like me, they couldn't believe that the People's

Liberation Army was shooting them. Or perhaps the decades of propaganda had warped their minds. Perhaps they were insane with anger. Or maybe after stopping an army in its tracks for days, armed only with moral certitude, they believed they were invincible. By now, I was recording heavy gunfire every six or seven minutes. It occurred to me that was about as much time as it took for people to run two blocks, calm down, regroup and creep back...

At exactly 4 AM, the lamps in the square snapped off. My heart froze. I could still see the students' tents near the edge of the square. Inside the Great Hall of the People, the lights blazed. I wrote in my notes: "'This is it. They're going to kill all the students. Are China's leaders watching from inside the GHOP?" I concentrated on counting a convoy of more than five hundred trucks as it rumbled into the square from the west. I could hear the thunder of distant gunfire to the south. By now, I was too tired to sit in the chair, so I slumped on the cement floor of the balcony, wrapped in a hotel blanket. By 4:30 AM, the soldiers had sealed off the northeast corner of the square. Below me, a few thousand die-hards lingered. I couldn't believe my ears when they began singing revolutionary songs and chanting slogans. Some cyclists hiked back and forth in the killing zone in front of the hotel.

I learned later that about five thousand students, many from the provinces, huddled that night around the Monument to the People's Heroes. Chai Ling led them in singing the *Internationale.* Many had joined the hunger strike as a springtime lark. Now they were sure they were going to die on a cool night in June. When the lights went out, many students started weeping.

At precisely 4:40, the lights snapped back on. A new broadcast tape started. "Classmates," said a metallic male voice. "Please immediately clear the square." The message was repeated. I heard shots ring out in the square. Were they killing the students in cold blood? I later found out the soldiers were blasting away the students' sound system.

The students took a hasty vote and decided to leave. At 4:50, I recorded more heavy gunfire and thick black smoke in the south. At 5:17, the soldiers allowed the frightened students to file out through the south side of the square, making them run a gauntlet of truncheons and fists. The students straggled past the Kentucky Fried Chicken outlet and then north. As they turned west onto the Avenue of Eternal Peace, they saw a row of tanks lined up between them and the square. A retreating student hurled a curse. Suddenly, one of the tanks roared to life and mowed down eleven marchers from behind, killing seven instantly.

Afterward, the government denied that tanks had crushed students at Tiananmen Square. But there were too many eyewitnesses, including an AP reporter. Eventually I tracked down two of the four survivors. One was a Beijing Sports Institute student whose legs were crushed when he pushed a classmate out of the tank's path. Another was a young factory technician whose right ear was torn off and right arm crushed. When I found him six months later, he was still afraid to leave his home because he knew he was a living contradiction of the government's Big Lie.

Dawn broke cold and gray on Sunday, June 4. As convoys of trucks and tanks rumbled in from the east, people frantically tried to push a bus into their path. One young man ran out and tossed a rock at the tanks. At 5:30, another convoy of a jeep and nine trucks went by, firing at random. People cowered in the bushes. At 5:36, a convoy of thirty trucks entered the square, followed by twenty armored personnel carriers and three tanks. At 5:47, two soldiers dismounted and started shooting their AK-47s into the crowd. I saw many fall to the ground, but I couldn't tell who had been hit and who was simply trying to take cover.

As Beijing awoke, ordinary people streamed toward the square, even as the pedicabs brought out more casualties. I saw a little girl and her parents take refuge behind a gray pickup truck in the Beijing Hotel parking lot. The thick smoke from a burning bus gave some protective cover. By now, I was aware of the bullets whistling past. Still, it seemed unthinkable to stay inside. Over the next hour, I counted dozens of armored personnel carriers and tanks. It was overkill. Whom were they fighting now? Some of the tank drivers seemed lost. I saw three make U-turns, change their minds, then turn around again.

With daylight, I could see better. At 6:40, a tank plowed into the Goddess of Democracy, sending her plaster torso smashing to the ground. I saw flames and lots of smoke. Chai Ling, in a dramatic video released in Hong Kong, later testified: "Tanks began running over students who were sleeping in tents. Then the troops poured gasoline on tents and bodies and torched them." (This turned out to be false. The tents *were* set on fire, but apparently no one was in them.) By 6:47, dozens of tanks had lined up in formation at the north end of Tiananmen Square. From a distance, the square looked solid green. The army had finally retaken the square. The broadcast stopped.

Cathy switched on the early-morning newscast. Through the open balcony door, we would still hear gunfire. "A small minority of hoodlums created chaos in Beijing," the government announcer said. "The army came in, but not to suppress the students and the masses." I left Cathy, an insomniac, to take notes of the broadcast while I fell into an exhausted stupor on the bed. I had been working day and night without a break for more than seven weeks, and had had almost no sleep in the past seventy-two hours. I awoke with a start a short while later as three military helicopters roared by our window on their way to the square to pick up wounded soldiers, casualties of friendly fire. More ambulances whizzed by. From the balcony, I recorded a lull as a crowd massed outside the hotel. Fifteen minutes later, the soldiers charged forward, firing directly into the crowd. Bodies littered the ground. I saw a couple of people use their own blood to smear slogans on a sheet of plywood propped against a barricade at the intersection. "Kill Li Peng!" said one slogan. "Blood debts will be repaid with blood," read another.

By then, I was numb. It seems strange in hindsight—perhaps it was my Chinese starvation genes—but I felt I had to eat. I could tell it was going to be a long, bloody Sunday, and without some food, I knew I would not last the day. When I suggested we try to get breakfast downstairs in the hotel dining room, neither Cathy nor Norman objected. We left Simon Long behind to take notes.

Downstairs, I discovered that many other journalists had spent the night on their balconies and seemed to have the same surreal craving for scrambled eggs. Mitch Farkas, a husky soundman for CNN, told us that we had just missed a fight. When the Chinese waitresses announced there was only coffee, no food, because the chef was too upset to cook, a couple of reporters became unhinged and started yelling that they would cook their own breakfast. Suddenly the chef appeared in the dining room. He was crying. "I've seen too many people killed last night," he said, his shaking hand resting on a doorknob. Everyone stared at the ground, ashamed of the boorish behavior of their colleagues. A waitress broke the silence. "We are all Chinese," she said. "We love our country."

Everyone began apologizing to everyone else, Mitch said, and the cook pulled himself together and announced that he would feed the reporters because "you are telling the world what happened."

As he recounted this, Mitch himself started crying. Like us, he was physically and mentally drained. When he broke down, Cathy and I did, too. I—who cried at the drop of a hat, when Beijing University was going to expel me, when I couldn't hack the labor at Big Joy Farm—realized that I hadn't shed a single tear all night. The enormity of the massacre hit home. So many people had been killed. Although it had been years since I was a Maoist, I still had harbored some small hope for China. Now even that was gone. I sat there weeping as the waitresses passed out plates of toast and fried eggs. None of us could eat.

For Discussion

1. By noting that she had forgotten Mao's statement that "political power grows out of the barrel of a gun," is Wong suggesting that she should not have been surprised by the Tiananmen Square massacre? (260)

2. Wong says that "the government might as well have issued engraved invitations" when warning people against going to Tiananmen Square. (260) Is she suggesting that the government intended to encourage the confrontation between the military and the demonstrators?

3. Why does the warning broadcast by the government prompt Wong to say, "History will be made tonight"? (260)

4. Why does Wong characterize the previous night's invasion of the square by foot soldiers as "harmless fun"? (262)

5. When she notices the armored personnel carrier burning in front of the Communist Party headquarters, why does Wong have to pinch herself to make sure she isn't dreaming?

6. Why does Wong begin to include the precise minute at which the events she reports occurred?

7. Does Wong's account support any one of the possible reasons she lists for the crowd repeatedly returning to its original position after being fired on by the military? (264–265)

8. Why does the massacre cause Wong to lose the small hope she had harbored for China?

9. Why does Wong often seem unaware of, or indifferent to, the danger that covering this story poses to her?

For Further Reflection

1. Once it became clear to the demonstrators that the military was willing to shoot and kill them, why do you think they continued to confront the soldiers?
2. Do you think that the government's responsibility for the massacre was affected by its broadcast warning demonstrators to stay away from Tiananmen Square?
3. Do you think that Tiananmen Square was a success for the demonstrators?

For Research

1. Research the history of Tiananmen Square, especially the significance of its name and physical features (i.e., the Gate of Heavenly Peace). What has been the fate of Tiananmen Square since the 1989 uprising?
2. Research the Chinese government's response to the massacre in Tiananmen Square. What did official government accounts of the events say?
3. Research prodemocracy activism in China today. How have the events in Tiananmen Square affected the prodemocracy movement?
4. Research the events that led up to the Tiananmen Square uprising. Identify the groups involved. What were their specific goals? What other means did they try or intend to use to achieve them?

Red Scarf Girl
(selection)

JI-LI JIANG (1954–)

In 1966, Chinese Communist leader Mao Zedong instituted the Great Proletarian Cultural Revolution—a sweeping ten-year campaign to reeducate the population and do away with all traces of pre-Communist China. Mao waged this campaign with the Red Guards, militant high school and college students, who pressured fellow students and others to conform to the new values and give up anything that suggested a bourgeois, or Western and capitalist, lifestyle. The Red Guards interrogated and terrorized, and in many cases imprisoned or killed, people who were not thought to be good Communists. Young people, especially those from middle-class or wealthy families, were sent to work in factories or on farms, performing manual labor as part of their reeducation.

Ji-Li Jiang was born in Shanghai and was only twelve years old when the Cultural Revolution began. Under the new values, her family was considered anti-Communist because her grandfather had been a landlord in prerevolutionary China and her family was relatively wealthy. Her memoir, Red Scarf Girl *(1997), from which this selection is taken, describes her and her family's experiences during the Cultural Revolution. Jiang emigrated to the United States in 1984. She lives in the San Francisco Bay area, where she cofounded a company that promotes cultural and economic exchange between China and Western countries.*

Red Scarf Girl
(selection)

why?

THE CLASS EDUCATION EXHIBITION

During math class a few days later, Teacher Hou from the Revolutionary Committee popped his head into my classroom. He barely glanced at Teacher Li before saying curtly, "Jiang Ji-li, come to our office right away. Someone wants to talk to you."

I stood up nervously, wondering what it could be. I felt my classmates' piercing eyes as I mechanically left the classroom. Teacher Hou walked ahead of me without seeming to notice my presence. I followed silently.

I tried not to panic. Maybe it was not bad. Maybe it was about the exhibition. Maybe Chairman Jin wanted me to help the others with their presentations. At the end of the long, dark hallway Teacher Hou silently motioned me into the office and then walked away.

I wiped my hands on my trousers and slowly opened the door. The thin-faced foreman from Dad's theater was right in front of me.

My face must have shown my dismay.

"Sit down, sit down. Don't be afraid." Chairman Jin pointed to the empty chair. "These comrades from your father's work unit are just here to have a study session with you. It's nothing to worry about." _re-education_

I sat down dumbly.

I had thought about their coming to my home but never imagined this. They were going to expose my family in front of my teachers and classmates. I would have no pride left. I would never be an educable child again.

Thin-Face sat opposite me, with a woman I had never seen before. Teacher Zhang was there too, his eyes encouraging me.

Thin-Face came straight to the point. "Your father's problems are very serious." His cold eyes nailed me to my seat. "You may have read the article in the *Workers' Revolt* that exposed your family's filthy past." I slumped down in my chair without taking my eyes off his face. "In addition to coming from a landlord family, your father committed some serious mistakes during the Antirightist Movement several years ago, but he still obstinately refuses to confess." His cold manner became a little more animated. "Of course, we won't tolerate this. We have decided to make an example of him. We are going to have a struggle meeting of the entire theater system to criticize him and force him to confess." He suddenly pounded the table with his fist. The cups on the table rattled.

I tore my eyes away from him and stared at a cup instead.

"As I told you before, you are your own person. If you want to make a clean break with your black family, then you can be an educable child and we will welcome you to our revolutionary ranks." He gave Chairman Jin a look, and Chairman Jin chimed in, "That's right, we welcome you."

"Jiang Ji-li has always done well at school. In addition to doing very well in her studies, she participates in educational reform," Teacher Zhang added.

"That's very good. We knew that you had more sense than to follow your father," Thin-Face said with a brief, frozen smile. "Now you can show your revolutionary determination." He paused. "We want you to testify against your father at the struggle meeting."

I closed my eyes. I saw Dad standing on a stage, his head bowed, his name written in large black letters, and then crossed out in red ink, on a sign hanging from his neck. I saw myself standing in the middle of the stage, facing thousands of people, condemning Dad for his crimes, raising my fist to lead the chant, "Down with Jiang Xi-reng." I saw Dad looking at me hopelessly, tears on his face.

"I . . . I . . ." I looked at Teacher Zhang for help. He looked away.

The woman from the theater spoke. "It's really not such a hard thing to do. The key is your class stance. The daughter of our former Party Secretary resolved to make a clean break with her mother. When she went onstage to condemn her mother, she actually slapped her face. Of course, we don't mean that you have to slap your father's face. The point is that as long as you have the correct class stance, it will be easy to testify." Her voice grated on my ears.

"There is something you can do to prove you are truly Chairman Mao's child." Thin-face spoke again. "I am sure you can tell us some things your father said and did that show his landlord and rightist mentality." I stared at the table, but I could feel his eyes boring into me. "What can you tell us?"

"But I don't know anything," I whispered. "I don't know—"

"I am sure you can remember something if you think about it," Thin-Face said. "A man like him could not hide his true beliefs from a child as smart as you. He must have made comments critical of Chairman Mao and the Cultural Revolution. I am sure you are loyal to Chairman Mao and the Communist Party. Tell us!"

"But my father never said anything against Chairman Mao," I protested weakly. "I would tell you if he did." My voice grew stronger with conviction. "He never said anything against the Party."

"Now, you have to choose between two roads." Thin-Face looked straight into my eyes. "You can break with your family and follow Chairman Mao, or you can follow your father and become an enemy of the people." His voice grew more severe. "In that case we would have many more study sessions, with your brother and sister too, and the Red Guard Committee and the school leaders. Think about it. We will come back to talk to you again."

Thin-Face and the woman left, saying they would be back to get my statement. Without knowing how I got there, I found myself in a narrow passageway between the school building and the schoolyard wall. The gray concrete walls closed around me, and a slow drizzle dampened my cheeks. I could not go back to the classroom, and I could not go home. I felt like a small animal that had fallen into a trap, alone and helpless, and sure that the hunter was coming. . . .

I did not know why Chang Hong wanted to talk with me.

I walked to school in the shade of the buildings. The sun was hot. In the still, heavy air my back was soaked with sweat before I had walked out of the alley. The whole city seemed to have slowed down. The few bicycles that passed seemed to be pedaling slowly through a murky oil. Even the cicadas chirped listlessly.

Three days after I had been thrown out of the exhibition, Chang Hong had sent a message to my home to insist that we meet at the Red Guard Committee office. "It's not convenient to have this conversation at your home or mine," she said. Obviously she had some official statement to pass on to me, but for once I did not care. I did not care about anything but Thin-Face's demands. I had no secrets, no goals, and no need to make any effort to impress anybody. I passed the police station where I had almost changed my name. Idly I wondered if anything would be different now if I had done it. The idea seemed to be just another fantasy, with no more reality than a dream of flying.

The Red Guard Committee office was on the sixth floor, the top floor, of the new building of the school. The doors of a few offices were open, but no voices drifted out of them. Through the hallway window, I could see the national flag on its flagpole. In the heat even it was drooping. Its five yellow stars were invisible.

Chang Hong opened the door to my knock. While she poured me a glass of cool water, I looked around the small office. It was full of red: red slogans, red posters, red armbands, and red flags. A huge poster of Chairman Mao in a green army uniform, waving to the Red Guards from the Tiananmen rostrum, covered almost an entire wall. There were posters of Chairman Mao's poems written in his own calligraphy, and a new poster of a group of Red Guards in belted army uniforms poised to march forward, waiting only for the Great Leader's order.

"I've been wanting to have a talk with you for a while, and now it seems even more important," Chang Hong said. We had not really talked for a long time, and I thought she looked a little depressed. How was her brother's epilepsy? I wondered suddenly.

"I was informed that you requested to do your summer labor in the factories instead of the countryside," she went on. "Is that true?"

"Yes. My mother has been quite ill recently, and Grandma is very old. If Mom had to go the hospital, Grandma and my brother and my sister wouldn't be strong enough to take her. That's why I asked to be assigned to a factory in the city this year. That way I'll be able to work and take care of Mom too." I was extraordinarily calm, I thought.

"I know about your family situation." Chang Hong crossed her arms and rested her elbows earnestly on the table. "I know you want to take care of your family. Undoubtedly there are difficulties. But Ji-li, have you considered the importance of your political life? It's not your fault that you were born into such a family, but the class influence of your family does have an effect. This makes your task of remolding yourself harder than other people's. A slight slackening could easily cause you to be recaptured by your family and turned into their follower.

"Chairman Jin told me that your father's work unit spoke to you about breaking with your black family. You hesitated, and that was why he replaced you in the exhibition. But Ji-li, it's not too late. If you go to the countryside to do your summer labor, the sweat of honest work will wash the black stain from your back and purify your mind so that you can follow Chairman Mao's revolutionary line. If you prove you are an educable child maybe Chairman Jin will put you back in the exhibition for the end of summer.

"This is a crucial moment for you! How could you ask to work in a factory instead? Ji-li, I was really worried for you when I heard that. I wanted to scold you for being so shortsighted. There is no difficulty, no matter how serious, that cannot be overcome, but if you miss this chance, it might ruin your whole political life. Then it will be too late to repent."

Chang Hong finally paused for breath. I could see that she was nearly in tears. She was so sincere, and she had so much faith in me. I was moved deeply by her caring. While other classmates were afraid of being too close to me, she still worried about me, felt sorry for me, and tried to think of what was best for me. I knew that she believed what she said: She wanted to help me, to rescue me from my black family.

"All right, I'll go," I said slowly.

"That's great! I knew you wanted to go forward. You'll thank yourself for taking advantage of this chance to follow Chairman Mao's revolutionary line."

I smiled at her with sincere gratitude. I did not want to disappoint her. I would go and try to prove myself. Maybe what she said was true, maybe they would accept me after I had done summer labor. More likely what she had told me was simply an order from Chairman Jin, and I had no choice but to remold myself. No matter what, there was one good thing about going to the countryside. I felt a sudden surge of relief. While I was there, Thin-Face could not come to make me testify against Dad.

"How's your brother?" I patted her arm and changed the subject.

As agreed, I went off with my classmates, resolved to do my share of the labor that fed us all.

We were sent to help with the "double rush," rush harvesting and rush planting. This was the busiest time of the year for the farmers, when they had to harvest the first crop of rice and immediately plant the second crop.

At five thirty in the morning we got up from our beds—straw mats in a storage room—and went to work harvesting the rice. In the still morning air, the rising sun turned the rice field into a golden sea. Each of us was assigned five rows, rows that seemed endless. We bent over the rice and concentrated on what the farmers had told us: Sickle in the right hand, grab six plants with the left hand, cut them at the roots, take one step forward. We slogged ahead.

The sun burned down on us with a force that seemed to press us deeper into the mud. In a few minutes, our thick jackets were soaked with sweat. The golden rice field stretched in front of us. We wielded our sickles mechanically, thinking of nothing but finishing our assigned rows. At noon lunch was sent to the rice fields. We gobbled our lunch in a few minutes and rushed back to work. By midafternoon our backs seemed about to break. Some people were forced to kneel in the mud and inch forward. As soon as we finished work, we threw ourselves on our mats and fell fast asleep, oblivious to our sweaty, filthy bodies and crying stomachs.

By the third day we were all exhausted.

I finally reached the low ridge that marked the end of the field and sat down. Another row finished! I closed my eyes. Every muscle, every joint in my body was aching. I wondered if the arthritis I had suffered as a child was returning. To force that thought out of my mind, I opened my eyes and took the towel from my neck to wipe my face. The stench of stale sweat on the cloth almost made me sick.

I slowly straightened my back and looked at the girl next to me. She had finished four rows and was already working on her fifth! I had done only three. I looked at the sun, already close to the horizon. It was probably five o'clock. Yesterday I had finished my fifth row in the darkness after everyone else had left the fields. I was even slower today. I felt a rush of alarm and picked up my sickle. I ran to the next row and began to cut frantically.

"Six plants, cut! Six plants, cut!" I repeated to myself, straining to make my arms and legs perform. Suddenly the sickle slipped out of my exhausted hand, and a two-inch gash appeared on my leg. Blood oozed out of the cut. I covered it with my muddy hand and cried with pain and frustration.

A weak breeze rustled the rice plants, and I could almost hear them talking to me. I raised my head. There was no one near me. No one would hear me crying. No one would come help me. It was getting dark, but no matter what, I still had to finish the five rows. Otherwise I would be disgraced. I stopped crying and took the towel off my neck to bind the wound.

It hurt badly. I clenched my teeth and took up the sickle again, forcing myself to think only of finishing the job. The pain slowly dulled.

Suddenly I heard something. I stopped cutting. A regular *swish, swish, swish* was moving in my direction. It did not sound like the wind rustling the grain. I looked around the field and saw no one; all the others had finished. The field was dark. I thought of how far I was from any house or any person, and my heart raced. *Swish, swish, swish.* I felt my legs growing weaker and weaker. If someone attacked me, I would never be able to fight him off. I sank to my knees, holding my sickle in my trembling hand, and waited.

The sound stopped, and someone stood up from the paddy. It was Bai Shan.

He put down the rice in his hand and straightened to ease his back. He was about to bend over again when he saw me rise. We stood about twenty yards apart and stared at each other.

"It's getting dark. I'm helping you cut a little." He smiled apologetically. His voice was low but clear in the quiet of the open field. Against the dusky sky he looked like a statue, tall and strong. I suddenly started to cry.

"Why are you crying?" He ran to my side. "Don't. . .don't cry. I'll help you. We'll finish in no time." His voice was affectionate but also flustered, like that of a child who had no idea what to do.

I only cried harder. I felt as if I were pouring out the whole year's grievances.

"Come on, you." He saw me wiping my tears with my muddy hands and held his own towel up to my face. "Just stop crying and take a break. I'll finish for you." Mumbling, he bent over and began to cut.

I cried and cried. Then a thought struck me. What was I doing? I was letting a boy help me. I did not need his pity. And if anyone found out, I would be criticized, and he would get in trouble too. I stopped crying and picked up my sickle. I walked over to his side and put my foot in front of the rice he was going to cut.

"Let me do it myself," I said.

"That's okay. I don't have anything else to do. Besides, I'm faster than you, and you'll get to go back sooner."

"No. What if somebody sees us?"

"It's dark. They won't see." He tried to nudge me out of the way.

I did not move.

"I said I don't want your help!" My voice was cold and stubborn.

He stood up. A clump of rice was still dangling from his left hand. His eyes were full of confusion, sympathy, and disappointment.

Everything was dark. His tall figure dissolved into the night, but I could still feel his eyes on me, shining despite the darkness.

I felt something new and unsettling, something I could not understand. I lowered my head and nervously said, "Please leave me alone."

When I looked up again, he had already vanished.

Early in the morning the work bell rang. I rubbed my sleepy eyes and looked out. Another sunny day. We would not get a day off after all. And last night after dinner, we had threshed until midnight because the forecast had been for rain.

I moved my body a little and almost groaned out loud. My head felt as if it were going to split, and my throat was swollen and sore. Every muscle in my body ached. The day before, I had started to feel sick, and I was sure I was coming down with a fever. I painfully turned over and closed my eyes.

Almost immediately I jerked myself upright. I could not go back to sleep. I had determined to face the challenge of the double rush, to remold myself, and I had to succeed. I had to go to work.

I struggled to my feet, took two of the painkiller pills I had brought with me, and trudged toward the threshing ground.

Bai Shan was there already, hard at work. I walked quickly to the thresher farthest from his and picked up a bundle of rice.

I held bundle after bundle into the mouth of the thresher and turned them over and over against a whirling drum to strip all the ripe kernels from the straw. Grains of rice jumped out of the machine and stung my face so often that in no time my whole face felt numb. The sun seemed determined to melt us. In a few minutes, I was dripping with sweat. I felt as if I were in a huge oven, scorched by the ever-increasing heat.

I thought of popsicles. Four fen apiece, cream, red bean, or lemon-flavored. I imagined holding one in my mouth and feeling each swallow of delicious icy water flow down my throat. I thought of resting in the shade, leisurely fanning myself. I thought of sitting in a tub full of cold water reading a novel.

I tried hard to imagine cool things to distract myself, but my legs began to tremble, and my eyes would not focus. I could not see clearly—not the thresher roller, not the bundle of rice in my hand. "Don't fall down, don't fall down. It will be all right after today," I told myself again and again. I repeated Chairman Mao's quotation, "Be resolute, fear no sacrifice, and surmount every difficulty to win victory."

Just before noon, when I turned around to get another bundle of rice, I lost consciousness. . . .

THE INCRIMINATING LETTER

It was good to be home, in spite of my worry about the summons from the theater. I lay in bed, my mind wandering and my body reveling in the softness. Every muscle and every joint in my body ached.

Someone knocked very softly at the door: two knocks, a pause, and three more. Mom opened the door without even asking who was there, and I heard Uncle Tian's voice. He and Mom disappeared into the bathroom.

Before long the bathroom door opened again, and Mom showed Uncle Tian out. "I'll let you know when I've finished revising it." She closed the door behind him and came back in. "It's late. Go to sleep," she said to me softly. She put some pieces of paper onto her nightstand and went back into the bathroom.

I turned off the light and closed my eyes. What were those papers? Why had she said, "I'll let you know when it's finished"? What was going on?

It was very quiet in the room. Ji-yong and Ji-yun had fallen asleep a while ago. Grandma was dozing on her bed, with her glasses on her nose and the newspaper on her chest. I heard Mom washing and knew she would be in the bathroom for at least fifteen minutes. Impulsively I slipped out of bed and, without even putting on my slippers, tiptoed over to Mom's bed.

Several sheets of paper were folded together on the nightstand. I picked up the one on top and held it under the soft light of Mom's bedside lamp. I held my breath as I read the first words: "Respected Comrades of the Municipal Party Committee."

I pressed the letter against my chest. The beginning of it made me too nervous to read any further. I heard Mom turning the water tap and looked guiltily over my shoulder. Then I read the rest of the letter as fast as I could.

The letter complained about the situation in the theater. The faction in power, the Rebels, did whatever they wanted, ignoring the policy directives from the Central Committee of the Party, the letter said. They treated people with nonpolitical problems, like Aunt Wu, as class enemies, and they had humiliated her, shaving half of her head in a yin-yang hairdo. They frequently beat their prisoners and had already beaten two to death. They even recorded the screams and moans of the prisoners being tortured, and played the tapes to frighten other prisoners under interrogation.

"We urgently hope," the letter concluded, "that the Municipal Party Committee will investigate this situation and correct it before it is too late." The letter was signed, "The Revolutionary Masses."

I tiptoed back to bed. My heart pounded inside my chest. Although the letter was merely reporting facts to a superior, it was a complaint about the Rebels at the theater. If they found out about it, Mom and Uncle Tian would be in serious trouble. And what would happen to Dad and Aunt Wu? What if Thin-Face found out? Would he blame me for not telling him?

I heard Mom go to bed. Lying in the darkness with my eyes open, I could not stop imagining all the horrors that could result from this letter. I was scared, and I did not know what to do.

It was dusk. I was shelling soybeans. Ji-yun and her classmate Xiao Hong-yin were laughing and chatting in the room, and Ji-yong was busy making a slingshot. Running water was gurgling from the roof. Grandma was washing clothes. Mom had gone to answer a telephone call.

The kitchen was getting dark, but I did not bother to turn the light on. I stared out the window. Another day had passed, and still Thin-Face had not shown up. What was he waiting for? What should I say when he came? What would he do to me?

I sighed and shelled more beans.

How was Dad? Surely they must have struggled with him enough. Had they beaten him? Since I had read Mom's letter two days ago, I had seen Dad in my mind, not just carrying concrete pipes and wiping away tears, but being tortured.

Had he really done something wrong? Why wouldn't he confess if he had? Was he really a rightist as they said? . . .

Suddenly pounding feet on the stairs jerked me back to reality. Mom ran up the stairs panic-stricken, yelling, "The letter, the letter." Grandma and I followed Mom into the room.

"The theater people are coming to search the house. The Dictatorship Group is watching the entrance to the alley. They wouldn't even let me answer the phone." We all stared at her as she reached under her pillow. "Quick!" Mom thrust a letter into my hand. "Hide this. We can't let them find it. I'll try to slow them down." She staggered downstairs. Xiao Hong-yin hurried out behind her.

I stood there dumbly. Searches were not allowed now without permission of the police. How could they be searching us? We had already been searched once before.

The loud voices on the stairs shook me awake. I looked at the letter—the thick, heavy letter that Mom and Uncle Tian had written to the Municipal Party Committee. My hand began to shake.

I rushed into the room and looked around desperately. No, the room would be thoroughly ransacked. I ran back out to the kitchen. Behind the sink? No. I dashed into the bathroom. Toilet tank? No. Where? Where should I hide it? I could not think. I could feel the blood throbbing in my temples.

Suddenly I remembered Little White's litter box. I dashed up to the roof. By the time I had smoothed out the ashes and walked downstairs, the searchers were already at the door.

Mom stood in the doorway, trying to keep Thin-Face from rushing in. "The Municipal Party Committee has directed that no searches are allowed without permission of the police."

Thin-Face sneered. He fished a piece of paper out of his pocket and thrust it in front of Mom's nose. "Read this. The authorities have determined that Jiang Xi-reng is a landlord who has escaped detection and gone unpunished. You're a damned landlord's wife." He threw the paper in Mom's face and rushed into the room with his crew.

What a ransacking!

They had brought big lights and thick wires from the theater and strung them through the room and on the roof and balcony. The whole apartment blazed like a movie set. We could hear the hubbub from the crowd of spectators outside in the alley.

Thin-Face and his crew were methodical and thorough. He emptied every trunk and every drawer, tore the beds and sofa apart, and even searched the dusty attic carefully.

One woman found the rags cut from Grandma's old gowns. "We can piece these together and use them for the Landlord Jiang Xi-reng's struggle meeting. It is excellent proof of his luxurious lifestyle," she said excitedly, and the whole box was carried away. Someone else saw the round porcelain stool under the window. It was cracked, so we had not been able to sell it like the other one. "This is a valuable antique from the Qianlong period," he said. The stool was taken away.

The search went on and on. Ji-yun, Ji-yong, and I sat in a corner of the room, trembling at the slamming of the wardrobe and the chests. My mind was entirely on the letter under the ashes. Suddenly Ji-yong stood up and walked toward one of the ransackers.

"I borrowed that book." He pointed toward a pile that the man was going to carry away.

"What? What did you say?" The young man turned around and arrogantly looked down on Ji-yong.

"I borrowed that book. I need to return it."

The young man pulled the book out of the pile. "*The Wild Animals I Have Raised,*" he read aloud. He scrutinized the book and then looked back at Ji-yong.

"Do you know what kind of book this is?"

"No. What kind is it?"

"It's a translation that propagates the bourgeois theory of humanitarism."

"I don't care what it propagates. I borrowed it, and I have to return it tomorrow." Ji-yong was feeling obstinate.

"You've got some nerve for a little black bastard. How dare you plead for this damned revisionist book?" He held the book in front of Ji-yong's face and very slowly began tearing the cover off.

Ji-yong rushed toward him and tried to grab the book. The man grabbed Ji-yong's collar and pulled my brother toward him, and then suddenly pushed away. Ji-yong staggered several steps backward and fell on a heap of clothes. He tried to stand up and rush at the man again, but Ji-yun and I jumped on him and held him down.

"He hit me! Let me go! Let me go!" His eyes were filled with tears. He struggled violently under our arms. I could feel his gasps against my face.

While we were struggling to hold Ji-yong down, Six-Fingers bustled in. He pulled Thin-Face into a corner and whispered something, then left.

Thin-Face watched us struggling like a hunter watching the animals in his trap. Ji-yong stopped fighting, and I straightened up.

"We've seen a lot of each other lately, haven't we?" He gave a grimace meant to suggest a smile. "According to reliable sources, you hid a very important letter just before we arrived." He paused and examined our reactions carefully. "Here is the opportunity for you to help Chairman Mao's revolution. Who can win the most honor by telling the truth."

I felt an intense rush of heat, as if my whole body were flushed.

"This was reported by a member of the revolutionary masses." He was talking only to me now. "We even know where it was hidden, but before I go get it, I'll give you one last chance to prove your loyalty to Chairman Mao. And then . . ."

It must have been Ji-yun's classmate Xiao Hong-yin, I thought. She was there when Mom gave me the letter. She must have reported it. But she didn't see me hide the letter. They couldn't know where it was.

Seeing that there was no response. Thin-Face took off his smiling mask. He stepped in front of me, bent over, and suddenly shouted in my face, "Don't you know, or is it just that you don't want to talk?"

I shivered. Ji-yun grasped my shirt and buried her face in my back. Thin-Face's head was only inches from mine. His bloodshot eyes bulged out so much that the whites seemed much larger than usual. His skin was red with rage. He looked so savage that I shrank back, sure that he was going to hit me. I shut my eyes and clenched my teeth. "I don't know."

My heart pounded. I waited. Nothing happened. I opened my eyes.

"So you don't want to talk," he snarled. "I think I can figure out a way to help you." He straightened up and shouted to the young man who had torn the book. "Bring the two landlords' wives in here!"

Grandma was leaning heavily on Mom as they came into the room.

Thin-Face was in front of them immediately. "Leniency for those who confess, severity for those who resist. I'm sure you remember that. Now. Where did you hide the letter? Confess!"

Mom's face changed color. Grandma looked at him and replied timidly, "Letter? What letter?"

"Damn you!" Thin-Face slapped her face with all his strength. Grandma staggered into Mom's arms.

"Grandma!" We all sprang to our feet and rushed to Grandma.

"She's over seventy, you — How could you?" Shielding Grandma with her own body, Mom shouted back at Thin-Face.

"Over seventy! So what? Damned old landlord's wife!" Thin-Face held his hand. He must have hurt it when he slapped Grandma. "Old landlord's wife, kneel down and face the wall. Stay there until you confess. You —" He turned to the rest of us. "You all sit here and watch. Don't go near her. If you care about her, confess. Otherwise she'll stay there forever. We'll see who's stronger." He walked out.

Grandma knelt down facing the wall. I could see the red marks of Thin-Face's fingers on her face. Her whole body was trembling so violently that I could see her linen shirt shaking.

"Grandma . . ." Ji-yun cried out suddenly. Tears were rolling down my cheeks too.

"Don't you cry for her. She's an exploiting landlord's wife." The young man stepped up to Ji-yun. "If you keep crying, I'll make your mother kneel down too."

I looked at Mom. Her face was terribly haggard. She looked as if she were about to faint. She took out her handkerchief and wiped Ji-yun's face. "Don't cry, dear, don't cry. Everything will be all right," she said softly.

Grandma was sitting limply on her legs now, supporting her weight on her hands just like Old Qian had that day. A few white hairs clung to her red cheek.

Maybe I should tell, I thought frantically. Grandma was so frail. . . . But then would we all get into bigger trouble? What should I do? What should I do, Mom? I stole several glances at Mom, but she hung her head and stared at the ground.

After a long while, the young man went into the bathroom. No one else was watching us. Mom whispered in my ear, "Where's the letter?"

"In Little White's litter box. Are you going to tell them?"

Mom shook her head hesitantly. She looked at Grandma and mur-mured, "I'm afraid she can't stand any more. It looks like they won't give up till they find it."

We were interrupted by a hubbub. Heavy footsteps rushed up to the roof. For a few minutes there was silence. Then suddenly we heard a crowd of people pounding down the stairs, roaring with coarse laughter.

"The cat did a great job. We should give her a reward."

"But the letter stinks of cat piss."

The letter!

I sagged weakly to the chair. Little White must have revealed the letter by raking up the ashes after she had used her box.

Thin-Face dashed into the room, his face lit with a sinister smile of vic-tory. "What did I say? Who won? Who was stronger, you or the iron fist of the Proletarian Dictatorship? Humph!" He waved the letter in Mom's face. "So you thought you could reverse the verdict, did you? Hah!" he grunted in satisfaction. "Chen Ying, tomorrow you will report to your work unit that you are a landlord's wife now. We will inform them of what happened today and will invite you as a companion to your husband's struggle meeting."

He stood over Grandma, who was still on the floor. "Old landlord's wife, starting tomorrow you will sweep the alley like the other landlords' wives. You have been lucky that we didn't expose you earlier. Go register at the Neighborhood Dictatorship Group at eight."

He turned and was about to walk out when he saw me.

"You," he snorted. Even in his elation his eyes froze me. "You have just missed your opportunity to be an educable child. Too bad. We will let your school know all about your firm class stance."

It was now four thirty in the morning. The alley was deserted. The huge truck, loaded with most of our possessions, blew its horn in the deadly si-lence and triumphantly left.

The dark world became quiet, as quiet as the inside of a grave.

We gathered around Mom and Grandma. Song Po-po tiptoed up from her room and joined us. The furniture was gone, and most of our possessions, but at the moment we could not worry about that. The letter, the letter we had worried about all night, was gone. That was all we could think about....

For Discussion

1. Why is Ji-li's interrogation called a "study session" (273) and her father's condemnation called a "struggle meeting"? (274)
2. What does the woman from the theater mean when she says that "as long as you have the correct class stance, it will be easy to testify"? (275)
3. When the "study session" is over, why does Ji-li feel that "I could not go back to the classroom, and I could not go home"? (275)
4. Why are the authorities eager to turn Ji-li against her father?
5. Why is Chang Hong nearly in tears when she finishes her speech to Ji-li?
6. Why does Ji-li welcome the hardships of working in the rice fields as a way to remold herself?
7. Why is Ji-li so determined to refuse Bai Shan's help?
8. Why does the crew ransack the apartment with such energy and excitement?
9. Why does Ji-yong insist on keeping the book he needs to return?
10. Why is Thin-Face willing to hit and humiliate Ji-li's grandmother? Why does he say, "We'll see who's stronger"? (287)

For Further Reflection

1. Is the "iron fist of the Proletarian Dictatorship" stronger than Ji-li?
2. Why are people who believe that they are acting on behalf of the greater good willing to harm others in order to achieve their goals?
3. At what point does political conviction become fanatical?

For Research

1. Research Mao Zedong and the Cultural Revolution, especially the practice of sending young people to work in the fields and factories.
2. Research what the Chinese Communist Party under Mao taught about class warfare and "class stance." What did it mean to be declared a "landlord" or "landlord's wife"?

My Forbidden Face
(selection)

LATIFA (1980–)

Latifa was born in Kabul, Afghanistan, not long after the Soviet Union had invaded the country to stabilize its fledgling, but unpopular, communist government. The Soviet occupation of Afghanistan fostered the unification of several regional resistance groups, together known as the mujahideen, who, with the help of Pakistan, the United States, and other countries, mounted an effective opposition. Soviet soldiers finally withdrew from Afghanistan in 1989, leaving behind fierce power struggles and civil war. Into this chaos, the Taliban emerged in 1994. The Taliban— a militant group consisting primarily of Afghan students who attended madrasahs, *or religious schools, in Pakistan—took control of most of the country in 1996 when it seized its capital, Kabul. Once in power, the Taliban proceeded to establish what they believed to be a pure Islamic state.*

Latifa (a pen name) was then a sixteen-year-old student interested in journalism. Like all women, she was forbidden by the Taliban not only from working or going to school, but from leaving her house without a head-to-toe veil, or chadri, *and a male relative to accompany her. Defying the regime, Latifa organized and ran an underground school, and her mother, who had been a doctor, continued to see patients in secret. In May 2001, she and her mother were invited to Paris to speak about the plight of women in Afghanistan under the Taliban. Along with Latifa's father, they made the trip in secret. In their absence, the Taliban issued a* fatwa, *or legal ruling, denouncing all women who spoke out against the regime, with death as a punishment. Latifa and her parents stayed in Paris, where she still lives. This selection is from* My Forbidden Face: Growing Up Under the Taliban: A Young Woman's Story *(2001), which Latifa wrote with Shékéba Hachemi, founder of Afghanistan Libre.*

This selection is taken from chapter 1, "The White Flag over the Mosque," and chapter 2, "A Canary in a Cage."

My Forbidden Face
(selection)

9 A.M., SEPTEMBER 27, 1996. Someone knocks violently on our door. My whole family has been on edge since dawn, and now we all start in alarm. My father jumps up to see who it is while my mother looks on anxiously, haggard with exhaustion after a sleepless night. None of us got any sleep: The rocket fire around the city didn't let up until two in the morning. My sister Soraya and I kept whispering in the dark; even after things quieted down, we couldn't fall asleep. And yet here in Kabul, we're used to being the target of rocket fire. I'm only sixteen years old, but I feel as though I've been hearing that din all my life. The city has been surrounded and bombarded for so long, the smoke and flames of the murderous fighting have terrified us so often, sometimes even sending us rushing down to the basement, that another night in this racket is just part of our daily routine!

Until this morning.

Papa returns to the kitchen, followed by Farad, our young cousin, who is pale and breathless. He seems to be shaking inside, and his face is taut with fear. He can hardly speak, stammering out words in a series of strange gasps.

"I came...to find out how you were. Are you all right? You haven't seen anything? You don't know? But they're here! They've taken Kabul! The Taliban are in Kabul. They haven't come to your place yet? They haven't demanded that you hand over any weapons?"

"No, no one's been here, but we saw the white flag waving over the mosque—Daoud spotted it a few hours ago. We were afraid the worst had happened...."

This morning, around five o'clock, my young brother Daoud went downstairs as usual to fetch some water from the tap in the courtyard of our building, but came hurrying back up with the basin still empty.

"I saw a white flag over the mosque and another one over the school."

The flag of the Taliban. It had never before flown over Kabul. I had seen it only on television or in newspaper photographs....

Even after my brother told us he'd seen the white flags, I didn't want to believe the truth. The government forces must have pulled back to prepare for another attack on the Taliban, or else they've taken refuge more to the north, in a suburb of the city. The mujahideen can't have abandoned Kabul. So many times I've heard, read, and preferred to ignore what the government has been telling us about the Taliban: "They imprison women in their own homes. They prevent them from working, from going to school. Women have no more lives, the Taliban take away their daughters, burn the villagers' houses, force the men to join their army. They want to destroy the country!"

Just yesterday, despite the civil war, life was "normal" in Kabul, even though the city is in ruins. Yesterday I went to the seamstress with my sister to try on the dresses we were going to wear to a wedding today. There would have been music, we would have danced. Life can't stop like this on the twenty-seventh of September in 1996. I'm only sixteen and still have so many things to do—I have to pass the entrance examination to study journalism at the university.... No, it's impossible that the Taliban could remain in Kabul; it's just a temporary setback....

This morning, my father and I will not be going jogging with Bingo, our dog. This morning, my father is silently wondering about a thousand things he keeps to himself so as not to distress our mother any further. She has already been sorely tried by seventeen years of war. War, fighting—that's all I've ever known since I was born on March 20, 1980, the first day of spring. But even under the Soviets, even under the rocket fire of the feuding military factions, even in the ruins, we were still living in relative freedom in Kabul.

What kind of life will our father be able to offer his loved ones? What will happen to his children? I was lucky to be born into a united and affectionate family, one both liberal and religious. My oldest brother, Wahid, lives in Russia. My oldest sister, Shakila, is married and lives with her in-laws, following the custom of our people. She's in Pakistan, waiting to join her husband in the United States. Soraya, who is twenty, is unmarried and has been a flight attendant for Ariana Afghan Airlines for three years now. She came home two days ago from a routine trip to Dubayy and was to have left again this morning. Daoud is studying economics. I just passed the first part of a university entrance examination to study journalism. That has always been my dream. My father and everyone else in my family hope to see me complete my studies and become a reporter, traveling around the country, earning my living. Will all this come to an end in a single moment? . . .

Finally, at 11 a.m., the radio station—rebaptized Radio Sharia—comes back on the air, with a long period of religious chanting, followed by a man's voice reciting a verse of the Qur'an. Then the Taliban decree:

> The Prophet told his disciples that their work was to forbid evil and promote virtue. We have come to restore order. Laws will be established by religious authorities. Previous governments did not respect religion. We have driven them out, and they have fled. But all those who belonged to the former regime will now be safe with us. We ask our brothers to hand over their weapons, to leave them outside the front doors of their buildings or at a mosque. And for reasons of security, we ask that women stay in their homes during this first period of transition.

This speech, delivered in a harsh, singsong voice, is followed by religious chanting until noon. Then there is silence again. We'll have to wait until this evening, when we might be able to learn more from the Persian-language broadcast of the BBC or the Voice of America.

What can we do in the meantime, except assume the worst, going over and over the awful things we've seen? We even forget to eat lunch.

✄

I try to think about cheerful, frivolous things, like my dress that Papa promised me he'd pick up from the seamstress. Mama gave him a reproachful look—she thinks he lets me get away with too much. I adore my father, and I can wheedle just about everything I want from him. When Daoud was a student, even he came to me if he needed something from Papa. Whenever I ask for money to buy a tape or some nail polish, Mama lectures me.

"Don't be silly, Latifa! We have to stick to our family budget!"

Yesterday, she was sincerely shocked that I could still think about the wedding at a time like that. But I hadn't even gotten to see the finished dress yet. . . .

Maybe I'm revealing a shallow side to my character, but I need to cling to the "normality" of my life as an ordinary girl. It's a way of denying the imprisonment that is lying in wait for me, lying in wait for every Afghan girl and woman. It's inevitable.

I can always just stay here staring at that cardboard rose. It's like an obsession, like an iron band around my forehead: I won't be going to classes anymore; I passed that exam for nothing; I'll remain shut up inside our apartment, without any goal or plan for the future. For how long? Weeks, months will go by before the resistance can chase away these white carrion crows. Years, perhaps. No one knows where General Massoud and his men have gone. "They have been driven out," announced Radio Sharia, and it will be a long time before we learn anything more.

Breakfast is a dreary affair; Radio Sharia isn't at all like Radio Kabul. It doesn't have a news program anymore; the broadcast will begin at eleven o'clock, as it did yesterday, with religious chants and decrees by the mullahs.

I hate this empty, meaningless morning. Before, it was a pleasure to breakfast on warm bread and sweet tea while listening to the program *Payam Sobhgahan* on Radio Kabul: the daily news, Persian poetry, music. Around eight o'clock, Daoud and Soraya would leave for work, and I'd go off to my classes. Only Mama would stay home, with Bingo for company. On certain days she would give free consultations to neighborhood women whose husbands were very strict and refused to let them be taken care of by male doctors at the hospital. For precisely this reason, most of the doctors in Kabul are women, especially the gynecologists.

Waiting for Radio Sharia to deign to inform us of the new regime's orders, we're allowed to hear nothing from eight to nine except religious chanting, a reading of verses from the Qur'an, and prayers. Daoud will turn on the radio periodically, in the unlikely event that there's something worth hearing.

I go back to my room to lie down while Soraya washes the dishes. Papa will attempt a cautious foray into the neighborhood to do some shopping, go to the bank, and try to pick up scraps of information in the homes of trusted friends. Mama stretches out on the living room sofa and is soon dozing. The life has gone out of her eyes. She didn't even scold me when she saw Soraya doing the dishes for me. She seems to have no interest in anything this morning.

When Papa returns, he brings bad news. The banks are still closed, stores and offices as well. Only the Ministries of Defense and the Interior are functioning. Papa has seen shattered TV sets lying all over like garbage and tangles of cassette tape hanging in trees, swaying in the autumn breeze like sinister wreaths. The streets are full of gloomy people, and there are long lines in front of the few stores that are open.

My father is going to the mosque now to hand over the family's antique arsenal, wrapped in a rag. My poor Papa, so sturdy, so resilient, so respectable—what a humiliation! He hasn't shaved this morning; his face is gray, sad, and the stubble on his cheeks makes him look ill.

Eleven o'clock. Radio Sharia comes back on to announce that the prime minister of the interim government, which is composed of six mullahs, has issued the following statement.

> From now on the country will be ruled by a completely Islamic system. All foreign ambassadors are relieved of their duties. The new decrees in accordance with Sharia are as follows.
>
> Anyone in possession of a weapon must hand it in to the nearest mosque or military checkpoint.
>
> Women and girls are not permitted to work outside the home.
>
> All women who are obliged to leave their homes must be accompanied by a *mahram*: their father, brother, or husband.
>
> Public transportation will provide buses reserved for men and buses reserved for women.

Men must let their beards grow and trim their mustaches according to Sharia.

Men must wear a white cap or turban on their heads.

The wearing of suit and tie is forbidden. The wearing of traditional Afghan clothing is compulsory.

Women and girls will wear the *chadri.*

Women and girls are forbidden to wear brightly colored clothes beneath the *chadri.*

It is forbidden to wear nail polish or lipstick or makeup.

All Muslims must offer ritual prayers at the appointed times wherever they may be.

As the days go by, decrees rain down on us at the same hour from Radio Sharia, chanted with the same threatening voice in the name of Islamic law.

It is forbidden to display photographs of animals and human beings.

A woman is not allowed to take a taxi unless accompanied by a *mahram.*

No male physician may touch the body of a woman under the pretext of a medical examination.

A woman is not allowed to go to a tailor for men.

A girl is not allowed to converse with a young man. Infraction of this law will lead to the immediate marriage of the offenders.

Muslim families are not allowed to listen to music, even during a wedding.

Families are not allowed to photograph or videotape anything, even during a wedding.

Women engaged to be married may not go to beauty salons, even in preparation for their weddings.

Muslim families may not give non-Islamic names to their children.

All non-Muslims, Hindus, and Jews must wear yellow clothing or a piece of yellow cloth. They must mark their homes with a yellow flag so that they may be recognizable.

All merchants are forbidden to sell alcoholic beverages.

Merchants are forbidden to sell female undergarments.

When the police punish an offender, no one is allowed to ask a question or complain.

All those who break the laws of Sharia will be punished in the public square.

This time, they're really killing us, killing all girls and women. They're killing us stealthily, in silence. The worst prohibitions, which have already been established throughout the great majority of the country, annihilate us by locking us outside of society. All women are affected, from the youngest to the oldest. Women may no longer work: This means a collapse of medical services and government administration. No more school for girls, no more health care for women, no more fresh air for us anywhere. Women, go home! Or disappear under the *chadri*, out of the sight of men. It's an absolute denial of individual liberty, a real sexual racism.

As a last insult to all Afghans, men and women, a new minister has been appointed. He bears the ridiculous title of Minister for the Promotion of Virtue and Prevention of Vice, or *AMR Bel Mahrouf* in Afghan.

I go to my room to look at all my things: my books, clothes, photos, comics, music tapes, videos, and posters. My nail polish, Soraya's lipstick... We'll have to pack all this up in cardboard boxes and hide it in the closet. I'm crushed, at moments enraged, in tears a second later. My mother and sister and I find this petty tyranny over our personal lives intolerable. Mama has begun to wrap up forbidden items, family albums, baby pictures, photos of weddings—hers and Shakila's. Mama has taken down her lovely portrait painted by her brother, the picture of a woman in full bloom, an image of liberty the Taliban cannot stand. While Soraya and I pile our girlish treasures into the closet, our mother hides her own keepsakes from her years as a student, young woman, wife, and mother, concealing them in the back of a kitchen cupboard. I pack my prettiest dresses into a suitcase, keeping only pants and black running shoes. Soraya does the same thing. Her pretty Ariana Airlines uniform, her short, colorful skirts, her spring blouses, her high heels and rainbow hued sweaters, now "indecent." Then Soraya helps Mama go through the apartment to hunt down forbidden pictures, including calendars and the football and music posters in Daoud's room.

And I break down and cry, alone in the middle of our bedroom with the last books to be packed away. I feel faint. While I was busily filling boxes, I was acting as if I were just temporarily putting my things into storage. Now I feel as though I were coming apart. I happen to notice a cartoon I cut out of a newspaper last year. It shows two scientists bending over a microscope, studying some *talibs* swarming on a specimen slide. The scientists seem perplexed and wonder what kind of germ they're looking at.

A nasty germ, a dangerously virulent microbe that propagates by spreading a serious disease insidiously fatal to the freedom of women. This microbe is highly infectious. The Taliban need only declare themselves through force the absolute masters of Sharia, the precepts of the Qur'an, which they distort as they please without any respect for the holy book. In my family, we are deeply religious; my parents know what the Sharia means for a good Muslim. And the injunctions of the Qur'an have nothing to do with what the Taliban want to impose on us.

The Taliban have already forbidden us to keep photos of animals; soon they will forbid us to keep the animals themselves, I'm sure of it. We have a canary in a cage on the living room balcony, which Papa converted into a glassed-in porch to protect us from the cold and from prying eyes. Our bird sings so sweetly at sunrise.

Returning from the mosque, Papa finds me sobbing in my room.

"Calm down, Latifa! Nobody knows yet how things will turn out. You must be patient. This won't last, you'll see."

"Papa, we have to let the canary go. I want him, at least, to be free!"

Opening this cage is a vital symbolic gesture. I watch the canary hesitate before this unfamiliar freedom, take flight in a flurry of wings, and disappear into the distance in the cloudy September sky. It's my liberty he carries away with him. May God guide him safely to some peaceful valley! . . .

The days are endless tunnels of inactivity. I spend most of my time lying down in my room, staring at the ceiling or reading. No more jogging in the morning, no more bike riding—I'm slowly going to seed. No more English classes, or newspapers; I stupefy myself with the simpering sentimentality of the Indian films Daoud brings home. So that the Taliban won't see the glow of the TV screen after curfew, my uncle came over to paint the windows of our bedrooms, the living room porch, and the dining and family rooms, which overlook the street. Now only the kitchen window affords a glimpse of the mosque and the school, where there's nothing to see anymore but a circle of boys around the mullah, reciting the Qur'an.

I can't think of anything to do. Sometimes I wander around my home like a convict taking a tour of her cell. I go sit in an armchair, then on a couch or on the rug. I stroll down the hall to the kitchen, then back to my room. Sit down, stretch out, study the designs on the carpets for a while, try the TV again, go lie down once more. I have never before paid such close attention to the furnishings of the apartment. A bread crumb on the table attracts my notice. A bird in the sky fascinates me. Without realizing it, I'm already becoming depressed, deprived of all focus. Mama is far away, dozing, and no longer takes any real interest in what Soraya and I are doing, since we're not doing anything.

Saber visits me occasionally. Sometimes Mama sees patients, who arrive in their *chadris*. They're from the neighborhood, always uneasy, always in a hurry. I let them in; they disappear into the living room with Mama. Their husbands wait for them downstairs.

One day, at the end of the winter, I open the door to a woman in a *chadri*, thinking she's another patient who has come for a secret consultation. But the woman begins to ask me strange questions.

"You really are Latifa? Alia's daughter? Saber's friend?"

Put off by her behavior, I'm about to shut the door in her face when she insists on coming into the apartment.

"Yes, yes—it really is you!"

Suddenly she bursts out laughing, raises her *chadri*, and I recognize Saber's sister.

"Farida! It's you? You almost frightened me! Whatever are you going around in that thing for?"

"My older sister is here visiting us: I certainly fooled her! And now I've pulled the same trick on you! Not only that—I'm going to go out in it. Here, try it on."

It's a shock to see her dressed like that. I know what a *chadri* is; I'd seen them long before the Taliban came. Some women from the villages used to wear these traditional garments—of their own free will—when they came to consult Mama. In Kabul itself, however, one rarely saw them. On the other hand, during the civil war, the *chadri* could be quite useful to men and women passing along information. These anonymous feminine silhouettes with hidden faces sometimes concealed resistance fighters in pants. When we encountered such figures in the street, my friends and I would giggle at them. We called them "bottles" or "upside-down cauliflowers" or "grocery bags." When there were several of them, they were "paratroops."

I look at this *chadri*, a shapeless cloth tent sewn to a tight-fitting cap and covering the entire body. Some *chadris* are much shorter, certainly less inconvenient. The small embroidered openwork peephole covering the eyes and nose frightens me.

"My father bought us some. They're not as long as yours.

"My sister found this one at an aunt's house," explains Farida. "It's old, and my aunt was tall. Try it on. If you ever want to go outside, you'll have to wear one."

I put it on to humor her but also to find out what it feels like inside one of these things. The cloth sticks to my nose, it's hard to keep the embroidered peephole in front of my eyes, and I can't breathe.

"Well? Can you see me?" asks Farida.

I can see her—if I stay right in front of her. To turn your head, you have to hold the cloth tightly under your chin to keep it in place. To look behind you, you have to turn completely around. I'm hot, and I can feel my breath inside the tent. I'm tripping over the hem. I'll never be able to wear such a garment. Now I know why the "bottle-women" walk so stiffly, staring straight ahead or bending awkwardly over unexpected obstacles. I understand why they hesitate before crossing a road, why they go upstairs so slowly. These phantoms now condemned to wander through the streets of Kabul must have a hard time avoiding bicycles, buses, carts. And a hard time escaping from the Taliban. This isn't clothing, it's a jail cell.

If I want to go outside, however, I'll have to give in and wear one. Unless I disguise myself as a boy, cut my hair, or try to grow a beard, I have no other choice. At the moment, there's no way I can bring myself to hide beneath that thing. That tiny barred window grid looks like a canary cage. And I'd be the canary.

I come out from under there angry and humiliated. My face belongs to me. And the Qur'an says that a woman may be veiled, but should remain recognizable. The Taliban are trying to steal my face from me, to steal the faces of all women. It's outrageous! I'm not going out with Farida.

"You can't spend the rest of your life shut up at home!"

"All right, I'm scared. Scared of stumbling in it, of drawing attention to myself, of being beaten in the street because I let something show or I lifted this thing up to sneeze. . . . If I had to run to save myself, I'd never manage it."

"This one's too long, wear yours."

"No. I've heard they're kidnapping girls to marry them by force to Taliban soldiers."

"Well, I can't stay cooped up. My brother's going with me; you don't risk anything if you're with your brother. Ask Daoud to come along!"

"Absolutely not, I'm not going out. Anyway, I've no desire to see long lines of women scuttling through the streets. I'd be too depressed when I got home, if I did get home. . . ." . . .

Farida and Saber occasionally drop in to visit me. They go out, they're more adventurous than I am, but I just don't dare risk setting foot outside. I feel as though the only way I can still resist is to shut myself in, refusing to see *them.*

It isn't until the very beginning of 1997, four months after the Taliban takeover, that Farida persuades me to venture into the streets of Kabul with her, under the pretext of retrieving the latest issue of our review from our friend Maryam, who recently borrowed it from me. I don't see why I have to go along on this errand.

"You must come outside!" insists Farida. "You look awful, and there's no better way to confront reality. If you stay shut in any longer, you'll go crazy."

I vanish under my *chadri*. Then Saber, Farida, and I begin our strange "walk." I haven't been outdoors for months. Everything seems strange to me, and I feel lost, as if I were a convalescent still too weak to be up and about. The street looks too big. I feel as though I were constantly being watched. We whisper under our *chadris* to avoid attracting attention, and Saber sticks close to our sides.

On the way to Maryam's, we pass our former high school; there are Taliban guards at the entrance. On the adjacent sports field, ominous garlands of cassette tape have been draped on the volleyball net, the basketball hoop, and the branches of trees. My father had already mentioned them, but I'd thought these displays were temporary. Apparently, they are systematically renewed, streamers of forbidden pleasures: no images, no music.

A bit farther on, we pass four women. Suddenly a black 4 x 4 brakes to a halt next to them with a hellish screech. *Talibs* leap from the vehicle brandishing their cable whips and without a word of explanation begin flogging these women even though they're hidden by their *chadris*. They scream, but no one comes to their rescue. Then they try to run away, pursued by their tormentors, who keep whipping them savagely. I see blood dripping onto the women's shoes.

I'm frozen, I can't move, I've been turned to stone—and they're going to come after me next. Farida grabs my arms roughly.

"Run! We have to get away! Run!"

So with one hand I clamp the peephole of the *chadri* over my face, and we race off like lunatics until we're completely out of breath. Saber stays behind us, our helpless bodyguard—he knows there's nothing he could do to protect us. I have no idea if the *talibs* are following us; I seem to feel them breathing down my neck and keep expecting every second to feel their whips, to stagger beneath their blows.

Fortunately we're not far from home, so within five minutes we're scrambling up the stairs of our building. On the landing I sob uncontrollably, gasping for air, unable to speak. Farida painfully catches her breath, muttering who knows what, probably cursing the Taliban. She's much more of a rebel than I am.

Saber has caught up with us. Horrified, he explains what happened.

"Farida, they beat those women for wearing white shoes."

"What? That's some new decree?"

"White is the color of the Taliban flag, so women are not allowed to wear white. White shoes mean they're trampling on the flag!"

Even though they seem to follow one another without rhyme or reason, these decrees have a certain logic: the extermination of the Afghan woman. . . .

But you don't even need to go outside to find yourself face to face with horror.

Early in the winter of 1997, we hear a woman wailing in the street.

"My son is innocent, he's innocent!"

Looking out the window, I recognize the mother of Aimal, a boy who lives in the building next door. Three *talibs* are beating her son with the butts of their Kalashnikovs. They strike methodically, especially on his ribs. Soraya and I move quickly back from the window to avoid being seen, but we can't escape the boy's pain. His shrieks are heartrending.

Then, silence. The *talibs* have gone, leaving Aimal's mother sobbing over the motionless body of her son. When the doctors arrive to take him to the hospital, it's too late: Aimal has been dead for almost an hour.

Daoud finds out what has happened. Aimal had invited some pals over to watch a film on his VCR, in spite of the prohibition in effect. The *talibs* had burst into the apartment and caught the boys, aged fifteen to seventeen, red-handed. After breaking the television and the VCR and ripping out the cassette tape, the *talibs* ordered everyone outside. Then they demanded to know which boy owned these forbidden things, and Aimal stepped forward. As punishment, they made the boys slap one another, which is very humiliating for an Afghan, even for a boy. When Aimal didn't hit hard enough for their taste, a *talib* went over to him and said, "I'll show you how to do it."

And he attacked him first with his hands, then with his weapon. Aimal's mother tried to shield him with her body, but a *talib* slapped her and hurled her into some barbed wire. Then they all battered the boy with their rifle butts.

When the Taliban entered Kabul, Aimal's family was among those who waved scarves from their windows to celebrate the victory. Since she lost her son, Aimal's mother has been endlessly begging pardon of everyone for having welcomed the Taliban. She has gone out of her mind: She could never have imagined that they could murder her son, in cold blood, before her very eyes. Now she gathers stones to hurl at their cars when they drive by. They have caught and whipped her more than once, but she always does it again. She doesn't care if they flog her—what has she got left to lose?

In February 1997, I venture outside for the second time. Although they have forbidden women to work, the Taliban have promised to pay them their salaries for a few more months. Daoud and I accompany Soraya to the offices of Ariana Airlines, which are about a mile from our apartment. Since it's quite cold out, my sister and I are wearing long black dresses over dark sweaters and jogging pants. Our socks and running shoes are black, and our brown *chadris* are firmly anchored on our heads, so in theory there's no reason for the Taliban to be suspicious of us. The avenue has greatly changed since I last saw it. The television and airline company buildings are still closed and gloomy. Corrugated tin shacks have been set up a few yards from the entrances to the buildings, simple bins with doors cut out of them, doors reserved for women. That's where the *chadris* line up, going one at a time to have documents verified and to receive the appropriate compensation. I notice a small opening on one side, a sort of spy hole, and while we're waiting, I realize what it's for. A woman enters the container through the large opening and stands in front of the Judas hole, through which she hands her papers to a *talib* on the other side, who checks them and returns them to her along with a stack of afghanis.

The *chadri* isn't enough: They also have to have this shield of sheet metal between them and a woman. Just what is it they are afraid of? We are impure—but that doesn't stop them from slapping a woman with their bare hands and shoving her into barbed wire!

The women who have come today to get the money owed them begin to protest. Why are they being humiliated, refused entry into the building? Why are they being relegated to a tin shack?

One of the armed *talibs* sitting on the ground by the entrance to the container stands up to shoot a few rounds into the air and scare us. As far as I'm concerned, he succeeds. But Narguesse, a colleague of Soraya's and one of her best friends, is so infuriated that she rips off her *chadri* and screams, "It's disgraceful to treat us like this!"

Utter astonishment. She has dared signal her rebellion by showing in broad daylight the pretty face of an out-of-work flight attendant.

Then the other women become caught up in her fervor: Shouting angrily, they close in on the *talib*, who is quickly joined by other men who push us roughly inside the shack and drag away Narguesse, who struggles like a demon.

Once inside, we take off our *chadris*, shouting, "We won't leave here until you bring her back!"

There are only about twenty of us. I don't know if Daoud saw the disturbance—I don't think so. He probably thought the paperwork would take a long time and strolled off down the avenue. Everyone is talking at once inside the shack: We're all afraid for Narguesse and are wondering what punishment she's suffering. Our sole means of exerting pressure is to stay here, with our faces uncovered, so that they hesitate to throw us out. It doesn't give us much leverage.

At last Narguesse reappears, extremely agitated; she is wearing her *chadri* again, but refuses to say anything. The *talibs* scream at us to get out.

Eight of us head back to Mikrorayan. Along the way, Narguesse tells us what happened. The *talibs* took her to the former personnel office on the ground floor of the building and made her put her *chadri* back on.

"Why did you remove your *chadri*? Why are you trying to defy and offend us?"

"Because you have no right to keep women from working. No right to receive us today like dogs in that shack. We helped make this company a success and we didn't wear *chadris* in the planes or in the offices!"

"You're nothing but a woman! You have no right to speak, no right to raise your voice. You have no right to take off your *chadri*. The days when you could travel and walk around without a *chadri* are over!"

Twice Narguesse tried to take off her *chadri* again, she tells us, and twice they stopped her.

"If you try that once more, we'll kill you."

Luckily for her, one of the *talibs* guarding the shack came to warn his superiors that we were refusing to leave until she returned. After hesitating a moment, they pushed her outside.

"Get out! And keep quiet!"

She escaped severe punishment, perhaps even death, for having rebelled like that, but why did they let her go? Because they were afraid of having to control a handful of women? True, there weren't a lot of them, either. . . . Perhaps they'd received instructions? We'll never know.

Narguesse is still upset, seething with anger. She has always been willful and independent.

"We have to fight back. Today we couldn't do much because there weren't enough of us. But if tomorrow there are thousands of us, then we'll be able to overthrow these Taliban!"

We agree with her, but how can we rebel? Where can we meet? We risk endangering our families. We have no weapons, no freedom of expression, no press, no television. To whom can we appeal? How can we obtain outside help when we have no voices, no faces? We're ghosts.

This has been our first protest demonstration since the Taliban took over five months ago. I'm afraid. I'm still shaking inside when Daoud catches up with our little group on the way back to Mikrorayan.

This evening, in the apartment with its painted-over windows, in the gloom of the kerosene lamp, Soraya and I finally have something to tell our mother. But Mama, who used to be so defiant, places her tired hands sadly on her daughters' heads and sighs, "I'm sure you were very brave."

And with a sharp pain in my heart, I realize that she doesn't ever want to hear about war or rebellion again. Every night she swallows her sleeping pills to take refuge in a dreamless sleep. . .where the Taliban can't touch her.

For Discussion

1. What is Latifa's attitude toward religious tradition?

2. Why does Latifa call the prohibitions against women and girls "this petty tyranny over our personal lives"? (299)

3. After putting away her forbidden possessions, why does Latifa feel as though she is "coming apart"? (299)

4. Why does Latifa consider not leaving her house a form of resistance to the Taliban? Why is she eventually persuaded to go outside wearing a *chadri*?

5. Why does Latifa consider Farida much more of a rebel than she is?

6. Why are the women successful when they refuse to leave until Narguesse is released? Does Latifah think this incident shows there is a way for the people to fight back?

7. Why isn't Latifa's once defiant mother cheered by her daughters' resistance?

For Further Reflection

1. If you were forced to live under laws you found intolerable, on what basis would you decide whether to risk your life in order to express your opposition?

2. Is clinging to the "normality" of life a way of resisting a totalitarian regime?

For Research

1. Research the rise of the Taliban in Afghanistan.

2. Research the range of Islamic beliefs about the proper place of women in society.

The Perplexities
of the Rights of Man

HANNAH ARENDT (1906–1975)

Hannah Arendt, one of the most important political philosophers of the twentieth century, was born and educated in Germany. Her life and intellectual concerns were profoundly shaped by the events surrounding World War II, particularly the rise of the Nazi Party in Germany and the Stalinist regime in the Soviet Union.

Arendt studied with several of the leading philosophers of her time, including Martin Heidegger and Karl Jaspers. Because she was Jewish, Arendt was prevented from pursuing an academic career in Germany. In 1933, Arendt moved to France and worked for Jewish refugee organizations until the German occupation of that country forced her to flee to the United States in 1941. In New York City, Arendt joined the intellectual circle associated with the Partisan Review.

In 1951, Arendt published her first major work, The Origins of Totalitarianism, *from which the following excerpt is taken. Throughout her career, Arendt produced works that combine a deep understanding of how real-world political situations evolve with a profound grounding in the philosophies of Plato, Aristotle, Locke, Kant, and Marx. In her most controversial book,* Eichman in Jerusalem *(1963), a carefully crafted report of the trial of former Nazi official Adolf Eichmann, Arendt coined the phrase "the banality of evil."*

The historical background of the following selection is the predicament of people left without citizenship in any country following World War I, the result of the dissolution of the Russian and Austro-Hungarian empires. Arendt asks if the concept of human rights has any significance for people apart from citizenship in a nation with its legal structures and protections.

The Perplexities
of the Rights of Man

THE DECLARATION OF the Rights of Man at the end of the eighteenth century was a turning point in history. It meant nothing more nor less than that from then on Man, and not God's command or the customs of history, should be the source of Law. Independent of the privileges which history had bestowed upon certain strata of society or certain nations, the declaration indicated man's emancipation from all tutelage and announced that he had now come of age....

Since the Rights of Man were proclaimed to be "inalienable," irreducible to and undeducible from other rights or laws, no authority was invoked for their establishment; Man himself was their source as well as their ultimate goal. No special law, moreover, was deemed necessary to protect them because all laws were supposed to rest upon them. Man appeared as the only sovereign in matters of law as the people was proclaimed the only sovereign in matters of government. The people's sovereignty (different from that of the prince) was not proclaimed by the grace of God but in the name of Man, so that it seemed only natural that the "inalienable" rights of man would find their guarantee and become an inalienable part of the right of the people to sovereign self–government.

In other words, man had hardly appeared as a completely emancipated, completely isolated being who carried his dignity within himself without reference to some larger encompassing order, when he disappeared again into a member of a people. From the beginning the paradox involved in the declaration of inalienable human rights was that it reckoned with an "abstract" human being who seemed to exist nowhere, for even savages lived in some kind of a social order. If a tribal or other "backward" community did not enjoy human rights, it was obviously because as a whole it had not yet reached that stage of civilization, the stage of popular and national sovereignty, but was oppressed by foreign or native despots. The whole question of human rights, therefore, was quickly and inextricably blended with the question of national emancipation; only the emancipated sovereignty of the people, of one's own people, seemed to be able to insure them. As mankind, since the French Revolution, was conceived in the image of a family of nations, it gradually became self-evident that the people, and not the individual, was the image of man.

The full implication of this identification of the rights of man with the rights of peoples in the European nation-state system came to light only when a growing number of people and peoples suddenly appeared whose elementary rights were as little safeguarded by the ordinary functioning of nation-states in the middle of Europe as they would have been in the heart of Africa. The Rights of Man, after all, had been defined as "inalienable" because they were supposed to be independent of all governments; but it turned out that the moment human beings lacked their own government and had to fall back upon their minimum rights, no authority was left to protect them and no institution was willing to guarantee them. . . .

The stateless people were as convinced as the minorities that loss of national rights was identical with loss of human rights, that the former inevitably entailed the latter. The more they were excluded from right in any form, the more they tended to look for a reintegration into a national, into their own national community. . . .

The failure of all responsible persons to meet the calamity of an ever-growing body of people forced to live outside the scope of all tangible law with the proclamation of a new bill of rights was certainly not due to ill will. Never before had the Rights of Man, solemnly proclaimed by the French and the American revolutions as the new fundament for civilized societies, been a practical political issue. During the nineteenth century, these rights had been invoked in a rather perfunctory way, to defend individuals against the increasing power of the state and to mitigate the new social insecurity caused by the industrial revolution. Then the meaning of human rights acquired a new connotation: they became the standard slogan of the protectors of the underprivileged, a kind of additional law, a right of exception necessary for those who had nothing better to fall back upon.

The reason why the concept of human rights was treated as a sort of stepchild by nineteenth-century political thought and why no liberal or radical party in the twentieth century, even when an urgent need for enforcement of human rights arose, saw fit to include them in its program seems obvious: civil rights—that is the varying rights of citizens in different countries—were supposed to embody and spell out in the form of tangible laws the eternal Rights of Man, which by themselves were supposed to be independent of citizenship and nationality. All human beings were citizens of some kind of political community; if the laws of their country did not live up to the demands of the Rights of Man, they were expected to change them, by legislation in democratic countries or through revolutionary action in despotisms.

The Rights of Man, supposedly inalienable, proved to be unenforceable—even in countries whose constitutions were based upon them—whenever people appeared who were no longer citizens of any sovereign state. To this fact, disturbing enough in itself, one must add the confusion created by the many recent attempts to frame a new bill of human rights, which have demonstrated that no one seems able to define with any assurance what these general human rights, as distinguished from the rights of citizens, really are. Although everyone seems to agree that the plight of these people consists precisely in their loss of the Rights of Man, no one seems to know which rights they lost when they lost these human rights.

The first loss which the rightless suffered was the loss of their homes, and this meant the loss of the entire social texture into which they were born and in which they established for themselves a distinct place in the world. This calamity is far from unprecedented; in the long memory of history, forced migrations of individuals or whole groups of people for political or economic reasons look like everyday occurrences. What is unprecedented is not the loss of a home but the impossibility of finding a new one. Suddenly, there was no place on earth where migrants could go without the severest restrictions, no country where they would be assimilated, no territory where they could found a new community of their own. This, moreover, had next to nothing to do with any material problem of overpopulation; it was a problem not of space but of political organization. Nobody had been aware that mankind, for so long a time considered under the image of a family of nations, had reached the stage where whoever was thrown out of one of these tightly organized closed communities found himself thrown out of the family of nations altogether.

The second loss which the rightless suffered was the loss of government protection, and this did not imply just the loss of legal status in their own, but in all countries. Treaties of reciprocity and international agreements have woven a web around the earth that makes it possible for the citizen of every country to take his legal status with him no matter where he goes. . . . Yet, whoever is no longer caught in it finds himself out of legality altogether. . . .

One of the surprising aspects of our experience with stateless people who benefit legally from committing a crime has been the fact that it seems to be easier to deprive a completely innocent person of legality than someone who has committed an offense. Anatole France's famous quip, "If I am accused of stealing the towers of Notre Dame, I can only flee the country," has assumed a horrible reality. Jurists are so used to thinking of law in terms of punishment, which indeed always deprives us of certain rights, that they may find it even more difficult than the layman to recognize that the deprivation of legality, i.e., of *all* rights, no longer has a connection with specific crimes.

This situation illustrates the many perplexities inherent in the concept of human rights. No matter how they have once been defined (life, liberty, and the pursuit of happiness, according to the American formula, or as equality before the law, liberty, protection of property, and national sovereignty according to the French); no matter how one may attempt to improve an ambiguous formulation like the pursuit of happiness, or an antiquated one like unqualified right to property; the real situation of those whom the twentieth century has driven outside the pale of the law shows that these are rights of citizens whose loss does not entail absolute rightlessness. The soldier during the war is deprived of his right to life, the criminal of his right to freedom, all citizens during an emergency of their right to the pursuit of happiness, but nobody would ever claim that in any of these instances a loss of human rights has taken place. These rights, on the other hand, can be granted (though hardly enjoyed) even under conditions of fundamental rightlessness.

The calamity of the rightless is not that they are deprived of life, liberty, and the pursuit of happiness, or of equality before the law and freedom of opinion—formulas which were designed to solve problems *within* given communities—but that they no longer belong to any community whatsoever. Their plight is not that they are not equal before the law, but that no law exists for them; not that they are oppressed but that nobody wants even to oppress them. Only in the last stage of a rather lengthy process is their right to live threatened; only if they remain perfectly "superfluous," if nobody can be found to "claim" them, may their lives be in danger. Even the Nazis started their extermination of Jews by first depriving them of all legal status (the status of second-class citizenship) and cutting them off from the world of the living by herding them into ghettos and concentration camps; and before they set the gas chambers into motion they had carefully tested the ground and found out to their satisfaction that no country would claim these people. The point is that a condition of complete rightlessness was created before the right to live was challenged.

The same is true even to an ironical extent with regard to the right of freedom which is sometimes considered to be the very essence of human rights. There is no question that those outside the pale of the law may have more freedom of movement than a lawfully imprisoned criminal or that they enjoy more freedom of opinion in the internment camps of democratic countries than they would in any ordinary despotism, not to mention in totalitarian country. But neither physical safety—being fed by some state or private welfare agency—nor freedom of opinion changes in the least their fundamental situation of rightlessness. The prolongation of their lives is due to charity and not to right, for no law exists which could force the nations to feed them; their freedom of movement, if they have it at all, gives them no right to residence which even the jailed criminal enjoys as a matter of course; and their freedom of opinion is a fool's freedom, for nothing they think matters anyhow.

These last points are crucial. The fundamental deprivation of human rights is manifested first and above all in the deprivation of a place in the world which makes opinions significant and actions effective. Something much more fundamental than freedom and justice, which are rights of citizens, is at stake when belonging to the community into which one is born is no longer a matter of course and not belonging no longer a matter of choice, or when one is placed in a situation where, unless he commits a crime, his treatment by others does not depend on what he does or does not do. This extremity, and nothing else, is the situation of people deprived of human rights. They are deprived, not of the right to freedom, but of the right to action; not of the right to think whatever they please, but of the right to opinion. Privileges in some cases, injustices in most, blessings and doom are meted out to them according to accident and without any relation whatsoever to what they do, did, or may do.

We became aware of the existence of a right to have rights (and that means to live in a framework where one is judged by one's actions and opinions) and a right to belong to some kind of organized community, only when millions of people emerged who had lost and could not regain these rights because of the new global political situation. The trouble is that this calamity arose not from any lack of civilization, backwardness, or mere tyranny, but, on the contrary, that it could not be repaired, because there was no longer any "uncivilized" spot on earth, because whether we like it or not we have really started to live in One World. Only with a completely organized humanity could the loss of home and political status become identical with expulsion from humanity altogether.

Before this, what we must call a "human right" today would have been thought of as a general characteristic of the human condition which no tyrant could take away. Its loss entails the loss of the relevance of speech (and man, since Aristotle, has been defined as a being commanding the power of speech and thought), and the loss of all human relationship (and man, again since Aristotle, has been thought of as the "political animal," that is one who by definition lives in a community), the loss, in other words, of some of the most essential characteristics of human life. This was to a certain extent the plight of slaves, whom Aristotle therefore did not count among human beings. Slavery's fundamental offense against human rights was not that it took liberty away (which can happen in many other situations), but that it excluded a certain category of people even from the possibility of fighting for freedom—a fight possible under tyranny, and even under the desperate conditions of modern terror (but not under any conditions of concentration-camp life). Slavery's crime against humanity did not begin when one people defeated and enslaved its enemies (though of course this was bad enough), but when slavery became an institution in which some men were "born" free and others slave, when it was forgotten that it was man who had deprived his fellow men of freedom, and when the sanction for the crime was attributed to nature. Yet in the light of recent events it is possible to say that even slaves still belonged to some sort of human community; their labor was needed, used, and exploited, and this kept them within the pale of humanity. To be a slave was after all to have a distinctive character, a place in society—more than the abstract nakedness of being human and nothing but human. Not the loss of specific rights, then, but the loss of a community willing and able to guarantee any rights whatsoever, has been the calamity which has befallen ever-increasing numbers of people. Man, it turns out, can lose all so-called Rights of Man without losing his essential quality as man, his human dignity. Only the loss of a polity itself expels him from humanity.

The right that corresponds to this loss and that was never even mentioned among the human rights cannot be expressed in the categories of the eighteenth century because they presume that rights spring immediately from the "nature" of man—whereby it makes relatively little difference whether this nature is visualized in terms of the natural law or in terms of a being created in the image of God, whether it concerns "natural" rights or divine commands. The decisive factor is that these rights and the human dignity they bestow should remain valid and real even if only a single human being existed on earth; they are independent of human plurality and should remain valid even if a human being is expelled from the human community. . . .

Humanity, which for the eighteenth century, in Kantian terminology, was no more than a regulative idea, has today become an inescapable fact. This new situation, in which "humanity" has in effect assumed the role formerly ascribed to nature or history, would mean in this context that the right to have rights, or the right of every individual to belong to humanity, should be guaranteed by humanity itself. It is by no means certain whether this is possible. For, contrary to the best-intentioned humanitarian attempts to obtain new declarations of human rights from international organizations, it should be understood that this idea transcends the present sphere of international law which still operates in terms of reciprocal agreements and treaties between sovereign states; and, for the time being, a sphere that is above the nations does not exist. Furthermore, this dilemma would by no means be eliminated by the establishment of a "world government." Such a world government is indeed within the realm of possibility but one may suspect that in reality it might differ considerably from the version promoted by idealistic-minded organizations. The crimes against human rights, which have become a specialty of totalitarian regimes, can always be justified by the pretext that right is equivalent to being good or useful for the whole in distinction to its parts. (Hitler's motto that "Right is what is good for the German people" is only the vulgarized form of a conception of law which can be found everywhere and which in practice will remain ineffectual only so long as older traditions that are still effective in the constitutions prevent this.) A conception of law which identifies what is right with the notion of what is good for—for the individual, or the family, or the people, or the largest number—becomes inevitable once the absolute and transcendent measurements of religion or the law of nature have lost their authority. And this predicament is by no means solved if the unit to which the "good for" applies is as large as mankind itself. For it is quite conceivable, and even within the realm of practical political possibilities, that one fine day a highly organized and mechanized humanity will conclude quite democratically—namely by majority decision—that for humanity as a whole it would be better to liquidate certain parts thereof. Here, in the problems of factual reality, we are confronted with one of the oldest per-plexities of political philosophy, which could remain undetected only so as a stable Christian theology provided the framework for all political and philosophical problems, but which long ago caused Plato to say: "Not man, but a god, must be the measure of all things."

These facts and reflections offer what seems an ironical, bitter, and be-lated confirmation of the famous arguments with which Edmund Burke opposed the French Revolution's Declaration of the Rights of Man. They appear to buttress his assertion that human rights were an "abstraction," that it was much wiser to rely on an "entailed inheritance" of rights which one transmits to one's children like life itself, and to claim one's rights to be the "rights of an Englishman" rather than the inalienable rights of man. According to Burke, the rights which we enjoy spring "from within the nation," so that neither natural law, nor divine command, nor any con-cept of mankind such as Robespierre's "human race," "the sovereign of the earth," are needed as a source of law.

The pragmatic soundness of Burke's concept seems to be beyond doubt in the light of our manifold experiences. Not only did loss of national rights in all instances entail the loss of human rights; the restoration of human rights, as the recent example of the State of Israel proves, has been achieved so far only through the restoration or the establishment of national rights. The conception of human rights, based upon the assumed existence of a human being as such, broke down at the very moment when those who professed to believe in it were for the first time confronted with people who had indeed lost all other qualities and specific relationships—except that they were still human. The world found nothing sacred in the abstract nakedness of being human. And in view of objective political conditions, it is hard to say how the concepts of man upon which human rights are based—that he is created in the image of God (in the American formula), or that he is the representative of mankind, or that he harbors within himself the sacred demands of natural law (in the French formula)—could have helped to find a solution to the problem.

The survivors of the extermination camps, the inmates of concentra-tion and internment camps, and even the comparatively happy stateless people could see without Burke's arguments that the abstract nakedness of being nothing but human was their greatest danger. Because of it they were regarded as savages and, afraid that they might end by being considered beasts; they insisted on their nationality, the last sign of their former citizenship, as their only remaining and recognized tie with humanity. Their distrust of natural, their preference for national, rights comes precisely from their realization that natural rights are granted even to savages. Burke had already feared that natural "inalienable" rights would confirm only the "right of the naked savage" and therefore reduce civilized nations to the status of savagery. Because only savages have nothing more to fall back upon than the minimum fact of their human origin, people cling to their nationality all the more desperately when they have lost the rights and protection that such nationality once gave them. Only their past with its "entailed inheritance" seems to attest to the fact that they still belong to the civilized world.

If a human being loses his political status, he should, according to the implications of the inborn and inalienable rights of man, come under exactly the situation for which the declarations of such general rights provided. Actually the opposite is the case. It seems that a man who is nothing but a man has lost the very qualities which make it possible for other people to treat him as a fellow man. This is one of the reasons why it is far more difficult to destroy the legal personality of a criminal, that is of a man who has taken upon himself the responsibility for an act whose consequences now determine his fate, than of a man who has been disallowed all common human responsibilities. . . .

The more highly developed a civilization, the more accomplished the world it has produced, the more at home men feel within the human artifice—the more they will resent everything they have not produced, everything that is merely and mysteriously given them. The human being who has lost his place in a community, his political status in the struggle of his time, and the legal personality which makes his actions and part of his destiny a consistent whole, is left with those qualities which usually can become articulate only in the sphere of private life and must remain unqualified, mere existence in all matters of public concern. This mere existence, that is, all that which is mysteriously given us by birth and which includes the shape of our bodies and the talents of our minds, can be adequately dealt with only by the unpredictable hazards of friendship and sympathy, or by the great and incalculable grace of love, which says with Augustine, "*Vola ut sis* (I want you to be)," without being able to give any particular reason for such supreme and unsurpassable affirmation.

Since the Greeks, we have known that highly developed political life breeds a deep-rooted suspicion of this private sphere, a deep resentment against the disturbing miracle contained in the fact that each of us is made as he is—single, unique, unchangeable. This whole sphere of the merely given, relegated to private life in civilized society, is a permanent threat to the public sphere, because the public sphere is as consistently based on the law of equality as the private sphere is based on the law of universal difference and differentiation. Equality, in contrast to all that is involved in mere existence, is not given us, but is the result of human organization insofar as it is guided by the principle of justice. We are not born equal; we become equal as members of a group on the strength of our decision to guarantee ourselves mutually equal rights.

Our political life rests on the assumption that we can produce equality through organization, because man can act in and change and build a common world, together with his equals and only with his equals. The dark background of mere givenness, the background formed by our unchangeable and unique nature, breaks into the political scene as the alien which in its all too obvious difference reminds us of the limitations of human activity—which are identical with the limitations of human equality. The reason why highly developed political communities, such as the ancient city-states or modern nation-states, so often insist on ethnic homogeneity is that they hope to eliminate as far as possible those natural and always present differences and differentiations which by themselves arouse dumb hatred, mistrust, and discrimination because they indicate all too clearly those spheres where men cannot act and change at will, i.e., the limitations of the human artifice. The "alien" is a frightening symbol of the fact of difference as such, of individuality as such, and indicates those realms in which man cannot change and cannot act and in which, therefore, he has a distinct tendency to destroy. If a Negro in a white community is considered a Negro and nothing else, he loses along with his right to equality that freedom of action which is specifically human; all his deeds are now explained as "necessary" consequences of some "Negro" qualities; he has become some specimen of an animal species, called man. Much the same thing happens to those who have lost all distinctive political qualities and have become human beings and nothing else. No doubt, wherever public life and its law of equality are completely victorious, wherever a civilization succeeds in eliminating or reducing to a minimum the dark background of difference, it will end in complete petrifaction and be punished, so to speak, for having forgotten that man is only the master, not the creator of the world.

The great danger arising from the existence of people forced to live outside the common world is that they are thrown back, in the midst of civilization, on their natural givenness, on their mere differentiation. They lack that tremendous equalizing of differences which comes from being citizens of some commonwealth and yet, since they are no longer allowed to partake in the human artifice, they begin to belong to the human race in much the same way as animals belong to a specific animal species. The paradox involved in the loss of human rights is that such loss coincides with the instant when a person becomes a human being in general—without a profession, without a citizenship, without an opinion, without a deed by which to identify and specify himself—*and* different in general, representing nothing but his own absolutely unique individuality which, deprived of expression within and action upon a common world, loses all significance.

The danger in the existence of such people is twofold: first and more obviously, their ever-increasing numbers threaten our political life, our human artifice, the world which is the result of our common and coordinated effort in much the same, perhaps even more terrifying, way as the wild elements of nature once threatened the existence of man-made cities and countrysides. Deadly danger to any civilization is no longer likely to come from without. Nature has been mastered and no barbarians threaten to destroy what they cannot understand, as the Mongolians threatened

Europe for centuries. Even the emergence of totalitarian governments is a phenomenon within, not outside, our civilization. The danger is that a global universally interrelated civilization may produce barbarians from its own midst by forcing millions of people into conditions which, despite all appearances, are the conditions of savages.

For Discussion

1. According to Arendt, what are "the perplexities of the rights of man"?

2. Why doesn't Arendt seem to think that human rights exist "independent of citizenship and nationality"? (315)

3. Why does Arendt consider the rights to action and opinion more fundamental than freedom and justice?

4. What does Arendt mean when she says that the alien "reminds us of the limitations of human activity—which are identical with the limitations of human equality"? (323) What implications do these limitations have for the securing of human rights?

For Further Reflection

1. Do you agree with Arendt that human rights do not exist apart from citizenship in a nation that can guarantee them through its laws and customs?

2. Is there a fundamental human right to have rights?

3. How can the public sphere and the private sphere, as Arendt describes them, coexist? Are they always at odds with each other, or are they necessary complements in any society?

4. Are human rights inherent in being human, or are they part of what Arendt would call "the human artifice" of highly developed civilizations?

For Research

1. Research the events in Europe following World War I, when the breakup of the Russian and Austro-Hungarian empires led to the situation of stateless people that Arendt addresses. Report on the ways in which these people were dealt with by other European nations.

2. Investigate the social, political, and philosophical background of the drafting of the Declaration of the Rights of Man in the eighteenth century (see this document elsewhere in *Citizens of the World*). Report on whether or not this document recognizes the possibility of rightless people that Arendt discusses.

The Cancer of Human Rights
(selection)

JOHN A. GENTRY (1949–)

John A. Gentry is a retired U.S. Army Reserve Lieutenant Colonel who was an analyst in the CIA's Directorate of Intelligence from the late 1970s until 1990. Until his retirement in 1998, Gentry worked on intelligence and special operations assignments, particularly in East Asia and Bosnia. Since then he has worked in a variety of national security–related positions for the U.S. government. He received a PhD in political science from George Washington University in 2008 and was a professor at the National Defense University for a year. Gentry's writings have been mainly concerned with intelligence issues, including his book, Lost Promise: How CIA Analysis Misserves the Nation *(1993).*

A basic issue in defining human rights is determining which aspects of life should be brought under its umbrella. Constitutional democracies generally include such things as freedom of speech and religion, equal treatment under the law, and freedom from arrest and punishment without due process of law. However, since the adoption of the Universal Declaration of Human Rights by the General Assembly of the United Nations in 1948, with its greatly expanded enumeration of rights, there has been a tendency, especially in the United States and Western Europe, to multiply greatly those rights endorsed as basic. This tendency is perhaps born of a genuine impulse to be as inclusive as possible in recognizing the greatest number of situations in which the well-being of individuals and groups might be in jeopardy. However, in the opinion of Gentry and others, the result has been to vitiate the power of what they consider the most basic human rights and to undermine the interests of nations by weakening their intelligence operations, military forces, and foreign policy positions, as well as their private economic sectors.

The Cancer of Human Rights
(selection)

THE DEVELOPMENT OF a broad variety of rights is a prominent feature of social and political life in the late second millennium. The establishment of political rights in the U.S. Constitution and its first ten amendments were a radical break from the political norms of the late eighteenth century. The growth and spread of these rights, and the philosophy they embodied, had a profound influence on the development of the United States and on ideas throughout the world.

The notion that good countries grant specific rights to their citizens has evolved to the point that many persons believe that innate "human rights" belong to all people—and that these rights transcend and subordinate national governments and social norms. Governments exist to provide resources to actualize the promises of human rights. Not surprisingly, ostensibly universal rights look much like those that developed in North America and Europe.

Elemental political rights, such as freedoms of speech and religion of the sort embodied in the U.S. Constitution, are political forces that largely define democratic societies. They allow much opportunity for individual growth and personal freedom. Many persons thus see such rights as powerful forces for good. I will not argue differently.

The expansion of rights from beyond elemental guarantees of personal opportunity and protections from state tyranny to much more numerous, tailored rights that guarantee results in narrow aspects of life, however, is causing problems. Rights are costly and dangerous when they disrupt traditional and effective organizational structures, contradict religious and secular moral values, and unbalance previously functional social systems. They render ineffective or incompetent the foreign policies of states led or strongly influenced by strong human-rights adherents. They lead to and prolong conflicts rather than resolve them. The unbridled growth of human rights accentuates differences among persons and groups, threatens internal order and social cohesion, and transforms nations into mere states. In the worst cases the uncontrolled growth of rights, like cancer cells, can kill the hosts that nurture them—and thereby kill themselves.

The United States most clearly reflects an advanced development of human rights, both domestically and in foreign policies, but it is not unique. Other countries and a powerful international group of human rights advocates—in and out of national governments—have altered the conduct of international affairs.

COSTS OF U.S. DOMESTIC RIGHTS

The proliferation of rights in the United States is pandemic. Once restricted to the major rights embodied in the Constitution, the legal, regulatory, cultural, and commercial rights of residents of the United States are massive and growing. Creation of rights has accelerated since the 1960s, when Great Society social programs were based in part on rights-based arguments. These benefits are part of the entitlement structure of the U.S. federal government and its mandates on state and local governments. This phenomenon helped generate what is known as an entitlement ethic—the notion that receipt of government services and cash is a right. This view, evident in many ways, permeates U.S. society.[1]

---

1. Traditional welfare payments go to a small share of citizens. But entitlements through the redistributive effects of Social Security (tens of billions of dollars annually in de facto payments through tax exemptions, deductions, and credits) and a host of other programs benefit the vast majority of citizens regardless of social status or need.

The creation of rights has spread from fundamental political guarantees to economic safety nets, consumption-support programs, government administrative procedures, and trivial matters of personal convenience. The creation of rights has shifted toward narrow functional issues and the assurance of outcomes rather than processes, opportunities, and protections. New legislative, administrative, and court-ordered rights in recent years gave handicapped persons rights to access to public transportation and buildings, often at substantial private and public financial cost. Partners of homosexuals won rights to medical insurance coverage similar to legally married persons in some jurisdictions. The U.S. Congress embodied a second "taxpayer bill of rights" in legislation in 1998 to modestly reform the Internal Revenue Service. Many people argue that respect is an entitlement right, not something that is earned. Commercial firms see the appeal of rights and offer variations of "consumers' rights." The list is long.

The establishment of rights creates high standards for acceptable performance that society and government cannot achieve. Because rights as entitlements are not things to be earned or purchased at market prices, people demand immediate consumption of lots of them. People expect the rights to meet absolute standards of quality and timeliness that usually are not attainable. Resources are scarce. Moreover, some rights grant persons changes in the behavior of people with whom they associate, even casually. As animals with limited intellectual capacities and abundant sociopolitical teachings or prejudices embodied in their cultures, people cannot and often do not want to perform to the standards of contemporary Western idealism.

The complex of alleged rights is internally inconsistent. So many rights exist that all U.S. citizens now are victims of discrimination—the failure of government or society to assure one or more explicit or perceived rights. The United States now has true equality of victimization. Further, the gap between slowly rising resources and more rapidly increasing demands to satisfy rights-rationalized agendas is growing. This amounts to a new variant of the "revolution of rising expectations" that originally referred to the political consequences of the slow realization of economic ambitions.

The proliferation of human rights is a boon for rights-oriented bureaucracies and trial lawyers, but it damages the social fabric that turns groups of people into communities and communities into a nation. Because the only asset any government ultimately has is its legitimacy, the cost of a government's inability to satisfy rights-based demands is overwhelming. That cost rises further when governments, and the political parties that seek to control them, favor some rights over competing claims to please political backers or to curry favor with voters.[2]

Excessive human rights are anathema to nationhood because they denigrate the compromise, discipline, and sacrifice needed for collective work in pursuit of common goals in favor of the immediate gratification of individual desires. With personal desires enshrined as rights through justifications of ideology or theology, there is no need to share them or to compromise on their definition, cost, or speed of actualization. Rights are absolute by definition. With claims to rights clear, the shared community values and goals that helped bond society when rights were fewer and resource constraints more obvious are much less important. There is less need to work together and thus less of the glue of nationhood. Even when nationhood is diminished or destroyed, however, government structures remain to service the rights of individuals and small groups, including the employment rights of bureaucracies and unions built to provide services justified by rights.

Although initially created as individual properties, human rights are easily aggregated to become collective assets of groups of similar individuals. The logical step is small, but the consequences of this action are sometimes very large because group rights are different from and greater than the sum of rights of individuals. Just as individuals have alleged rights of opportunity and sometimes results, activists often claim that the collective ambitions of groups deserve actualization as rights. The variously defined performances of groups in society—be they consumption levels, unemployment rates, or inmate populations—must in aggregate be at least equal

---

2. These predictable costs are exacerbated by the unintended costs of incompetent implementation of rights-generated government programs. There is a now-extensive history of ostensibly well-intended laws, regulations, policies, and programs that have unintended ramifications, including the establishment of new incentives that either prevent achievement of goals or cause other problems.

to that of other groups without consideration of troublesome distractions such as historical and cultural factors, labor force participation rates, and work ethics. As in Lake Wobegon, everyone must be at least average. Subpar performance by any of a host of measures is allegedly evidence of discrimination.

As for individuals, the rights of groups allegedly are immutable and merit immediate gratification. Because they too are absolute, there is no appropriate compromise among the demands for group rights. The result is proliferation of strident social subgroups of special interests little inclined to work constructively with one another except for reasons of tactical expediency. The degeneration of U.S. society into narrow interest groups further diminishes the nationhood of the United States. Countless commentators have identified symptoms; single-issue groups constitute a growing share of politically active citizens, for example.

Samuel Huntington made the point differently by observing that, in the name of multiculturalism, powerful forces in the United States are accentuating the differences among U.S. residents and encouraging their preservation. By so doing, these persons attack the identity of the United States as a member of Western civilization. Failure to assimilate immigrant groups risks transformation of the United States into what Huntington calls a cleft country, with potentially dire consequences for political stability. This amounts to an attack on the whole in the name of the perceived rights of groups that refuse to assimilate.

Countries that are not nations can survive a long time in the absence of a crisis. They are prone to fail in the face of external threat but may explode, however, if the crisis is internal. They are especially likely to fail if disparate groups, bolstered by the certainty that they hold rights to their goals, strive for self-gratification at the expense of other groups. If groups threaten the perceived vital interests of other groups, including perceived human rights, civil war may result. This happened in Bosnia in 1992 and in Kosovo in 1998. Although not an immediate threat, it could happen in California, too.

A United States that protects and advances under the rubric of rights the parochial interests of discrete but politically powerful groups, including bureaucratic constituencies, must damage the traditional freedoms of small groups and individuals, either absolutely or by relative deprivation compared with favored groups. Disregard for, or subordination of, the rights of the politically weak generates substantial unhappiness among persons and groups personally aggrieved or disillusioned with the failure of the country to honor its promises. Antigovernment groups thus flourish in the late twentieth century in the United States. Timothy McVeigh swore allegiance to the United States as an U.S. Army soldier but became angry enough with its government to attack it physically in Oklahoma City in 1995.

Even in the absence of civil war, part of government in an age of human rights must become impersonal and disconnected from the lives of citizens, that is, the part that through taxation fills the economic trough that feeds people who are transformed from taxpayers to rights holders. Obtuse tax systems enable governments to accomplish this magic by separating the pleasures of receiving baskets of entitlements—and the benevolence of politicians for providing them—from the magnitude and timing of the pain of taxation.

Lee Kuan Yew, prime minister of Singapore from 1959 to 1990, and others have noted the deleterious effects of the proliferation of individual rights in the West in general and the United States in particular. Lee has noted that the proliferation of rights in the United States is dysfunctional because it places the freedom of individuals above the interests of society as a whole. This damages the coherence of society and eventually those same individual freedoms, broadly defined to include freedom of individual action and personal safety.[3]

A key consequence of the proliferation of human rights is the deterioration of personal responsibility. When the government guarantees rights, there is no need for personal responsibility in those aspects of life the rights cover. There is no personal responsibility to pay for rights that states exist to deliver. Thus the idea of a personal payment, denominated in money, time,

JOHN A. GENTRY

---

3. Excessive personal freedoms damage the ability of social organizations, especially corporations, to create wealth. Social disincentives potentially are numerous, including a host of regulations, taxation, and liability to lawsuits for alleged product or workplace deficiencies.

or blood, for rights-based objectives is offensive. Virtually any price is too high, hence the need for an obtuse, federal fiscal policy. In a world dominated by human rights, humans should expect to get what they want without paying. Rights come without strings. Rights do not bear the symmetrical burdens of duty and responsibility that privileges carry. In a rights-based society, privileges have little value and compel correspondingly modest obligations.

Personal irresponsibility borne in part by the proliferation of human rights has spread to many aspects of life in the United States. The decay of national fiscal responsibility, interrupted temporarily in the late 1990s by a booming economy and a movement toward budget balance, is caused largely by demands on the resources of a distant impersonal state. Many people presume that this state has deep pockets filled with resources that are numerous and free.[4] At the personal level, the penchant to satisfy desires immediately is a major cause of the long-term decline in personal savings at rates that long have been below other industrialized countries and that in late 1998 and 1999 was negative for the first time since the 1930s.[5] Personal irresponsibility aided by lax bankruptcy laws surely is a major cause of the otherwise incongruous surge in personal bankruptcies during the boom years of the late 1990s.

The attitudes of U.S. citizens toward human rights and responsibilities have changed significantly in a relatively short time. Presidents and the citizenry have long felt that something special about the United States makes the advancement of good an ideal that the United States should pay to advance. President John Kennedy eloquently said in his inaugural address that his administration would not permit "the slow undoing of those human

---

4. Note that the U.S. federal budget, claims of both major political parties notwithstanding, did not balance in the 1990s except with the help of a large surplus in the Social Security trust fund. Non–Social Security tax receipts did not match non–Social Security spending.

5. Commentators have offered many explanations for this phenomenon, including the rise in tax-sheltered investments and the rise in wealth that booming capital markets have provided. The trend of the consistently defined measure of personal savings has been steadily downward for years, however, and is the lowest among all industrialized nations.

rights to which this nation has always been committed, and to which we are committed today at home and around the world. Let every nation know, whether it wishes us well or ill, that we shall pay any price, bear any burden, oppose any foe to assure the survival and success of liberty."

But in recent years, support for human rights has evolved toward carping. The United States has been little inclined to pay much of a tangible price for human rights, even for clear national interests.

A focus on rights, and a collective confidence that the United States knows better than the rest of the world what human rights are and how they are rank-ordered, has led the government to a growing extent to pontificate, cajole, exhort, and extort through sanctions political action from countries around the world. Across the political spectrum, from religious conservatives to radical secular leftists, Americans criticize the performances of foreign governments in those parts of the human-rights spectrum that are their own personal interest. They also criticize U.S. leaders who fail to advocate the brand of ethical imperialism that advances their favorite human rights.

The United States has embodied human rights firmly in the institutional framework of its foreign policy. Human rights are prominent in the national security strategies of presidents. The U.S. Department of State has an assistant secretary who manages issues related to human rights and an ambassador for war crimes. Policymakers both pay lip service to and embody human rights into policy decisions.

Congress, reflecting the activism of constituents with narrow interests across the political spectrum, pushes the executive branch to be yet more active in human-rights arenas. When foreign governments fail to heed their advice, members of Congress increasingly impose economic sanctions to force action. By its own count, Congress through mid-1998 imposed sanctions 104 times since World War II, including 61 times since Bill Clinton became president. State and local governments have jumped on the bandwagon by banning their purchasing agents from buying goods and services from allegedly offending nations ranging from Myanmar to Switzerland. They have ordered government employee pension funds to sell shares of companies doing business in "bad" places. These mini–foreign policies have prompted many legitimate foreign complaints and undoubtedly caused consternation at the State Department.

Americans appear to support strongly such actions in most cases. They evidently care little that economic sanctions rarely change the behavior of foreign governments but regularly damage the well-being of the citizens of target countries. Since 1991, for example, many reputable Western organizations and United Nations agencies estimate that sanction-induced deprivations have killed several hundred thousand Iraqis, mainly children and old people. Advocates for these victims argue without effect that deprivation sponsored by the United States violates their rights. But Americans, if they know the human cost of sanctions, typically claim piously that it is all Saddam Hussein's fault, that all would be well if Saddam only did as Washington properly demands.

For Discussion

1. What does Gentry mean when he says that "the unbridled growth of human rights . . . transforms nations into mere states"? (330)
2. According to Gentry, do the "elemental political rights, such as freedom of speech and religion of the sort embodied in the U.S. constitution" apply universally? (329)
3. Does Gentry question the proliferation of rights because he considers additional rights illegitimate or because "much more numerous, tailored rights that guarantee results in narrow aspects of life" are too difficult to satisfy? (329–330)
4. What part, if any, does Gentry think human rights considerations should play in the formation of U.S. foreign policy?

For Further Reflection

1. Among the greatly extended array of human rights now claimed, are some more essential than others? If so, are there criteria that could be used to rank them in importance?
2. Is it desirable to increase human rights in order to provide protection in as many different situations and for as many special interests as possible? Or does doing so diminish the effectiveness of safeguarding a smaller core of generally recognized human rights?
3. To what extent should democratic governments allow human rights considerations to influence their foreign, fiscal, and military policies?
4. Is Gentry correct in arguing that "a key consequence of the proliferation of human rights is the deterioration of personal responsibility"?

For Research

1. Research the history and drafting of the 1948 Universal Declaration of Human Rights. Find the arguments that were made at the time for the greatly expanded array of human rights included in this document.
2. Find information about the consequences of economic sanctions by the United States and Western European countries against other countries for their abuses of human rights. Report on whether or not these sanctions achieved their stated goals.

Promoting Human Rights

WILLIAM F. SCHULZ (1949–)

Some of the most influential initiatives to safeguard human rights have been advanced by nongovernmental organizations. Among the most prominent is Amnesty International, founded in 1961, whose mission is to campaign for internationally recognized human rights for all. Amnesty International was awarded the 1977 Nobel Prize for Peace.

William F. Schulz, an ordained Unitarian Universalist minister, was the executive director of Amnesty International USA from 1994 to 2006 and accompanied many international missions to places including Sudan, Liberia, Cuba, Tunisia, Mongolia, and Northern Ireland. In addition, Schulz traveled widely in the United States, bringing the message of Amnesty International to schools, civic and religious organizations, and corporations, and frequently appearing on television shows such as 60 Minutes, The Today Show, *and* Nightline. *He has received numerous awards and honorary degrees for his humanitarian work. Schulz is currently a fellow at the Center for American Progress in Washington, D.C.*

In the following selection, Schulz offers a point-by-point refutation of the "realist" political position, which generally denies that human rights issues have a place in considerations of national interest. In so doing, Schulz raises fundamental questions about the relation of political interests to overarching humanitarian standards, a central part of the ongoing debate about the nature of human rights.

Promoting Human Rights

Let us not underrate the value of a fact;
it will one day flower in a truth.
HENRY DAVID THOREAU

THE YOUNG CATHOLIC MAN killed at that street corner in Portadown, Northern Ireland, by a Protestant mob, while the police sat across the street in their Land Rover and did nothing, was named Robert Hamill. I visited his family at their modest row house in 1999. Later, when I had occasion to meet with David Trimble, leader of the Ulster Unionist Party, first minister of Northern Ireland, and one of Protestantism's most ardent defenders, I raised the case with him. The Hamill killing had become emblematic for the Catholic republican community of their mistreatment by Protestant unionists and of the indifference of the Royal Ulster Constabulary. But more than that, the Hamills were Trimble's constituents.

David Trimble is an enigmatic man. A co-winner of the Nobel Peace Prize (with the Catholic leader John Hume), he is given to legendary bouts of temper. A key figure in forging the compromises with republicans, including Sinn Fein, that allowed Northern Ireland to regain self-governance, he built his reputation on his credentials as a member of the rabid Protestant Orange Order and once danced a jig with the hate-filled extremist Ian

Paisley. A former law professor, Trimble took no compunction in assuring me that the principle of "innocent until proven guilty" was no more than a "theoretical construct." David Trimble is a tough, hard-nosed realist when it comes to politics in Northern Ireland.

For this reason, when an Amnesty International colleague and I met with him in 1999, we did not have high expectations that he would make a priority of combating human rights violations against Catholics. Indeed, Trimble put on his customary show of temper at republican outrages (of which of course there have been many) and at one point slammed a book down on a table to make his point. When I raised the Hamill case, the unionist leader was quick to aver that Hamill himself had been guilty of various vague infractions. "You're not saying, are you," I asked, "that Hamill brought his death upon himself by simply walking down that street?"—a question that elicited another tirade. So I decided to change my tack. "Mr. Minister," I said as quietly as I could, putting my hand gently on his forearm, "I don't know the whole facts of the Hamill incident. Perhaps none of us ever will. But I *do* know that there are a mother, father, and sister in that house who are in deep mourning for a beloved child. And I *do* know that as first minister, you are now not just leader of the Ulster Unionist Party. You are the leader of this *entire* country, this *whole* community. If Northern Ireland is ever to heal, it will be because people in your position reach out across the barriers of the mind to the regions of the heart. Can you find it in *your* heart to reach out to a suffering family, even though they be of a different political or religious faith, as simply one frail human being to another?"

With that, something absolutely remarkable happened. The room became still and for an instant David Trimble's eyes filled with tears. The tears didn't spill over; they were so brief that my colleague, sitting across the room, didn't even notice them, and Trimble quickly caught himself and reverted to his more familiar style. So stunned was I at what had just transpired, even uncertain that it had, that I decided to test the matter once again. After thirty more minutes of conversation, just before the meeting was drawing to a close, I once again turned quietly to Trimble. In similar words to those I had spoken before, I asked if he would consider visiting the Hamill family, his own constituents, as just one scarred and suffering human being to another. Once again Trimble's eyes became misty and he averted his head. "Yes," he said. "I will consider it," and the meeting drew to a close.

I have thought of this interaction with Trimble many times since then. If he were asked if our conversation had affected him emotionally, I'm sure he would deny it, assuming he even remembered it had occurred. I don't think he has ever made it to the Hamills' door and I didn't really expect him to. But the incident provoked three thoughts in me, the first being the obvious observation that occasionally it is possible to cut through political and cultural barriers to touch a strain of our common humanity. The second observation is that the reason we must remain so vigilant about human rights, embedding them in law and pursuing them in practice, is because we cannot rely on the persistence of our governors' tears.

The philosopher Martin Buber tells of an emperor who was presented with an edict banning Jews from his country. The emperor took up his pen, was interrupted, took up his pen again, and again was interrupted. Finally he signed, but reaching out for the sandbox to dry his signature, he spilled the inkwell all over the paper. In the face of this final obstacle, the emperor tore up the edict. "Never bring it to me again," he instructed. A just order, we reflect, but can we stake our lives on our "emperors' " clumsiness?

My third observation about David Trimble's tears, however, is the most important. I think his bombast is not so much a sign of insensitivity as it is a protection against feeling all the pain he sees around him—the Hamills' and everybody else's. Of the aphorist E. M. Cioran, it has been said: "He didn't see Auschwitz and despair. He despaired as a way of not seeing Auschwitz." I think Trimble is like many other so-called pragmatists, "realists": he is afraid that if he allows himself access to the true terror of *everybody's* suffering in Northern Ireland, he will be both emotionally overcome and forced to revise his worldview. So when the tears break through, he has to be quick to choke them. Not only would he lose credibility with his unionist allies if he were thought to be going "soft" on republicans but, even more frighteningly, he would come face-to-face with his own limitations—moral limitations ("How have I contributed to this carnage?") and political limitations ("Maybe I don't have the power to stop this").

Trimble's dilemma is that of all political realists, where "realist" refers to those who counterpose "morality" to "national interest" and assure us that rarely the twain do meet. I grant it is not easy to learn of slaves in Mauritania whose legs are tied to the sides of parched camels and whose legs, thighs, and groins are slowly dislocated as the camel drinks and its sides expand. It is not pleasant to read Harry Wu's description of a Chinese prisoner so famished that he licked soup from a mud floor even after a guard had split open his head so that "bean sauce, blood and mud [were] smeared across his face." It is disheartening to know that every twelve seconds in the United States a man beats up a woman.

We are tempted to deny these unpleasant truths, to push them away. When a puff adder plays dead, a tiny trickle of real blood drops from its mouth. Perhaps this human blood too is only pretense. How frustrating that we powerful ones can sometimes do so little, even if we would do much, and how hollow perhaps sound Gandhi's words to those who are accustomed to triumph, "What you do will be insignificant, but it is very important that you do it." How much easier it is to declare this suffering "terrible, terrible, yes," but not as important as other things—our national security, our economic welfare. How complicated life might be if in fact the suffering and the "other things" are one.

The arguments by which foreign policy "realists" try to stave off human rights claims follow a pretty consistent pattern. First, as we have seen, the "realist" will claim that Americans must make a choice between promoting human rights and pursuing our national interest. Then they will warn that promoting human rights is tantamount to imposing our values on other people—something we Americans have been taught never to abide. Third, they will suggest that even if we want to support human rights, there is either very little we can do or, conversely, we run the risk of getting entangled in military ventures that could cost American lives. And finally, when all else fails, the "realist" will issue a dire warning about our American independence, implying that to accommodate an international human rights regimen may ultimately be to sacrifice our own freedom and sovereignty as a people to some vague but terrifying "new world order." It is necessary to respond to each of these arguments in turn to clear the way for a "new realism."

When it comes to characterizing human rights and U.S. national interests as fundamentally at odds with one another, some "realists" resort to caricature. "I maintained," says Alexander Haig of his years as secretary of state, "that an American foreign policy which is preoccupied solely with the achievement of ephemeral values such as human rights will ultimately . . . offend our sense of reality." Because no serious observer has ever contended that human rights (which, in Haig's view, presumably include such "ephemeral" values as free speech and the right to a fair trial) should be the "sole" goal of U.S. foreign policy, Haig's comment is as overblown as his personality. Other analysts, however, put the point in more sophisticated terms. Ronald Steel of the University of Southern California has said that "a workable foreign . . . cannot indulge in flights of rhetoric, dedicating itself to the pursuit of vague objectives like 'democracy' and 'pluralism' [which he calls "quixotic goals"] in lands inhospitable to these values and of no threat to the United States." Richard N. Haass of the Brookings Institute has written:

> The principal focus of American foreign policy should be on interstate relations and the external conduct of states—discouraging classic aggression, acquisition of weapons of mass destruction by rogue states, protectionism. . . . These matters have the greatest potential to affect the most important U.S. interests most deeply. . . . Considerations of "justice"—democracy, human rights, human welfare—would . . . ordinarily be of a lower priority. . . . The reasoning here is simple. Order is the most basic concern. One can have order without justice but not the other way around.

As I have shown in this book, "interstate relations and the external conduct of states" are very much related to human rights conditions in those states. If democratic communities that respect rights are less likely to wage war on other such communities, as is almost universally agreed, what better way to prevent "classic aggression" than to encourage the creation of such communities? Does Haass really believe that whether Afghanistan, Iraq, Libya, or any other "rogue state" acquires weapons or uses terrorist tactics bears no relationship to their degree of respect for human rights? Foreign policy analyst Steven R. David has warned that "as central governments weaken and fall, weapons of mass destruction may fall into the hands of rogue leaders and anti-American factions," but the stability of "central governments" rests in good measure on whether they create a rights-friendly atmosphere. Furthermore, the extent to which a country adheres to the rule of law and other human rights–related variables has a direct bearing on how open it will be to economic relations that truly benefit U.S. interests. Tell the former leaders of South Africa, Indonesia, and the former Soviet Union, Mr. Haass, how lasting order is without justice.

Indeed, when Steel and Haass list what they consider "vital national interests" (as opposed, presumably, to "quixotic goals"), Steel includes protection of natural resources, quelling regional disorders, and defending U.S. borders against illegal aliens and terrorists. Haass adds such things as preventing disease, promoting U.S. exports, and preventing domination of Europe and elsewhere by a hostile power—every one of which is related to issues of human rights.

Haass for one seems to be uncomfortable with the false dichotomy he has established, for in the very next paragraph following on that quoted above, he writes: "Under this doctrine, the United States would act . . . to shape the behavior . . . of governments . . . so that they are less likely to act aggressively either beyond their borders *or toward their own citizens.*"[1] But what does it mean to act aggressively toward one's own citizens but to violate their human rights?

Haass's self-correction is a wise one of course. A failure to take internal repression seriously can indeed have drastic consequences for the United States. When Saddam Hussein saw that he could get away even with using chemical weapons against his own Kurdish citizens in 1988, it emboldened him to think the world would little balk at an invasion of Kuwait. More than one former political dissident has ended up a leader of his country—Vaclav Havel and Nelson Mandela are the most prominent—and it hardly makes for warm relations if the United States has supported their

WILLIAM F. SCHULZ

1. [Emphasis added by the author.]

oppressors. "Were the Persian Gulf oil fields destroyed in a Saudi civil war," says Steven R. David, something that might well eventuate from the Saudi Arabian government's brittle repression of its political opposition, "the American economy . . . would suffer severely." And then again, as British Foreign Secretary Robin Cook has testified, "Countries which observe the rule of law at home are more likely to accept their international obligations to fight the drugs trade or halt weapons proliferation." To insist that we must choose between supporting human rights and defending our national interests is not only a phony choice but a foolish one.

What Churchill said of Munich applies far more often today than we think: "The moment came when honour pointed the path to duty and when . . . the facts . . . reinforced its dictates."

The "realist's" second line of defense is one that superficially appeals to many Americans. Because we are taught to be tolerant of other cultures, the argument that to advance human rights around the globe is to try to impose American values on other people and hence should be avoided has a certain logical ring to it. Mao was raised in the Chinese tradition. The Chinese tradition has no concept of human rights. To expect Mao to abide by them, therefore, is not only unfair but reflects an attempt to foist Western values on a different culture. The Chinese Communist Party may decree, as indeed it has, that Mao's merits outweigh his mistakes by a proportion of 7 to 3, but making judgments like that is not up to outsiders.

This argument has been popularized by Singapore's Lee Kuan Yew, who has claimed that "Asian values" place the interests of the community ahead of those of the individual and that economic development requires sublimation of personal liberties to the achievement of the collective good. Many Americans found themselves quite sympathetic to Lee's approach, when in 1994 an American teenager, Michael Fay, was caned four times for allegedly spray painting graffiti on cars and traffic signs in Singapore. I appeared on dozens of talk shows about the Fay case, and many a caller would insist that "it is not up to us to tell Singapore how to run its civic life," expressing a tolerance for brutality Fidel Castro and Saddam Hussein would no doubt be thrilled to hear. I always asked such interlocutors whether, since they supported the caning of Fay because they so respected the sanctity of law, they also supported the caning of vendors in the Sudan whose licenses had expired or the stoning to death of women in Saudi Arabia who are accused by men of adultery, since those punishments were prescribed by those two nations' laws. The best I ever got for an answer was that those situations were (somehow) different.

The idea that contemporary concepts of human rights, including the fundamental notion that governments ought not practice cruelty, have no basis in non-Western traditions is nonsense, as economist Amartya Sen has gone to great lengths to show. Confucius himself asserted that "an oppressive government is worse than a tiger." Moreover, it has always struck me as odd that when Lee and his disciples speak on behalf of Asians and what Asians presumably value, they seem always to have in mind only those Asians who are wielding the stick and never the ones on the receiving end. Do we truly believe that all those Chinese who were tortured or died in Mao's prisons would agree that they deserved their ill treatment because it was consistent with "Asian values"?

The fact is that human rights, as articulated in the Universal Declaration of Human Rights, are not "Western values," no matter what their origin, but universal values that transcend any particular culture. "Realists" seem to have no problem promoting the Western value of "private property" even though that concept may be a foreign one to millions of the world's people. Why, then, are they so reluctant to support values (like the right not to be tortured or imprisoned for one's nonviolent beliefs) that have been affirmed by nearly every nation in the world?

Human rights represent the boundaries of the acceptable, the limits beyond which an international consensus agrees that we may not go, regardless of the proclivities of a culture or tradition. "If you practice slavery, torture suspects, castrate girl children, we will not abide or sanction it no matter how loudly you proclaim it a custom of your society"—that is the message human rights deliver. The strict cultural relativist has no grounds for criticizing any practice undertaken in the name of tradition. The human rights advocate believes not necessarily that values are absolute but that we have in hand a global vision of "best practices" with which to order our common life together.

Some "realists" will acknowledge that support for human rights is a valid goal of U.S. foreign policy but will then go on to argue that there is very little we can do short of trying to become that notoriously dreaded gendarme, "the world's policeman." Richard Haass warns that "promoting democracy and human rights may be important interests, but U.S. foreign policy can only rarely accomplish this." That will be news to the millions of people in Eastern Europe, the former Soviet Union, South Africa, Latin America, Korea, Taiwan, the Philippines, Thailand, and now Indonesia, who over the past decade or so have experienced, in relation to their own histories, unprecedented levels of respect for human rights and democratic institutions. It is true that sometimes U.S. foreign policy has actually thwarted the emergence of those new impulses (as, for example, in parts of Latin America or in our stubborn support for Suharto). But unless Haass is prepared to say that we are nothing but a sleeping giant, the idea that the United States played little or no role in those developments is surely wrong-headed.

I remember a cartoon that was very popular back in the "radical 1960s." It showed a much-beribboned U.S. general talking on the phone to some hapless dictator. The general was saying, "Become a democracy tomorrow or we bomb the shit out of you." But the U.S. government and its allies have wide-ranging resources with which to entice, cajole, badger, and boost other countries into greater respect for human rights short of bombing them, and those resources begin with the diplomatic table. Imagine how different the situation in Sudan might be, for example, if the United States put as much effort and prestige into resolving that conflict as it has into settling differences in Northern Ireland or the Middle East. (One cannot help but speculate that racism may play a role in our choice of priorities, or worry what impact those choices have on the confidence of African Americans in the U.S. government.) Imagine what impact we could have on Myanmar or even China if we put as much energy into cracking the information shield in which those countries have enveloped their citizens as we did in Cold War Eastern Europe—something that with new communications technologies is far easier to do today than in the 1950s. Training in how to institutionalize the rule of law and other elements of civil society is far from inconsequential.

In as globally interdependent a world as ours, we need not rely only on such relatively paltry goals as academic or cultural exchanges to define our leverage over other countries. Controlling the trade in arms or in those commodities that support that trade (such as diamonds in West Africa) can be a highly effective tool to further human rights. Travel bans and support for extradition of those who may be guilty of human rights crimes to countries where they will be put on trial are other measures. Most countries are desperate for international respectability. Why else would the Chinese spend millions of dollars in foreign aid each year to bribe developing countries that sit on the UN Human Rights Commission to vote against resolutions of censure of China's human rights record—resolutions that carry little, if any, practical consequences at all? Playing on that desire for respectability can be a productive ploy. Those same countries are desperate for economic integration with the global economy, be it through private investment or grants and loans from international financial institutions with which the United States holds considerable sway. Clever use of economic carrots and sticks can bring remarkable change, as we discovered most dramatically in the case of apartheid South Africa.

But to play with carrots and sticks is to be willing under certain circumstances to withhold the carrot or wield the stick, and it is exactly because they shy away from employing or withholding economic incentives that "realists" are sometimes reluctant to admit the degree of influence we can wield over human rights developments if we choose to. Their modesty parallels the tongue-tiedness that strikes many corporate executives when they are asked to help promote human rights overseas. At some point a CEO will inevitably say, "We'd like to help, but we just don't have the power you think we do." I always get a kick out of watching a mighty CEO play the shrinking violet. We know that of the world's one hundred largest economies today, fifty are corporations, not countries, and that if we combine the sales of the top two hundred corporations, that figure exceeds the combined economies of one hundred eighty-two nations—all nations in the world, in fact, except the nine largest. We also know that many corporations are more powerful even than intergovernmental organizations—and a lot wealthier. The total United Nations budget in 1995 and 1996 was $18.2 billion, while Lockheed Martin alone took in more than $19 billion that year. One of the few advantages of running a trade deficit with China is that we buy up about 40 percent of China's exports, and it wouldn't be a piece of cake for China to make that loss up overnight from others. That is clout the United States has proven to have in its negotiations over piracy of intellectual property.

But more telling than many of these statistics is the fact that much of what corporations are asked to do to promote human rights requires no confrontations with government; only decisions about how to run their own businesses. They can be mindful of human rights when it comes to setting wages, working conditions, and production standards for subcontractors and suppliers or granting labor rights (including even where trade unions are forbidden, recognition of workers' associations that can negotiate with management) or meeting environmental protection requirements. They can insist that security forces working in tandem with the corporation respect human rights or pay attention to the company's impact on a community. Indeed, dozens of corporations, to their credit, have adopted codes of conduct and terms of engagement without risking government ire (though their willingness to allow independent monitoring of these codes often leaves much to be desired). Furthermore, many retailers or mail-order houses that may not operate directly in repressive countries can support human rights simply by insisting that their products be free of the taint of child labor or slavery.

Even when a human rights–friendly approach requires resistance to a government (when, for example, an employee is arrested for free expression or a company objects to the holding of political indoctrination sessions on its premises), it is more than possible in most circumstances to raise objections, preferably with the support of one's own government and others in the industry, without risking fatal animus. Some business leaders have even gone so far as to advocate release of prisoners of conscience without ill consequence. Former president of the U.S. Chamber of Commerce in Hong Kong, John Kamm, for example, has done so on numerous occasions and swears his business connections have never suffered for it. In 1999, Paul Fireman, president of Reebok, wrote a moving letter to President B. J. Habibie of Indonesia, citing his company's decade-long investment in Indonesia and seeking the release of human rights activist Dita Sari—a gesture that may well have played a part in winning her freedom. There were no negative repercussions for Reebok's operations. Of course nothing precludes corporations from being far more generous and supportive of human rights organizations themselves, both domestic and international, thereby accomplishing indirectly what the corporations may be hesitant to do themselves. The U.S. government can certainly be proactive in encouraging steps like these.

When it comes to economic sanctions, the record of success is decidedly mixed. Economic sanctions alone rarely, if ever, topple a government and often lead to humanitarian catastrophes, but sanctions as part of a larger strategy, particularly sanctions targeted to affect the power brokers, may well have a salutary impact, as they did in ridding Cambodia of Khmer Rouge influence and in helping bring an end to apartheid in South Africa. The key is whether those sanctions are strictly enforced and, because they so rarely have been, it is hard to know just how effective economic sanctions would be if they were taken seriously by all parties involved. The larger point is, however, that both governments and businesses have far more options than "realists" generally acknowledge with which to bend other parties to international will.

One of those options of course is military intervention. English critic Cyril Connolly once said, "If attacked by a lion, thrust your arm down his throat. This takes some practice." "Realists" find the notion of using military force for human rights purposes equally impractical and are quite adept at invoking the specter of Somalia to prove it so. Unless there is a direct and obvious connection with U.S. national security or economic interests, "realists" oppose intervention to stop slaughter. Commentators of that ilk fell all over themselves declaring the Kosovo War unwise and unwinnable. Even after the war had ended and most of the Kosovars returned to their homes, journalist Michael Hirsh could write, "By the middle of May, despite two months of bombing . . . , it should have been obvious to even the dullest observer that, no matter what the strategic outcome, America had lost the war in Kosovo." Hirsh will presumably forgive those thousands of Kosovars whose lives may have been saved by the NATO bombing and who are now back in their homes for being such dull observers as not to have taken notice of NATO's loss. And we will forgive him for not being prescient enough to see how that "defeat" ultimately set the stage for Milosovic's departure.

Advocating military intervention for humanitarian purposes is always a tricky call for human rights advocates. Amnesty International never takes a position on such matters and, although the organization had steadfastly criticized dictator Slobodan Milosovic's actions in Kosovo, it also accused NATO of war crimes after the war was over. But governments and intergovernmental organizations do not have the luxury of such studied neutrality, and to rule out military action even in the face of genocide or its potential is to tread a line both morally ambiguous and imprudent.

No one would disagree that military intervention should always be a last resort, employed only after all other options have failed. It goes without saying that the lives of young Americans are immensely precious. But to wave the red flag of U.S. casualties, to haul out the image of the United States as "the world's policeman," every time the possibility of military action for humanitarian ends is contemplated is tragically misleading. First, it is by no means true that Americans must always be on the battle lines in such ventures. Although the United States must usually encourage or support (and certainly not block) international interventions if they are to be successful, regional powers can often be called on to carry the military responsibility, as witness ECOMOG (Economic Community of West African States Cease-Fire Monitoring Group) in West Africa and Australia in East Timor. A standing military force under United Nations control would further decrease need for unilateral U.S. involvement. Second, even if the United States should commit its own troops, casualties are far less likely if action is taken early before bloodshed gets out of hand. Whether American or other troops had intervened in Rwanda in response to General Romeo Dallaire's call for reinforcements early in the conflagration, it would not have taken many of them. Finally, we must ask ourselves how many foreign lives one American life is worth. National security analyst Alan J. Kuperman has argued that had the United States intervened in Rwanda late in the genocidal rampage, we might have saved seventy-five thousand lives, a number that, compared with the eight hundred thousand killed, he implies, would not have been worth the effort. But on what grounds are we willing to contend that the lives of seventy-five thousand Rwandans are not worth the risk to a few hundred Americans?

Military intervention is never a happy choice, and under some circumstances it would be a disastrous one. No sensible observer, for example, has ever suggested such action by outside parties to put an end to Russia's misadventures in Chechnya. The idea that post-Kosovo the United States is going to run around committing troops willy-nilly to faraway places to combat human rights infractions is a scare tactic of the most scurrilous kind. As journalist Michael Ignatieff has written: "Stopping genocide doesn't commit America to intervene everywhere. It actually sets the bar to intervention very high and justifies the use of force only when large numbers of civilians are facing extermination, mass deportation, or massacre and where force can actually turn the situation around.

Ought force remain an option when it comes to supporting human rights as it does when it comes to protecting national security or promoting U.S. economic welfare? Given how intimately linked human rights are to those and other interests, quite apart from our moral obligations, the answer should be obvious. After all, we put Americans in harm's way to topple a ruler in Grenada and to capture a drug-dealing thug in Panama. What kind of people would we be if we were utterly unwilling to consider doing that to stop the massive slaughter of the innocent?

When all other arguments fail, the "realist" will wave the flag of American "exceptionalism," the doctrine that the rules that apply to the rest of the world do not apply to us. "Realists" will claim that if we conform our own laws and practices to international human rights standards, we will be in danger of sacrificing our sovereignty. Thus, in describing a "conservative" foreign policy, Professor Samuel P. Huntington can say, "Conservatives give their highest loyalty to their country. . . . Unlike most liberals, they see international institutions not as good in themselves but good only insofar as they contribute to furthering the well-being of the American nation." And John Bolton of the American Enterprise Institute, in decrying criticism of the use of the death penalty in the United States by a UN special rapporteur, warns darkly that "to whatever extent the rapporteur's work has an impact, it represents a shift away from a [U.S.] constitution-based decision-making structure toward one that subjects us to the vagaries of world opinion."

When I hear comments such as these, I often wonder what world their vocalists are living in. On a globe as interdependent as ours, how can American interests possibly be divorced from those of our trading partners, our cyberspace neighbors, and indeed even our would-be adversaries? What breathtaking self-pride to believe that we can reap the benefits of interconnectedness—lower trade barriers, bans on weapons, military alliances, environmental cooperation, holding others accountable for crimes—but refuse, whenever we wish, to play by the rules ourselves, rules that in many cases, including that of the Universal, Declaration of Homan Rights, we have been instrumental in making. "Realists" like to say that the United States must lead by example, but what kind of example do we set by such an attitude? What kind of a world would we live in if every nation took the tack that "international institutions [are] ... good only insofar as they contribute to furthering the well-being of [our] nation?" Let Americans just try to solve our environmental and health problems, maintain a healthy economy, and preserve the peace in such a world as that.

The United States is a mighty power, but it is not omnipotent. If history is any guide, it will not remain even a mighty power forever. Wouldn't it be wiser, then, while we have the power, to enter wholeheartedly into the creation of international norms, be they legal or behavioral, that best reflect our values and then respect those norms and their attendant procedures even when we may be found in violation? This is not to sacrifice our Constitution but, at most, to adapt its interpretation to the changing nature and values of the world—something that we have always done, when, for example, we outlawed slavery or child labor. European countries have managed thus far to conform their laws to the strictures of the European Court of Human Rights without abrogating their national identities. How "realistic" is it to think that we can thumb our noses at the rest of the world forever and truly suffer no ill consequences?

If foreign policy "realists" have their illusions, human rights advocates do too, perhaps the greatest of which is an unwillingness to acknowledge the moral ambiguity that often accompanies hard policy decisions. It is simply not true that human rights concerns trump every other. To refuse to negotiate with human rights violators when the consequence may be widespread violence; to refuse to make alliances with distasteful regimes to counter even greater evil; to insist that all human rights criminals must be brought to justice even if that means continuing upheaval for most of a nation's people; to show no sympathy for policy makers who must balance competing interests—this is also to live in a dream world (as playwright Bertolt Brecht famously said of the Spanish Civil War: "My food I ate between battles/To sleep I lay down among murderers"). It is to risk the kind of moral myopia that the Marxist historian Eric Hobsbawn displayed when he was asked whether had he known in 1934 that fifteen million to twenty million people would die for the Soviet experiment, he would have renounced Communism. "No," he said. "The chance of a new world being born in great suffering would still have been worth backing." It is hard to come up with a better moral compass for decision-making than a utilitarian calculation as to how many people will endure how much suffering. This means that addressing human rights claims will sometimes have to be a lower priority than negotiating an arms control agreement, for example.

The problem of course is that it is often impossible to make such calculations with any sense of assurance that they are accurate. That is why we resort to rules for the protection of human rights and must tread warily on their breach. Nor is it the case that human rights must inevitably be violated to reach our larger objective. Crime can be fought without abusing citizens' rights. Drugs can be interdicted without targeting innocent people. Wars can be fought without committing war crimes. In fact, all of these goals can be achieved even *more* readily if they are accomplished in a manner that honors human rights. Among the reasons to exclude torture from a government's bag of tricks is that the information received under such duress is rarely reliable. The resentment capricious torture spawns in the affected community, to say nothing of the affected individual, inevitably makes relations with the governing authority even worse.

Take an illustration provided unwittingly by political observer Robert Kaplan. In a casual little essay written for the *Atlantic Monthly*, Kaplan inveighs against those who would introduce moral scruples into policy making and praises the ruthlessness of those Machiavellian-like political leaders who adopt a "warrior" mentality on behalf of just causes. He cites Yitzhak Rabin admiringly and specifically Defense Minister Rabin's 1988 order to Israeli soldiers to "go in and break bones" in response to the Palestinian intifada. It was Rabin's toughness, Kaplan avers, that got him elected prime minister in 1992 and allowed him to start peace talks with the Palestinians. What Kaplan doesn't mention is that as a result of Rabin's order, Israel was convulsed in turmoil when it learned that its soldiers had with no cause at all mercilessly beaten groups of passive Palestinians in the West Bank villages of Beita and Hawara; that an Israeli court found the soldiers commander, Col. Yehuda Meir, guilty of issuing a manifestly illegal order; and that Rabin subsequently denied having told anyone to break any bones at all. How can Kaplan know that loss of Israeli moral stature—in the eyes of Israelis, of Palestinians, and of the rest of the world—caused by Israeli mistreatment of the Palestinians has not done the country more harm than good? How can he be sure that had the Palestinians been treated more equitably (which in no way excludes their criminal acts from being punished), they might not have come to negotiations even earlier? How can he tell that it was Rabin's association with a policy both the court and he himself had repudiated that changed voters' minds, rather than his status as a war hero? How can Kaplan measure the degree to which Rabin's endorsement of gratuitous violence may have contributed to the "warrior" mentality in Israeli society that ultimately struck him down when he was assassinated?

So although human rights advocates ought not claim supremacy for our values in every instance, those who would downgrade their importance risk facing more than a moral quandary; they risk damage to the very interests (in Rabin's case, Israel's security and stature, peace with one's adversaries, and the preservation of his own life) that presumably motivated them in the first place.

⊱⊰

Ending human rights abuses is not easy, and it does not happen quickly. When the guru Sri Ramakrishna was asked why God allowed evil to flourish in the world, he replied, "To thicken the plot." But the plot is now quite thick enough, and it takes a long-term commitment to unravel it. What I have offered in this book is not a replacement for "realism" but a corrective to it. That is why I call for a "new realism"—a recognition not that human rights are the only or even necessarily the primary consideration that either Americans or American foreign policy makers must take into account, but that they are entwined in a far more complicated way with matters of safety, trade, health, and progress than has ever been acknowledged.

A new realism would insist, for example, that human rights concerns be understood as matters of morality, legality, *and* utility, rather than sloughed off as a subsidiary interest unrelated to the truly "serious questions" of the day. A new realism would take human rights out of the box marked "preferences" and place it solidly in the box marked "strategic interests." It would recognize that human rights have implications for nearly every other policy concern our leaders must address. It would view human rights as more than the release of prisoners of conscience or an end to torture but as a comprehensive effort to shape democratic communities of rights that will be peaceful neighbors, fair trading partners, and collaborators in the effort to preserve a green planet. It would be flexible in its choice of tactics, recognizing that we cannot deal with a nuclear power in the same way we deal with a developing state, but it would insist that the same rules apply to all, including ourselves, even if the enforcement is uneven. It would recognize that short-term expediencies often lead to long-term catastrophes, and it would act with an eye cocked toward the future. If a new realism is successful, human rights will come to be understood as a "hard" concern, not a soft one, and its pursuit just as much a function of gumption, fortitude, and courage as any other national interest. Ronald Reagan, after all, was a champion of the rights of those oppressed by Russian Communism and in that sense was an unreconstructed Wilsonian—and no one ever considered Reagan soft on anything,

Are all human rights violations of equal threat to the United States? Of course not and, as I said earlier, some may not directly affect Americans' interests at all. But you can be pretty sure that one set of violations signals the possibility of others. If a country employs child soldiers or persecutes gay, lesbian, bisexual, and transgendered people or intimidates religious minorities or tolerates acid burnings of women, for example, it is a good bet that that country will be guilty of other abuses—that it may tolerate environmental toxins, fail to regulate cyberfraud, or ignore treaty commitments at will. A new realism will understand human rights violations in a holistic fashion.

What is an acceptable living wage? When should sanctions be applied? How "democratic" must an election be to be recognized as legitimate? Is there a reasonable transition phase from authoritarianism to democracy during which limited human rights compromises are appropriate? What are the warning signals of genocide, and at what point is the United States obligated to intervene? These and many other questions about how to implement human rights policies are complicated ones, but we will never answer them satisfactorily if we are content to adopt the traditional "realist" posture that human rights are compelling only when they are convenient.

And we will never transcend traditional "realism" until the American people recognize how abidingly their own interests are entangled with respect for other people's human rights around the world—so abidingly that they cannot be left to foreign policy technocrats alone. Fortunately, many women at least are apparently getting it. A recent poll showed that American women are more likely than men to decide issues based on their global implications. "American women understand," says the director of the project that commissioned the poll, "that the well-being of themselves, their families, and their communities are . . . intimately connected with the well-being and stability of other countries."

Foreign policy rarely sways national elections, nor do issues like police brutality, prison conditions, or the death penalty usually affect state and local elections. But even modest-sized numbers of people can have an impact on foreign governments and international corporations as well as legislation, policy making, and a politician's image here in the United States. At least forty thousand political prisoners have been freed thanks at least in part to the letter writing to foreign governments (and now the faxing and e-mailing) of Amnesty International's members. Retailers are supremely sensitive to how they are perceived in the activist student community, and the threat of consumer boycotts can have a major impact. When Senator Patrick Leahy of Vermont inserted a ground breaking amendment into the Foreign Assistance Act in 1999 that banned U.S. military assistance to any foreign military or police units associated with human rights violations, he rejoiced in the grassroots support that helped get it passed.

To convince jewelers not to trade in diamonds that fuel the grotesque brutality in Sierra Leone, or American diplomats to be as wily in lobbying in *favor* of a UN Human Rights Commission resolution condemning China's human rights record as the Chinese are in opposing it, or the U.S. Senate to ratify a treaty establishing an International Criminal Court, or a police commissioner to crack down on the misbehavior of his officers—all this can be accomplished by a determined constituency. The environmental movement provides an inspiring model. Not only are few politicians today willing to be labeled "enemies of the environment," but environmentalists have often made an ally of business. The Forest Stewardship Council, for example, certifies which forests are being logged at a sustainable rate and hence which derivative consumer products support ecologically sound practices. The timber industry (and, increasingly, fisheries as well) supports this program because they want to avoid litigation and bad public relations and because they know that sustainable forests are ultimately in their own best interests. Environmentalists support this program because they know that logging is here to stay and business will be either an ally or an agitator. How has the environmental movement been able to leverage its power with both politicians and corporate chieftains? By connecting the globe's future to our own, by supplementing our love of nature with the need to protect our children's health. The human rights movement will learn to link the moral to the pragmatic as well, or we will remain irritants rather than influentials carrying plenty of passion with but a thimbleful of weight.

Finally, a confession. When I was preparing this book, I summarized its thesis to a friend. "Oh, what a shame!" she exclaimed. "To think that we need selfish reasons to care about our fellow human beings." I understood what she meant. I wish it were enough to tell people that in early twentieth-century Congo, Belgian labor bosses cut off the right hands of boys who did not meet their mining quotas for diamonds. To show off their strictness, they kept baskets full of those hands on display in their offices. I wish the revulsion that story evokes were enough to motivate people to stop parallel atrocities committed today in Sierra Leone. But it is not.

I wish everybody responded with chills down their spines when they read Loung Ung's reflections on her father's murder by the Khmer Rouge when she was a small child. Her Pa was "loved for his generous heart," "a teddy bear, soft and big and easy to hug," who "smiles not only with his mouth but also with his eyes." After months of hiding from the Khmer Rouge, the Loungs were finally discovered. Two men in black came for Pa. " 'My beautiful girl,' he says to me as his lips quiver into a small smile, 'I have to go away with these men for awhile.' " Ung never saw her Pa again, never knew exactly what happened to him, but she imagines:

> I have heard many stories about how the soldiers kill prisoners and then dump their bodies into large graves. How they torture their captives, behead them, or crack their skulls with axes so as not to waste their precious ammunition. I cannot stop thinking of Pa and whether or not he died with dignity. I hope they did not torture him. Some prisoners are not dead when they are buried. I cannot think of Pa being hurt this way, but images of him clawing at his throat, fighting for air as the soldiers pile dirt on him flood my mind. I cannot make the pictures go away! I need to believe Pa was killed quickly. I need to believe they did not make him suffer. Oh, Pa, please don't be afraid.

I wish that story made everybody shudder, that we each could feel as if we knew Pa too, but it does not.

I wish all of us identified with Aleksandr Tvardovsky, the editor of the Russian journal *Novy Mir*, who, the first time he read *Ivan Denisovich*, Aleksandr Solzhenitsyn's staggering account of life in Stalin's camps, got out of bed and put on a coat and tie, saying that it would have been an insult to the victims had he read the book in his pajamas. But we do not.

I have spent a professional lifetime trying to convey the truth about human suffering that it might touch another's heart. I am a reasonably good writer; I can give a fair public speech; I can occasionally call on some skein of authenticity with which to reach into a soul to find that little corner out of which one human can respond to another's brokenness. And once in a while I have been successful, even in evoking David Trimble's tears. All of it is good, I think. But it is not enough. Not to enough rescue the tortured and the dying from the throes of perfidy. On some level I accept my failure and my limitations. It would be the height of hubris if I did not. But what I will *not* accept is those who tell us that it doesn't matter, that other things are more important, that we ought to offer a hand to anguish only in the narrowest of circumstance.

This book has argued that those circumstances are far wider than we think. But it is a mere footnote to the reason we ought offer that hand in the first place: because to look on human agony and consistently remain unmoved is to be dead in all the ways that truly matter, dead to the mystery of pulse and breath, dead to the gifts of grace and kindness, dead to the fragility of Creation.

Ultimately I do not care why we staunch another's suffering. Only that we do what we can to stop it. Only that we not remain indifferent. This book is a polemic against those who would cloak indifference in the raiment of "interests." It is an appeal to Americans to judge their interests wisely. A similar book could be written for every country in the world. But it is meant as nothing more than a supplement to a much more abiding conviction: that if we would live in the world with honor, we must not let misery go unmet. A world worth keeping sleeps ill with the torn unmended.

For Discussion

1. What does Schultz mean when he says, "How complicated life might be if in fact the suffering and the 'other things' are one"? (344)

2. What authority does Schulz think a nation such as the United States should appeal to in deciding to use military intervention in another country to prevent abuses of human rights?

3. What assurances, if any, does Schulz offer that his "new realism," in acknowledging "the moral ambiguity that often accompanies hard policy decisions," will not lapse back into the "realism" that he criticizes? (356)

4. If David Trimble read Schulz's argument for the "new realism," how might he respond?

For Further Reflection

1. Should order or justice be the most basic political concern?

2. How can human rights advocates effectively recommend the widespread adoption of values as "best practices" that they know are neither absolute nor universally accepted?

3. Should outside military intervention ever be used to prevent human rights abuses by a nation against its own inhabitants?

4. What should be the relation between nongovernmental organizations such as Amnesty International and the governments of the nations in which these organizations are headquartered?

For Research

1. Research which Amnesty International initiatives have been most successful, which have been least successful, and what criteria have been used to evaluate the results.

2. Find documentation for circumstances in which official United States concerns over human rights abuses in another nation have come into conflict with U.S. foreign policy regarding that nation. How were the conflicts resolved, if at all?

Let's Fight Terrorism, Not the Constitution

Confusing Freedom with License

DAVID COLE *(1958–)*
DOUGLAS W. KMIEC *(1951–)*

David Cole is a professor of law at Georgetown University, focusing on constitutional law relating to the First Amendment. He was a staff attorney at the Center for Constitutional Rights and successfully litigated cases establishing First Amendment protection for flag burning and challenging content restrictions for federal arts funding. Cole is the legal affairs correspondent for the Nation *and a regular commentator on National Public Radio. His books include* Enemy Aliens: Double Standards and Constitutional Freedoms in the War on Terrorism *(2003), which received an American Book Award.*

Douglas W. Kmiec is professor of law at Pepperdine University. Previously he directed the Thomas J. White Center on Law and Government at Notre Dame and was dean of the law school at Catholic University of America. Under President Reagan, Kmiec was Assistant Attorney General Office of Legal Counsel in the U.S. Department of Justice. He is often a guest commentator on television and radio programs.

One of the great ideological debates in recent politics concerns how democratic governments can provide for the security of their citizens while guarding against the erosion of constitutional principles guaranteeing basic rights. The following selections present opposing points of view regarding the USA Patriot Act, which was passed in 2001 and renewed in 2006, and is likely to be at the center of this debate for some time.

Let's Fight Terrorism, Not the Constitution

THE TERRORIST ATTACKS of September 11 have shocked and stunned us all and have quite properly spurred renewed consideration of our capability to forestall future attacks. Yet in doing so, we must not rashly trample on the very freedoms that we are fighting for. Nothing tests our commitment to principle like fear and terror. But precisely because the terrorists violated every principle of civilized society and human dignity, we must remain true to our principles as we fashion a response.

Three principles in particular should guide our response to the threat of terrorism. First, we should not overreact in a time of fear, a mistake we have made all too often in the past. Second, we should not sacrifice the bedrock foundations of our constitutional democracy—political freedom and equal treatment—absent a compelling showing of need and adoption of narrowly tailored means. And third, in balancing liberty and security, we should not succumb to the temptation to trade a vulnerable minority's liberties, namely, the liberties of immigrants in general or Arab and Muslim immigrants in particular, for the security of the rest of us.

Unfortunately, the USA Patriot Act, our government's first legislative attempt to respond to the threats posed by September 11, violates all three of these principles. It overreacts in just the way that we have so often overreacted in the past: by substituting guilt by association for targeted measures directed at guilty conduct. It violates core constitutional principles, rendering immigrants deportable for their political associations, excludable for pure speech, and detainable on the attorney general's say-so. And by reserving its harshest measures for immigrants—in the immediately foreseeable future, Arab and Muslim immigrants—it sacrifices commitments to equality by trading a minority group's liberty for the majority's security. In addition to being unprincipled, our response will in all likelihood be ineffective. Painting with a broad brush is not a good law enforcement tool. It wastes resources on innocents, alienates the very communities we need to be working with, and makes it all the more difficult to distinguish the true threat from the innocent bystander.

The Patriot Act's principal flaws are as follows: (1) It imposes guilt by association on immigrants, resurrecting a long-abandoned philosophy of the McCarthy era; (2) it authorizes executive detention on mere suspicion that an immigrant has at some point engaged in a violent crime or provided humanitarian aid to a proscribed organization; and (3) it resurrects ideological exclusion, denying admission to aliens for pure speech, resurrecting yet another long-interred relic of the McCarthy era.

A HISTORY OF MISTAKES

Before turning to the specifics of the Patriot Act, it is worth reviewing a little history and assessing what powers government already had in the fight against terrorism before September 11. Both assessments are critical to asking whether our immediate reactions to the events of September 11 were measured and likely to be effective.

This is not the first time we have responded to fear by targeting immigrants and treating them as suspect because of their group identities rather than their individual conduct. In World War I, we imprisoned "enemy aliens" for their national identity and dissidents for merely speaking out against the war. In the winter of 1919-1920, the federal government responded to a series of politically motivated bombings, including one of Attorney General A. Mitchell Palmer's home in Washington, D.C., by rounding up 6,000 to 10,000 suspected immigrants in thirty-three cities across the country—not for their part in the bombings but for their political affiliations. They were detained in overcrowded "bull pens" and coerced into signing confessions. Many of those arrested turned out to be citizens. In the end, 556 were deported, but for their political affiliations, not for their part in the bombings.

In World War II, we interned 110,000 persons, over two-thirds of whom were citizens of the United States, not because of individualized determinations that they posed a threat to national security or the war effort but solely for their Japanese ancestry. And in the fight against Communism, which reached its height in the McCarthy era, we made it a crime even to be a member of the Communist Party and passed the McCarran-Walter Act, which authorized the government to keep out and expel noncitizens who advocated Communism or other proscribed ideas or who belonged to groups advocating those ideas. Under the McCarran-Walter Act, which remained a part of our law until 1990, the United States denied visas to, among others, writers Gabriel García Marquez and Carlos Fuentes and to Nino Pasti, former deputy commander of NATO, because he was going to speak against the deployment of nuclear cruise missiles.

All these past responses are now seen as mistakes. Yet while today's response does not yet match these historical overreactions, it is characterized by many of the same mistakes of principle—namely, targeting vulnerable groups not for illegal conduct but because of their group identity or political affiliation.

In considering whether the new laws directed at immigrants are necessary, it is also important to know what authority the government had prior to September 11 to deny admission to, detain, and deport aliens engaged in terrorist activity. Before the Patriot Act, the government could detain without bond any alien with any visa violation if it had reason to believe that he posed a threat to national security or a risk of flight. It could deny admission to mere members of terrorist groups, and it could deport any alien who had in any way engaged in, furthered, supported, or facilitated terrorist activity, expansively defined to include virtually any use or threat to use a firearm with intent to endanger person or property. Moreover, the Immigration and Naturalization Service (INS) maintained that it had the power to expel, detain, and deport aliens using secret evidence that the alien had no chance to confront or rebut.

The extent of these preexisting powers is illustrated by the unprecedented incarceration of between 1,500 and 2,000 persons in connection with the investigation of the September 11 attacks. As of December 2002, the identity of the vast majority of these detainees was still a secret, as was even the total number detained. (The government stopped issuing a daily tally in early November 2001, when the number was 1,182.) The bulk of the detainees were held on immigration charges, and all the immigration detainees were tried in proceedings entirely closed to the public, a practice that three federal courts have declared unconstitutional. In October 2002, one court upheld the constitutionality of the closed hearings, and the matter is likely to be resolved in the Supreme Court. As of October 2002, not one person arrested since September 11 had been charged with any involvement in the attacks under investigation. The only person so charged was Zacarias Moussaoui, and he was arrested before September 11. Most of the detainees have been affirmatively "cleared" by the FBI of any involvement in terrorism. And most important for purposes of assessing the need for new powers, the government carried out this unprecedented program of secret mass detentions without even relying on the Patriot Act.

GUILT BY ASSOCIATION

The single most problematic feature of the Patriot Act is its adoption of the philosophy of guilt by association, which the Supreme Court has condemned as "alien to the traditions of a free society and the First Amendment itself." Under prior law, aliens were deportable for engaging in or supporting terrorist *activity*. The Patriot Act makes aliens deportable for wholly innocent *associations* with a "terrorist organization," regardless of any nexus between the alien's support and any act of violence, much less terrorism. And because the Patriot Act defines "terrorist activity" to include virtually any use or threat to use violence and defines a "terrorist organization" as any group that has used or threatened to use violence, the proscription on political association potentially encompasses every organization that has ever been involved in a civil war or a crime of violence, from a pro-life group that once threatened workers at an abortion clinic to the African National Congress (ANC), the Irish Republican Army (IRA), or the Northern Alliance in Afghanistan.

The law contains no requirement that the alien's support have any connection whatsoever to a designated organization's terrorist activity. Thus, an alien who sent coloring books to a day care center run by an organization that was ever involved in armed struggle would be deportable as a terrorist, even if she could show that the coloring books were used only by three-year-olds. Indeed, the law apparently extends even to those who seek to support a group in the interest of *countering* terrorism. Thus, an immigrant who offered his services in peace negotiating to the Real IRA in the hope of furthering the peace process in Great Britain and forestalling further violence could be deported as a terrorist.

Guilt by association, the Supreme Court has ruled, violates the First and the Fifth Amendments. It violates the First Amendment because people have a right to associate with groups that have lawful and unlawful ends, so long as they do not further the group's illegal ends. And it violates the Fifth Amendment because "in our jurisprudence guilt is personal." To hold an alien responsible for the military acts of the ANC, for example, because he offered a donation to the ANC's peaceful anti-apartheid efforts, or for providing peace-negotiating training to the Real IRA, violates that principle. Without some connection between the alien's support and terrorist activity, the Constitution is violated.

Some suggest that the threat from terrorist organizations abroad requires some compromise on the principle prohibiting guilt by association. But this principle was developed in connection with measures directed at the Communist Party, an organization that Congress found to be, and the Supreme Court accepted as, a foreign-dominated organization that used sabotage and terrorism for the purpose or overthrowing the United States by force and violence. Others argue that because money is fungible, even support of lawful activities may free up resources that can be devoted to terrorism. But, of course, the same argument could have been made of the Communist Party or indeed any organization that engages in legal as well illegal activity. Yet surely it cannot be the case the Congress could have simply reenacted all the anti-Communist laws struck down on guilty by association grounds simply by rewriting them to hinge their penalties on the payment of dues to the Communist Party instead of membership in that party.

DETENTION VERSUS DUE PROCESS

The Patriot Act also authorizes the INS to detain, potentially indefinitely, any alien certified by the attorney general as a "suspected terrorist." While "suspected terrorists" sounds like a class that ought to be locked up, the law defines the class so broadly that it includes virtually every immigrant who has been involved in a barroom brawl or domestic dispute, as well as aliens who have never committed an act of violence in their life, and whose only "crime" is to have provided humanitarian aid to an organization disfavored by the government. And the act provides that such persons may be detained indefinitely even if they are *granted* relief from removal—and therefore have a legal right to remain here.

This provision raises several constitutional concerns. First, it mandates preventive detention of persons *who pose no threat to national security or risk of flight.* The Supreme Court has upheld preventive detention of accused criminals and aliens in deportation proceedings, but only where the government demonstrates a specific need for the detention—by showing that the individual poses a danger to others or a risk of flight. In doing away with that minimal requirement, the legislation vests the attorney general with unprecedented and unconstitutional authority.

Second, the law allows the INS to detain aliens *indefinitely, even where they have prevailed in their removal proceedings.* This, too, is patently unconstitutional. Once an alien has prevailed in his removal proceeding and has been granted relief from removal, he has a legal right to remain here. There is no longer a legitimate immigration reason to detain such a person because immigration detention is permissible only as an aid to removing a person from the country. Yet the act provides that even aliens *granted* relief from removal may still be detained. This is akin to detaining a prisoner even after he has received a pardon. Once an alien has prevailed in his immigration proceeding, the INS has no legitimate basis for detaining the individual.

Third, and most important, it is critical to the constitutionality of any executive detention provision that the person detained have a meaningful opportunity to contest his detention both administratively and in court. The bill affords an alien no opportunity to make a case that he should not be detained within the administrative process. It relegates him to the filing of a habeas corpus petition. But due process requires that the agency depriving a person of his liberty afford him a meaningful opportunity to be heard, and the fact that one can sue the agency afterward is not generally sufficient.

Finally, the Patriot Act permits detention of certified aliens for up to seven days without the filing of any charges. The Supreme Court has ruled that individuals arrested in the criminal setting must be brought before a judge for a probable cause hearing within forty-eight hours except in the most extraordinary circumstances. This law extends blanket authority to detain an alien for seven days on mere certification that he or she was at one time involved in a barroom brawl. Such overbroad authority clearly does not meet the Supreme Court's requirement that any preventive detention authority be accompanied by heightened procedural protections and narrowly drawn laws.

IDEOLOGICAL EXCLUSION

The Patriot Act also revives ideological exclusion, denying entry to aliens for pure speech. It excludes aliens who "endorse or espouse terrorist activity" or who "persuade others to support terrorist activity or a terrorist organization" in ways that the secretary of state determines undermine U.S. efforts to combat terrorism. It also excludes aliens who are representatives of groups that "endorse acts of terrorist activity" in ways that similarly undermine U.S. efforts to combat terrorism.

Excluding people for their ideas and associations is flatly contrary to the spirit of freedom for which the United States stands. Moreover, such exclusions have a negative impact on free debate within the United States by denying those who live here access to those who might dissent from government policies. It was for that reason that Congress repealed all such "ideological exclusion" grounds in 1990 after years of embarrassing visa denials for political reasons. We are a strong enough country, and our resolve against terrorism is strong enough, to make such censorship wholly unnecessary.

CONCLUSION

We must respond to terrorism, but we must also ensure that our responses are measured and balanced. Is it measured to make deportable anyone who provides humanitarian aid to any organization engaged in a civil war? Is it measured to label domestic disputes or barroom fights with weapons acts of terrorism? Is it measured to subject anyone who might engage in such activity to mandatory detention without any procedural protections and without any showing that he poses any current danger? Is it measured to restore exclusion for pure idea?

The overbreadth of the Patriot Act reflects the overreaction that we have often indulged in when threatened and raises serious constitutional concerns even if it were shown that such measures would make us more secure. But there is also reason to doubt that the expansive authorities that the act grants will in fact make us safer. By penalizing even wholly lawful, nonviolent, and counterterrorist associational activity, we are likely to waste valuable resources tracking innocent political activity, drive other activity underground, encourage extremists, and make the communities that will inevitably be targeted by such broad-brush measures far less likely to cooperate with law enforcement. As Justice Louis Brandeis wrote nearly seventy-five years ago, the framers of our Constitution knew "that fear breeds repression; that repression breeds hate; and that hate menaces stable government."[1] In other words, freedom and security need not necessarily be traded off against one another; maintaining our freedoms is itself critical to maintaining our security.

The immigration provisions of the Patriot Act fail to live up to the very commitments to freedom that the president has said that we are fighting for. As the Supreme Court wrote in 1967, declaring invalid an anti-Communist law, "It would indeed be ironic if, in the name of national defense, we would sanction the subversion of one of those liberties—the freedom of association—which makes the defense of the Nation worthwhile."[2]

---

1. *Whitney v. California*, 274 U.S. 357 (1927).
2. *United States v. Rubel*, 389 U.S. 258 (1967).

Confusing Freedom
with License

THE EVENTS OF SEPTEMBER 11 remain ever present in the minds of American citizens. For thousands of families, a husband or wife or child will never return home because of what happened that day. The diabolical events of that morning will be forever etched in our consciousness. And yet, along with those mental pictures, it is important to grasp fully what happened: It wasn't a political rally, it wasn't a nonviolent speech protest, it wasn't an example of urban street crime, it wasn't even an attack by another sovereign state or nation. It was the deliberate murder of innocent men and women, not for a high political purpose or cause—or even a base one—but simply the random manifestation of hate intended to spread panic and fracture the civil order and continuation of American society.

As grievously wounded as we may be, American society and its principled understanding of freedom *with* responsibility does not fracture or panic that easily. But it does expect that justice will be done. It earnestly desires, along with our president, to see those who so mercilessly took sacred human life to be held accountable—not in a local criminal court but by the able men and women of the military and our law enforcement communities, working together either to eliminate on a field of battle these "enemies of mankind," as Blackstone called them, or to apprehend and punish them—presumably before the bar of a properly convened military tribunal, like those employed against Nazi saboteurs in World War II.

In considering the USA Patriot Act, it is useful to remember that our founders' conception of freedom was not a freedom to do anything or associate for any purpose but to do those things that do not harm others and that, it was hoped, would advance the common good. Freedom separated from this truth is not freedom at all but license. *Congress can no longer afford, if it ever could, to confuse freedom and license because doing so licenses terrorism, not freedom.* Those who have voiced opposition to the Patriot Act seem to have either a more extreme view of freedom, a less sober view of the threats we face, or both.

With due respect, such unrefined autonomy or complacency hides a basic confusion or underappreciation for the war against terrorism that now must be fought. The objectors think of the mass destruction of the World Trade Center and the Pentagon as the equivalent of murder, kidnapping, or bank robbery. They think the point is a criminal trial; it is not—it is the elimination of terrorism.

The primary authority for dealing with the terrorist threat resides both in the president, as commander in chief, and in Congress, as the architect of various specific legal authorities under the Constitution, to meet that threat. The president has courageously told the nations of the world that all are either for the United States in this or with the terrorists. There is no middle ground. Similarly, Congress, by joint resolution, has given President Bush authority to act against not only those wealthy and bloody hands that orchestrated the events of September 11 but also all cooperators in those cowardly actions or "any future act" of international terrorism. However, to ensure successful application of our military might, Congress needed to equip our law enforcement and intelligence communities with adequate and constitutional legal authority to address a war crime on a scale that previously was not seen in this generation or seen ever in peacetime.

The Patriot Act supplied the necessary authority and direction. The act gives due regard to the necessary balance between the civil liberties enjoyed by our citizens under the Constitution and the law enforcement authority needed. In particular, the act advances two fundamental purposes: to subject terrorism to at least the same rigorous treatment as organized crime and prosecution of the drug trade and to supply up-to-date law enforcement capabilities that address the technology of the day, which no longer observes some of the lines previously drawn under existing law. Terrorists don't stay in one place using only landline telephones and postcards, and it is folly to have a legal investigation authority that still assumes that.

While the Patriot Act's provisions are a bit arcane and complex, they incorporate the recommendations of virtually every commission in the last decade to study terrorism. Specifically, with respect to conducting intelligence gathering against a foreign power or their agents, the act ensures that the insights of the specialized foreign intelligence court are available to superintend the investigative process. There is no reason to deny the Justice Department this authority even if a given investigation has a significant criminal purpose as well. So, too, information gathered on the criminal justice side of an investigation or through a grand jury should be made available to those tasked with the difficult worldwide manhunt of shadowy and elusive terrorist cells. Such are matters of prudent legal reform and just plain common sense.

WIDENING THE NET

Turning to the immigration provisions, the broadened definition of "terrorist" is necessary to meet the current dangers we now face. Under past law, an alien was inadmissible and deportable for, among other reasons, engaging in a terrorist activity employing "explosives or firearms." The Patriot Act adds the words "or other weapon or dangerous device" to the applicable section of the U.S. Code.

Professor David Cole objects, arguing that expanding the term to include a residual category of other weapons trivializes terrorism. With due respect, this is not constitutional law but opinion—and not likely one shared by the families of the innocent men and women who were killed with a "box cutter" en route to crashing into the World Trade Center or the Pentagon or in rural Pennsylvania. Perhaps, prior to September 11, we could be lulled into the notion that not even terrorists would conceive of using innocent human beings as a weapon against other innocent human beings on our own soil, but sadly that is no longer our reality. Hypothetical objections that the statute might be contorted to apply to a barroom brawl or a domestic dispute are, in my judgment and the present context, too facetious to be credited as a legal objection.

Similarly, opponents of the new law expressed a concern that aliens who associate with terrorist organizations may be deported even when they supposedly kept their association to the nonterrorist functions of the organization. Yet this objection, too, seems overstated. The Patriot Act does not punish those who innocently may support a front organization. Moreover, the act even allows for giving support to an individual who had previously committed a terrorist act if the alien establishes that the individual had renounced his terrorist activity before the alien provided support.

Reality tells us that terrorists unfortunately gain financial and other support hiding behind the facade of charity. Those opposing this new immigration authority seem undisturbed by this. That is again a policy choice; it is not a constitutional one. A statute like the present one, aimed at supplying a general prohibition against an alien contributing funds or other material support to a terrorist organization (as designated under current law by the secretary of state) or to any nondesignated organization that the alien "knows or reasonably should know" furthers terrorist activity, does not violate the Constitution. Some civil libertarians have supported their opposition to this provision by loosely referencing older cases that wrongfully assigned criminal guilt to U.S. citizens for associating with the domestic cause of civil rights in the 1950s and 1960s; such analogies are simply inappropriate. Surely it is possible to draw distinction between nonviolent associations of American citizens, which are entitled to full First Amendment protection, and the fanatical planning of widespread mass destruction against innocents by noncitizens, which clearly is not.

CONSIDERING INTENT

Still unpersuaded and want the fine print? Well, here it is: "Engaging in terrorist activity" means committing a terrorist act or otherwise committing an act that "the actor knows, or reasonably should know, affords material support . . . [to any organization that the actor knows, or reasonably should know, is a terrorist organization, or] to any individual whom the actor knows, or reasonably should know, has committed or plans to commit any terrorist activity."[1] The specific intent requirements are not only explicit but multiple. This is not, as the objectors claim, "guilt by association" but rather guilt for associating with terrorists for terrorism purposes.

Critics of the Patriot Act have claimed that the First and Fifth Amendments apply without distinction to citizens and aliens residing in the United States. However, this cannot be said without qualification. American citizens enjoy certain privileges and immunities within our constitutional structure that noncitizens do not. Americans, for example, travel freely in and out of our sovereign borders. That same freedom is obviously not afforded noncitizens. With regard to exclusion of immigrants, U.S. authority is plenary, and such authority may be exercised by Congress to prohibit entry altogether. The Court has long held that "whatever the procedure authorized by Congress is, it is due process as far as an alien denied entry is concerned."

Terrorists or those seeking association with them clearly can be excluded from our nation without offending the First Amendment or any other provision of the Constitution. While additional rights do attend an immigrant granted admission, such rights are not necessarily on par with those of citizens. In *U.S. v. Verdugo-Urquidez*, for example, the Court opined that "[our] cases . . . establish only that aliens receive constitutional protections when they have come within the territory of the United States and developed substantial connections with this country."[2] Lower courts have thus upheld the deportation of an alien who associated with groups assisting Nazi persecution, even without proof that the alien himself engaged in the act of persecution.

More problematic is the question of how long those aliens subject to removal who also pose a terrorist threat can be detained by the attorney general. The detention provision was the subject of much debate. The Patriot Act ultimately provided that "the Attorney General *may* certify [for

---

1. Uniting and Strengthening America by Providing Appropriate Tools Required to Intercept and Obstruct Terrorism Act (USA Patriot Act), H.R. 3162, 107th Cong., 1st sess., October 24, 2001, Sec. 411.

2. *U.S. v. Verdugo-Urquidez*, 494 U.S. 259 (1990).

detention] an alien he has reason to believe may commit, further, or facilitate [terrorist] acts . . . or engage in any other activity that endangers the national security of the United States"[3] (emphasis added). This is authority that is reminiscent of that exercised by the United Kingdom against the Irish Republican Army (IRA). In that context in the 1970s, the British secretary of state could issue a detention order against those attempting or carrying out or organizing for the purpose of terrorist activity. In *The Republic of Ireland v. The United Kingdom*, the European Court of Human Rights found this similar—indeed, more sweeping—detention authority, applicable to those who were not always suspected of a crime but were sought to be interrogated for intelligence purposes, to be compatible with the European Convention on Human Rights. The individual right against deprivation of liberty, held the unanimous court, was subordinate to the emergency presented by the terrorist activity found at that point in Northern Ireland.

Is the less expansive detention authority given to the U.S. attorney general under the Patriot Act unconstitutional? Not even the opponents claim this; instead, they merely opine that it raises "constitutional concerns." They say, for example, that the Constitution would be transgressed if the detention power were used to detain those giving "peace training to the IRA." Any statute can be made to raise constitutional concerns if it is manipulated to apply against something other than its constitutional object. Congress is not tasked with drafting against the absurd. It is tasked with addressing the very real dangers of those who wish to kill us for no reason other than that we are American. The attorney general can be given authority to address such hatred. He can also be given the authority to address the risks posed by enemy aliens who may flee or who may seek to thwart our security by exchanging information or launching an additional attack.

But, claim the objectors, the attorney general cannot be given authority to detain persons he cannot deport. Perhaps, but that is not the question that needs to be answered. The attorney general did not ask for that authority. He sought and was given the power to detain those who have been found to be

3. USA Patriot Act, Sec. 412.

removable. An alien is removable principally when the alien has entered the nation illegally, is in present violation of a previously granted immigration status, or has been engaged in other criminal activity. But for various reasons—mostly related to international obligations that prevent deportation and repatriation to a country where torture is inevitable—being removable is not always the same as being capable of being removed immediately.

So, then, for how long can a removable alien be detained? Under the law prior to the Patriot Act, removable aliens could be detained when "determined by the Attorney General to be a risk to the community or unlikely to comply with the order of removal." This pre-Patriot Act postremoval detention authority was construed by the Supreme Court in *Zadvydas v. Davis*, and the Court suggested six months as a reasonable postremoval detention period.

Yet *Zadvydas*, as a case of statutory interpretation, did not rule out more indefinite detention where risk to community or flight risk is accompanied by special circumstance. The Court explicitly noted that in establishing a presumptive six-month period for detention, it was not denying the government detention beyond this point under unique circumstances. Wrote Justice Breyer for the Court, "Neither do we consider terrorism or other special circumstances where special arguments might be made for forms of preventive detention and for heightened deference to the judgments of the political branches with respect to matters of national security."[4]

The detention by attorney general certification under the Patriot Act should thus not be seen as anomalous or beyond constitutional limit. The attorney general is required to review his certification every six months. Moreover, even the opponents of this highly debated aspect of the act concede that it explicitly provides for judicial review of the attorney general's determination—"Judicial review of any action or decision relating to [detention] (including judicial review of the merits of a determination [by the attorney general that an alien presents a danger to national security]) is available by habeas corpus."[5]

---

4. *Zadvydas v. Dovis*, 533 U.S. 678 (2001).
5. USA Patriot Act, Sec. 412.

In addition to detention following a removal decision, the Patriot Act provides for short-term detention of a suspected terrorist for up to seven days *before* charging an alien with a crime or a basis for removal. If no charges are filed, the alien is released. Prior to the act, the Immigration and Naturalization Service could detain an alien for forty-eight hours before charging a crime or removable offense. Extending this time of detention without charge does present some legal questions that cannot be fully answered apart from the facts of individual cases. In this respect, whether a constitutional problem is presented by the act likely depends on the extent of due process protection the courts decide must be afforded an individual alien in light of the degree of his or her substantial connection with this country.

CONCLUSION

Raising civil libertarian objections to new law enforcement provisions is a healthy sign of a vibrant democracy committed to human rights. America should be justly proud of its temperate actions in response to September 11, including its ongoing debate over the proper protection of civil liberties. But no significant constitutional objections have been raised to the USA Patriot Act, either before or after its passage by Congress. Moreover, Congress should be commended for providing a sunset of some of the law enforcement and intelligence authorities that this legislation granted. As Congress has recognized, the possibility of abuse should not obscure the present need and the supposition of trust that one must have if our democratic order is to be safeguarded from those outside our borders who wish to subvert it.

For Discussion

1. Instead of measures such as the USA Patriot Act, which he calls an "overreaction," how does Cole think that the "bedrock foundations of our constitutional democracy—political freedom and equal treatment" can be balanced with the need to provide national security in times of crisis? (367)

2. According to Cole, why has the philosophy of guilt by association repeatedly been found to violate the First and Fifth Amendments of the U.S. Constitution? Why does he think that the rejection of this philosophy is so fundamental to preserving constitutionally guaranteed freedoms?

3. What does Kmiec mean when he says that opponents of the Patriot Act have "a more extreme view of freedom"? (376)

4. How would Kmiec respond to Cole's slippery slope apprehensions about how the provisions of the USA Patriot Act might be applied?

For Further Reflection

1. What circumstances justify sacrificing constitutionally guaranteed freedoms to provide for national security?

2. What is the relation of civil rights to human rights? Are the potential violations of civil rights that Cole attributes to the USA Patriot Act also violations of human rights?

3. How can legislation dealing with situations involving issues of civil liberties and human rights be drafted in such a way that the possibility of abuse is minimized?

4. Are Kmiec's arguments a convincing refutation of Cole's claim that the USA Patriot Act was an overreaction to the events of September 11?

For Research

1. Research the drafting, adoption, and provisions of the USA Patriot Act in 2001 and the Congressional debates surrounding its renewal in 2005 and 2006. Report on how the major provisions of the Act have been applied to specific circumstances and the controversies arising from these applications.

2. Investigate the history of Congressional acts that were passed in the heat of events thought to require emergency legislation. Find out how effective these pieces of legislation were in addressing the perceived crises.

3. Research the process of litigation by which laws such as the USA Patriot Act are challenged and brought before the courts for judicial review.

Moral Prohibition at a Price

Should We Fight Terror with Torture?

MICHAEL IGNATIEFF (1947–)
ALAN DERSHOWITZ (1938–)

*Michael Ignatieff is a Canadian writer and politician who has served since 2008
as the leader of the Liberal Party of Canada. His earlier academic career included
teaching posts at Harvard, Cambridge, Oxford, and the London School of Economics.
Ignatieff has written numerous books interpreting world political events for general
readers, including* Virtual War: Kosovo and Beyond *(2000) and* Human Rights as
Politics and Idolatry *(2001).*

*Alan Dershowitz is the Felix Frankfurter Professor of Law at Harvard Law
School. Dershowitz is the author of hundreds of articles and numerous books examin-
ing a vast array of civil rights issues. His topics include the challenges to civil liberties
posed by the urgent need to prevent terrorist activities and the policies of the government of Israel in its conflict with the Palestinians. Dershowitz is well-known to the
general public as a prominent criminal defense attorney whose clients have included
Patricia Hearst, Leona Helmsley, Michael Milken, and O. J. Simpson.*

*Torture has been used throughout history as a means of punishment and coercion
by regimes across the political spectrum. The debates about its legitimacy take on particular urgency in light of recent incidents at Abu Ghraib prison, at Guantánamo Bay
detention center, and in the ongoing Israeli–Palestinian conflict. Both Ignatieff and
Dershowitz are concerned with the moral and practical implications for liberal, democratic nations forced to deal with circumstances in which harsh methods of interrogation are part of the calculus for saving the lives of civilians—the so-called "ticking
bomb" situation.*

Moral Prohibition at a Price

IT IS DIFFICULT to think about torture honestly. In a recent article on the interrogation techniques employed by the United States, the writer Mark Bowden observed that few "moral imperatives make such sense on a large scale, but break down so dramatically in the particular." The moral imperative—do not torture, anytime, anywhere, in any circumstances—is mandated by the UN Convention Against Torture. "No exceptional circumstances whatsoever, whether a state of war or a threat of war, internal political instability or any other public emergency," says the Convention, can "be invoked as a justification of torture." The fact that terrorists themselves torture—i.e., that we face enemies who do not observe the Torture Convention—does not change these moral imperatives. Our compliance should not depend on reciprocity, on whether our enemies observe these rules or not.

As long as we stay on the high moral ground of unconditional moral prohibition, we seem to know where we are. Problems begin, as Mark Bowden observes, when we descend into the particular, when we ask what exactly counts as torture.

Since no state wants to be seen as torturing suspects but all states want to be able to extract information to protect their citizens, the key practical question for states is whether they can use methods of coercive interrogation that do not qualify as torture. When the Torture Convention was ratified by the U.S. Senate in 1994, maintaining a meaningful distinction between coercive but lawful interrogation and outright torture was a central concern. The Senate ratified the Convention on the understanding that torture should be reserved for "*severe* physical or mental pain or suffering" resulting in "*prolonged* mental harm."[1] Once the war on terror began, the parsing of the Convention went still further. In the now-notorious memos submitted by the Office of Legal Counsel to the Defense Secretary to the White House in the beginning of 2002, these definitions were stretched to the point that the threshold for torture "must be equivalent to the pain accompanying serious physical injury, such as organ failure, impairment of bodily function or even death." Any physical abuse below that standard counted as "coercive interrogation." Some forms of coercive interrogation, the lawyers admitted, might not be torture, but they would still be defined as "inhuman and degrading treatment."

When the European Court of Human Rights investigated British interrogation practices in Northern Ireland in 1978, they concluded that a range of painful practices constituted inhuman and degrading practice even if they did not qualify as torture. When the Israeli Supreme Court ruled against Israeli interrogation techniques in 1999—techniques that included holding suspects in painful positions with hoods, and vigorously shaking the head and shoulders—they also ruled against them as inhuman and degrading, but not as torture.

There is thus a conceptual and practical distinction between torture and coercive interrogation. There is a further distinction—at least in theory—between methods of coercive interrogation that are lawful and permissible and those that may be inhuman and degrading. While this distinction exists in theory, most human rights activists would deny that such a distinction can be maintained or observed in practice.

Human rights activists accept that in combating terrorists, reliable information is essential, and that interrogation is a central feature of any counterterrorist strategy. Kenneth Roth, the executive director of Human Rights Watch, argues that "respect for the Geneva Conventions does not

MICHAEL IGNATIEFF

---

1. [Emphasis added by the author.]

preclude vigorously interrogating detainees about a limitless range of topics." What work is the word "vigorously" doing in this sentence? It is intended to make it clear that a human rights defender takes seriously the necessity of getting from detainees real information that may prevent future terrorist attacks. But what, in specific terms, might "vigorous" interrogation actually entail? Clearly, Ken Roth and anyone else who cares about human rights wants absolutely to exclude any form of abuse. But what exactly counts as abuse in a "vigorous" interrogation?

In order to prevent vigorous interrogation from slipping down any slope, human rights activists want to collapse the distinction between "coercive interrogation" and "torture," and to maintain that any physical or psychological coercion in interrogation should be banned. But there does remain a significant distinction (significant, that is, to the victim) between the two. As legal theorist Richard Posner has argued, "almost all official interrogation is coercive, yet not all coercive interrogation would be called 'torture' by any competent user of the English language." As the philosopher Jean Bethke Elshtain has written, "when human rights groups label 'unpleasant or disadvantageous treatment of any kind' torture . . . they fail to discriminate between cases," for example, between "sleep deprivation and amputation or burning or some other horror."

Clear thinking about torture, therefore, is not served by collapsing the distinction between coercive interrogation and torture. Both may be repugnant, but repugnance does not make them into the same thing.

If coercion and torture are on a moral continuum, at what point on the continuum, to use the words of Richard Posner, does queasiness turn to revulsion? Vigorous interrogation might mean lengthy, exhausting, harassing exchanges with interrogators. Provided that there is no physical contact between interrogator and subject, no deprivation of food or water harmful to health, this might qualify as lawful interrogation. But at every ratchet of coercion, moral problems occur. Sleep deprivation will not leave physical or even permanent psychological scars, but as Menachem Begin, who was interrogated in Soviet Russia, remembered, "anyone who has experienced this desire [for sleep] knows that not even hunger or thirst are comparable to it."

It might be lawful to deceive a subject under interrogation, by stating or implying that all of their associates are already in detention when they are still at large. But other forms of deception can inflict excruciating psychological anguish. Threatening a subject with the imminent death or torture of those dearest to them may not leave any physical marks, but it rightly constitutes torture, not just coercion, in even the U.S. Senate's definition.

Both the philosopher Jean Elshtain and Richard Posner have argued against the moral perfectionism that elides the distinction between coercion and torture and have stressed the cruel if regrettable necessity of using coercive methods on a small category of terrorists who may have information vital to saving the lives of innocent people. Posner justifies coercive interrogation on utilitarian grounds: saving the lives of many counts more, in moral terms, than abusing the body and dignity of a single individual. Elshtain justifies coercive interrogation using a complex moral calculus of "dirty hands": good consequences cannot justify bad acts, but bad acts are sometimes tragically necessary. The acts remain bad, and the person must accept the moral opprobrium and not seek to excuse the inexcusable with the justifications of necessity.

My own work on "lesser evils" brings me close to the Elshtain position—in that I agree with her that necessity may require the commission of bad acts, which necessity, nevertheless, cannot absolve of their morally problematic character—but I still have a problem. If one enumerates the forms of coercive interrogation that have been judged to be inhuman and degrading by the Israeli and the European courts—hooding, holding subjects in painful positions, exposing them to cold or heat or earsplitting noise—these techniques also seem unacceptable, though at a lower threshold of awfulness than torture. Like Elshtain, I am willing to get my hands dirty, but unlike her, I have practical difficulty enumerating a list of properly coercive techniques that I would be willing to have a democratic society inflict in my name. While I can envisage interrogations that deceive subjects—for example, by pretending to have full knowledge of their networks—I could not approve the deception of threatening either them or their relatives with imminent death. I could envisage withholding sleep, but not the radical sleep deprivation of which Menachem Begin speaks. I could envisage interrogations that disorient and isolate subjects, but I cannot envisage accepting ones that bombard subjects with painful noise or that withhold from them all contact with medical or legal personnel. I accept that a slap is not the same thing as a beating, but I still don't want interrogators to slap detainees, because I cannot see how to prevent the occasional slap deteriorating into a regular practice of beating. The issue is not, as Elshtain implies, that I care overmuch about my own moral purity but rather that I cannot see any clear way to manage coercive interrogation institutionally so that it does not degenerate into torture.

On the issue of regulation, there are those—Professor Alan Dershowitz, for example—who believe that banning torture and coercion outright is unrealistic. Instead the practice should be regulated by court warrants. Judicialization of torture, in my view, would lead to its "banalization," to torture becoming routine rather than an emergency exception. I would take a similar position on coercive interrogation techniques involving stress and duress, physical abuse, psychologically damaging sleep deprivation, and so on. A position in favor of outright prohibition of both torture and coercive interrogation has gained strength from the abuses at Abu Ghraib and from the memos of the Office of Legal Counsel and the White House parsing the Torture Convention into permission for coercive interrogation. It seems clear from the dire experience of Abu Ghraib that outright prohibition of both torture and coercive interrogation is the only way to proceed. Clear rules for interrogations, with clear penalties in the Uniform Code of Military Justice, should be mandatory.

Absolute prohibition, however, is easy. Enforcement is hard, and even rules and punishment for infraction are not enough. The crucial element of enforcement of any set of rules and procedures against abuse of detainees is habeas corpus, the legal requirement of any detaining power in a democracy to produce detainees before a court of law and justify detention to a duly appointed legal authority. As long as the United States—or any state, for that matter—has the power to detain at pleasure and in secret, abuse of detainees is inevitable. International pressure, domestic mobilization, and finally Congressional legislation are all necessary to stop the practice of "ghost detainees": detainees held outside the United States, inside the United States, or in third countries, whose identities remain concealed. It should be mandatory that every single detainee held by the United States, whether a citizen or not, be publicly known. If operational necessity—keeping the enemy from knowing who is in our custody—requires that their names be kept secret, disclosure of their names to Congress and the courts can be undertaken *in camera*. It should also be mandatory that every detainee of the United States, whether citizen or not, whether held onshore or offshore, should have habeas corpus access to U.S. federal court, together with the legal capacity to make representations to that court about treatment and detention. Detention should be limited by law, and detainees who cannot be charged or lawfully detained as prisoners of war should be released. Detainees should not be deported to countries where torture is known to occur. Until recently, the British detained terrorist suspects in British prisons rather than deport them to countries where they might be tortured upon their return. Following House of Lords rulings critical of the practice of indefinite incarceration, the British government is proposing to keep these suspects under house arrest. This strikes me as a lesser evil than rendition.

I am not so naive as to suppose that federal court review of detention will always provide effective remedies for detainees. Evidence of the impact of recent Supreme Court rulings and federal court rulings on the tribunal review process at Guantánamo, and also on ordinary treatment of the detainees, does suggest, however, that court review and access, however imperfect, is the only reliable way to keep detention under the rule of law.

So I end up supporting an absolute and unconditional ban on both torture and those forms of coercive interrogation that involve stress and duress, and I believe that enforcement of such a ban should be up to the military justice system plus the federal courts. I also believe that the training of interrogators can be improved by executive order and that the training must rigorously exclude stress-and-duress methods.

Two significant problems remain. First of all, there is the problem of the exceptional case, one where lives can be saved by the application of physical methods that amount to torture. "Ticking bomb cases" cannot be wished away. They might arise, especially in connection with a weapons-of-mass-destruction threat against an American or European city. An outright ban on torture and coercive interrogation in these cases leaves a conscientious security officer with little choice but to disobey the ban. In this event, as the Israeli Supreme Court has said, even a conscientious agent, acting in good faith to save lives, should be charged with a criminal offense and be required to stand trial. At such a trial, a defense of necessity could be entered in mitigation of sentence, but not to absolve or acquit. This is the only solution that I can see that remains consistent with an absolute ban on torture and stress-and-duress coercive interrogation. Let us not pretend that the enforcement of this rule will be easy or pleasant. Where the threat can be shown to be genuine, it seems evident that few legal systems would punish such a conscientious offender. But let us be clear: an outright ban on torture creates the problem of the conscientious offender. This is a small price to pay for a ban on torture.

Does an outright ban on torture and coercive interrogation meet the test of realism? Would an absolute ban on torture and stress-and-duress coercive interrogation so diminish the effectiveness of our intelligence-gathering operations that it would diminish public safety? It is often said—and I have made this argument myself—that neither coercive interrogation nor torture is necessary, since entirely lawful interrogation can secure results just as effective as those produced by coercion. There must be some truth to this. Israeli interrogators have given interviews assuring the Israeli public that physical duress is unnecessary. We are grasping at straws if we think this is the entire truth. As Posner and others have tartly pointed out, if torture and coercion were both as useless as critics pretend, why is there so much of it going on? While some abuse and outright torture can be attributed to the sadism of individuals, poor supervision, and so on, it must be the case that other acts of torture occur because interrogators believe, in good faith, that torture is the only way to extract information in a timely fashion. It must also be the case that if experienced interrogators come to this conclusion, they do so on the basis of their experience. The argument that torture and coercion do not work is contradicted by the dire frequency with which both practices occur. I submit that we would not be "waterboarding" Khalid Shaikh Mohammed—immersing him in water until he experiences the torment of nearly drowning—if our intelligence operatives did not believe it was necessary to crack open the Al Qaeda network that he commanded. In other words, we must at least entertain the possibility that the operatives working on him—in our name—are engaging not in gratuitous sadism but in a good-faith belief that this form of torture—and it does qualify as such—makes all the difference.

If they are right, then those who support an absolute ban on torture and stress-and-duress had better be honest enough to admit it that moral prohibition comes at a price. It is possible, at least in theory, that subjecting interrogators to rules that outlaw torture and coercive interrogation—backed up by punishment if they go too far—will create an interrogation regime that allows some interrogation subjects to resist divulging information and prevents our intelligence services from timely access to information that may save lives.

If there is a significant cost to an outright ban on coercive interrogation and torture, what can possibly justify it? Many of the arguments that human rights activists make in justification amount to the claim that torture shames their moral identity as human beings and as citizens, and that they do not wish such acts to be committed in their name by their own democracies. Other citizens in a democracy are not likely to value their own moral scruple over the collective interest in having accurate security information, even if collected by dubious means. It may be obvious to human rights activists how to adjudicate these claims, but it is not obvious to me. That is, I do not see any trumping argument on behalf of the rights and dignity of security detainees that makes their claims prevail over the security interests (and human right to life) of the majority of the population. The best I can do is to relate the ban on torture to the political identity of the democracies we are trying to defend, i.e., by claiming that democracies limit the powers that governments can justly exercise over the human beings under their power, and these limits include an absolute ban on subjecting individuals to forms of pain that strip them of their dignity, identity, and even sanity.

We cannot torture, in other words, because of who we are. This is the best I can do, but those of us who believe this had better admit that many of our fellow citizens are bound to disagree. It is in the nature of democracy itself that fellow citizens will define their identity in ways that privilege security over liberty and thus reluctantly endorse torture in their name. If we are against torture, we are committed actually to arguing with our fellow citizens, not treating those who defend torture as moral monsters. Those of us who oppose torture should also be honest enough to admit that we may have to pay a price for our own convictions. *Ex ante*, of course, I cannot tell how high this price might be. *Ex post*—following another terrorist attack that might have been prevented through the exercise of coercive interrogation—the price of my scruple might simply seem too high. This is a risk I am prepared to take, but frankly, a majority of fellow citizens is unlikely to concur. The important point—going back to where I started on the difficulty of being honest on this subject—is that there is a price, and opponents of torture and coercive interrogation should not pretend that it might not be high. Abstaining from the evil of torture is itself an exercise in moral hazard and should be justified as such, rather than as an exercise in moral perfection.

Should We Fight
Terror with Torture?

THE GREAT AMERICAN JUSTICE Oliver Wendell Holmes Jr. once remarked that "it is revolting to have no better reason for a rule of law than that it was laid down in the time of Henry IV. It is still more revolting if the grounds upon which it was laid down have vanished long since, and the rule simply persists from blind imitation of the past." The rules of law regulating how civilized societies protect their citizens from aggression were not laid down as far back as the time of Henry IV. They were enacted, in significant part, following the two awful wars of the twentieth century in which massive numbers of civilians were targeted for death and murdered in cold blood. The human rights revolution of the mid-twentieth century was largely a reaction to the human wrongs of the Holocaust.

The period between the end of the Second World War and now has seen more profound changes in the nature of warfare than occurred from the time of Henry IV to the beginning of the First World War. Weapons of mass destruction in the hands of suicide terrorists with no fear of death and no home address have rendered useless the deterrent threat of massive retaliation. This threat has been the staple of military policy since the days of the Bible. Because suicide terrorists cannot be deterred, they must be preempted and prevented from carrying out their threats against civilians before they occur. This change in tactics requires significant changes in the laws of war—laws that have long been premised on the deterrent model.

Consider, for example, the United Nations Charter, drafted in the aftermath of Germany's aggressive war between 1939 and 1945. Article 51 confirms "the inherent right of individual or collective self-defence if an armed attack occurs against a member." The use of the word "occurs" would seem to require a nation, seeking to act in compliance with the charter, to wait until it is actually attacked before it responds in self-defense. But what should a democratic nation do if it becomes aware of an imminent threat of attack by a group of suicide terrorists in a distant part of the world? Surely it should not simply wait until an "armed attack occurs" and then engage in retaliatory self-defense. First, there is often no known entity to attack, since the suicide terrorists have died and the leaders who sent them have gone into hiding among civilians and may well be preparing renewed terrorist attacks. Second, there is no good reason for a democracy to have to absorb a first blow against its civilian population, especially if that blow can be catastrophic. Third, there is little possibility that potentially catastrophic first blows can be deterred by the threat of retaliation against a phantom enemy who welcomes martyrdom.

Despite these new realities, the old UN charter has not been changed, though it is currently in the process of being "redefined." A "High-Level Panel on Threats, Challenges and Change" has recommended that despite the "restrictive" language of Article 51, a nation should be free to take proportional military action against an "imminent" attack if no other means are available. But it also proposed that if a threat, though catastrophic and highly likely, is not imminent, a nation may not resort to preventive self-help. Instead it must seek the approval of the Security Council. In other words, preemptive self-defense against imminent threat is consistent with Article 51, but preventive self-defense against more distant, though equally certain, threats requires approval by the Security Council. While this distinction makes sense in theory, it fails to recognize that the Security Council is a highly politicized body, with veto power in the hands of nations that have long supported terrorism, at least on a selective basis. No nation, facing a highly likely catastrophic threat—even if it is not imminent—will rely on the whim of other nations with agendas different from its own. As the former U.S. Secretary of State Dean Acheson once, aptly, put it, "The survival of states is not a matter of law." States will do what they deem necessary, not only to ensure their own survival, but also to protect the lives of their citizens from catastrophic threats.

Consider, for example, the developing Iranian nuclear threat. The Iranian leadership has threatened to attack Israel and American targets. If Iran gets close to having a deliverable nuclear weapon, and if one of its target nations has the capacity to destroy its nuclear program the way Israel destroyed the Iraqi reactor back in 1981—with one air strike and a single casualty—it should have the legal right to do so. This would be especially so if the Security Council refused to do anything to stop Iran because of self-serving Russian or Chinese vetoes. We are not yet at that decision point, and it is unlikely that the Iranian nuclear threat can be ended by surgical air strikes, but international law should authorize preventive self-defense if the threat is cataclysmic and relatively certain, even if not imminent, and if it can be abated with few civilian casualties.

In any event, the UN report "sees no need to amend Article 51" since it can be reinterpreted to permit states to take preemptive action against imminent threat, but not to take preventive action against longer-term threats. Even the recommended reinterpretation does not have the force of law. It is merely the opinion of a high-level panel which has received no formal approval by the United Nations. It would be far better to change Article 51 so as to reflect the new realities, but there is an apparent allergy to changing old laws, whether they go back to Henry IV or to the post–World War II period.

The laws of preemptive and preventive self-defense are but one example of the legal sclerosis from which we are suffering in the war against terrorism. The human rights rules that were enacted to protect civilians are now being turned on their heads by self-proclaimed human rights groups. Instead of being a shield for innocent civilians, they are being used as a sword by terrorists against civilians. Terrorists deliberately hide among civilians, most often civilians who support them. In order to prevent the terrorists from carrying out their threats, democratic nations must often take actions that endanger some civilians. For example, when coalition forces targeted Abu Musab al-Zarqawi and his "spiritual adviser," Abu Abdul-Rahman, they inadvertently killed several civilians, including a child. This was not the first time that targeting terrorists has resulted in collateral casualties. When the United States targeted Abu Ali, known as Qaed Salim Sinan al-Harethi, in Yemen in 2002, they also killed five other people, at least some of whom were probably Al Queda members or supporters. Israel, as well, has caused the deaths of civilians in its efforts to preempt terrorist attacks by targeting "ticking bomb" terrorists as well as terrorist commanders who were the equivalents of Zarqawi and Rahman.

Human rights organizations often fail to distinguish between civilian deaths accidentally caused by democracies despite their best efforts to avoid them, and civilian deaths deliberately caused by terrorists who seek to maximize civilian casualties by constructing anti-personnel bombs, designed to kill as many innocent people as possible, and by specifically targeting crowded buses and other soft targets. These human rights organizations blink at the reality that terrorists seek not only to maximize civilian deaths among their enemies, but also to maximize civilian deaths caused by their enemies, even if the victims are their own supporters. As one European diplomat told the *New York Times*, the terrorists understand the "harsh arithmetic of pain." Enemy "casualties play in their favor" and casualties inflicted on their own people by the enemy "play in their favor."

By condemning all targeted killing of terrorists, human rights groups actually increase the risks to civilians. The law should permit the targeting of individuals who are actively engaged in terrorist planning and actions, so long as it is highly likely that the target is an actual terrorist, that the number of likely civilian deaths is proportional to the likely civilian deaths that would have been caused by the targeted terrorists, and that there is no other alternative—such as arrest—that is feasible under the circumstances. The law should also cast the blame for unintended civilian deaths caused by democracies on the terrorists who deliberately hide among civilians using them as "shields." The domestic law of most democratic nations does precisely that. If a bank robber takes a teller hostage and uses him as a shield against the police, and if the police, in an effort to shoot the robber who is firing from behind his shield, kill the shield, it is the robber who is guilty of murder, even though it was the policeman who fired the fatal shot. The same should be the case in international law.

Next, consider the problem of what to do with captured "prisoners" who are believed to be terrorists. This vague category of detainees comprises several different subgroups. There are those who were captured in the course of military action in a foreign country. The United States and its allies captured Taliban "soldiers" and those fighting alongside them in Afghanistan. A few wore ersatz uniforms; most did not. Some were just in the wrong place at the wrong time. Then there were admitted members of Al Queda, ranging from Khalid Shaikh Mohammed, the alleged number two or three man in the organization, to Zacarias Moussaoui, a terrorist wannabe who may or may not have been the "twentieth" September 11 hijacker. Some of the detainees are believed to have valuable real-time information that could save lives. Others are simply terrorist pawns willing to do whatever they are told, even if it entails suicide. Inevitably, some, probably, are completely innocent and not dangerous.

The problem is that the current laws regulating the detention of combatants are near useless when it comes to this motley array of detainees. These detainees simply do not fit into the old, anachronistic categories. Most are not classic prisoners of war. They were not part of a uniformed army under the command of a nation. But neither do they fit in to the classic definition of "unlawful combatants." They are not spies or saboteurs, as those terms have been understood in the context of conventional warfare. Nor are many of them simple "criminals," subject to ordinary trials under the domestic law of crimes. They comprise a new category—or set of categories—unto themselves. They cannot be held as POWs until the end of the war, because this is a war that will never end. They cannot simply be released, because many of them would quickly volunteer to engage in suicide terrorist missions against their former captors, as some already have done. Most cannot be tried as criminals, because their actions took place outside the jurisdiction of the detaining nation. Those who have valuable, real-time information will be interrogated, and—short of the absolute law against "torture"—there are few, if any, rules governing the nature of permissible interrogation when the object is not to elicit "incrimination confessions" for purposes of criminal prosecution, but rather to obtain "preventive intelligence" for the purpose of preempting future terrorist attacks.

Should the same rules that govern the interrogation of ordinary criminal suspects be applicable? Or should more latitude be afforded to interrogators in the preventive context? Should sleep deprivation be authorized? Loud music? Alternating heat and cold? Uncomfortable and/or painful seating? What about truth serum? False threats? We know that the United States has used "waterboarding"—a technique that produces a near-drowning experience but no physical aftereffects—on Khalid Shaikh Mohammed, a high-ranking Al Queda detainee. Is that categorized as torture? I certainly think so, but the United States government apparently does not. We need rules even for such unpleasant practices.

There is today a vast "black hole" in the law. It is this hole that accounts for Guantánamo, extraordinary renditions, and other phantom places and actions about which we know nothing. As a lifelong civil libertarian, I strongly oppose such gaps in the law. The rule of law requires that all governmental action be subject to legal constraints. The refusal to change old laws that do not fit new situations is bad for human rights and dangerous to democratic accountability.

Nor does it help the situation when Amnesty International and other human rights groups exaggerate the problems and cast all the blame on democracies that are seeking—sometimes by questionable means—to keep their citizens safe from terrorists. Anne Fitzgerald of Amnesty recently compared the alleged terrorists being detained by the United States and its allies to the "disappeared" in Argentina during the junta. The comparison is obscene. The disappeared in Argentina were mostly political opponents of the junta, many of whom were tortured to death and dropped into the ocean from aircraft. Credible sources estimate that as many as 30,000 people may have been killed. Pregnant women had their babies ripped from their wombs so they could be adopted by childless friends of the junta. There is no evidence of anything even close to this being done by the United States today in its sometimes excessive efforts to prevent terrorism. The problems are bad enough without the need to exaggerate them for political and ideological purposes.

Human rights groups undercut the real interests of human rights when they exaggerate the faults of democracies and minimize the faults of terrorists. Most democracies seek to operate within the rule of laws, and laws must realistically reflect the desirable balance between the legitimate needs of security and the equally legitimate claims of human rights. Striking this balance is a daunting task, and it is in the nature of such balances that few are ever satisfied that it has been properly struck. It is far easier to stick with the comfortable old ways, even if it produces hypocrisy and gaping holes in the law.

Laws must change with the times. They must adapt to new challenges. That has been the genius of the common law. Ironically, it is generally the left that seeks change in the laws, while the right is satisfied with Henry IV. Today it is many on the left who resist any changes in the law of war or human rights. They deny the reality that the war against terrorism is in any way different from conventional wars of the past, or that the old laws must be adapted to the new threats. The result is often an unreasonable debate of extremes: the hard left insists that the old laws should not be tampered with in the least; the hard right insists that the old laws are entirely inapplicable to the new threats, and that democratic governments should be entirely free to do whatever it takes to combat terrorism, without regard to anachronistic laws. Both extremes are dangerous. What is needed is a new set of laws, based on the principles of the old laws of war and human rights—the protection of civilians—but adapted to the new threats against civilian victims of terrorism.

The president of the Supreme Court of Israel, Aharon Barak, in deciding that torture could not be justified even for purposes of securing information that might prevent terrorism, wrote the following lines: "[It] is the destiny of democracy that not all means are acceptable to it, and not all practices employed by its enemies are open before it. Although a democracy must often fight with one hand tied behind its back, it nonetheless has the upper hand. Preserving the Rule of Law and recognition of an individual's liberty constitutes an important component in its understanding of security. At the end of the day, they [add to] its strength...."

But, while it may well be necessary for democracies to fight terrorists with one hand tied behind their backs, it is neither necessary nor desirable for a democracy to fight with two hands tied behind its back, especially when the ropes that bind the second hand are anachronistic laws that can be changed without compromising legitimate human rights. The laws must be changed to permit democracies to fight fairly and effectively against those who threaten its citizens. To paraphrase Robert Jackson, who served as the United States chief prosecutor at Nuremberg—the law must not be "a suicide pact."

For Discussion

1. What does Ignatieff mean when he says, "We cannot torture . . . because of who we are"? (394)
2. Would Ignatieff agree with Dershowitz that torture should be allowed, but only if it is legally regulated?
3. Does Dershowitz share Ignatieff's belief that the prohibition of torture is "an exercise in moral hazard and should be justified as such"? (395)
4. How does Dershowitz think laws should be changed so that a democracy does not have to fight threats to its citizens with "two hands tied behind its back"? (402)

For Further Reflection

1. How should torture be defined for the purpose of banning or legally regulating it?
2. What position should human rights organizations take on the use of torture?
3. Why is the use of torture to interrogate suspected terrorists a human rights issue?
4. Should the consideration of human rights issues and legal restraints affect "ticking bomb" situations? If an interrogator disregards these considerations in such a situation, what consequences should he or she have to bear?

For Research

1. Find studies claiming that torture elicits accurate and useful information from prisoners. Do the same for studies that claim the opposite. What evidence is there to support one position more than the other?
2. Investigate the ethical arguments that underlie absolute bans on torture, such as the UN Convention Against Torture and the Israeli Supreme Court's decision to prohibit torture.

Comparative
Discussion Questions

1. Compare Cato's and Seneca's attitudes toward slavery. Who has a more enlightened perspective? Why?
2. Compare Hortensia's protest with the transcript from *United States of America v. Susan B. Anthony*. What similarities and differences do you notice in each woman's strategy for arguing that women and men should be accorded the same rights?
3. How did the language and ideas in the selection by John Locke influence the authors of the Declaration of Independence?
4. Compare the selections by John Locke, Jean-Jacques Rousseau, and Eduardo Galeano. According to each of them, how does society corrupt what would otherwise be a natural state of freedom and happiness?
5. What assumptions do the Declaration of Independence and the Declaration of the Rights of Man and of the Citizen share about the proper relationship between government and individual citizens?
6. Compare the rights enumerated in the Bill of Rights (Constitution of the United States of America) with those in the Universal Declaration of Human Rights. In light of the differences, how would you describe the underlying philosophy of each document in terms of the rights each considers essential?

7. How do Mahatma Gandhi's andMartin Luther King Jr.'s attitudes toward the use of violence compare with that of Nelson Mandela?

8. How do Martin Luther King Jr. and Nelson Mandela justify their illegal activities? Do you find one argument more persuasive than the other?

9. Compare "A Few Remarks" and the Declaration of Independence. Based on these documents, what similarities do you see in the situations faced by the American colonists of 1776 and the Czech citizens of 1989?

10. Which selection makes the more powerful argument for freedom of expression: Luis Aguilar's "Defending Freedom and Freedom of Speech" or Luisa Valenzuela's "The Censors"? Why?

11. What do Webb Miller's and Jan Wong's accounts tell you about the relationship between journalists and the human rights abuses they write about?

12. As young women living under the rule of totalitarian regimes, how do Ji-li Jiang and Latifa both try to live according to their own values and beliefs?

13. How does Victor Klemperer's account of the erosion of rights in Nazi Germany illustrate Hannah Arendt's analysis of the perplexities of the rights of man?

14. What bearing does the Preamble to the U.S. Constitution have on the arguments presented by David Cole and Douglas W. Kmiec regarding the USA Patriot Act?

15. How would Michael Ignatieff and Alan Dershowitz interpret the application of Article 9 of the Declaration of the Rights of Man and of the Citizen and of Article 5 of the Universal Declaration of Human Rights?

16. Which of the human rights listed in the Universal Declaration of Human Rights would John A. Gentry consider legitimate?

17. What would William F. Schulz say to President Andrew Jackson about his support for the Indian Removal Act? Is it likely that Schulz could have elicited tears from Jackson?

Synthesis Questions

1. Based on your reading of these selections, what do you consider the most essential human rights?
2. Where do human rights come from?
3. What is the relation between freedoms and rights?
4. Can a person be said to have a right if there is no way for that right to be protected?
5. Are laws valid if they do not take into consideration their implications for human rights?
6. What resolution is possible when human rights come into conflict with religious beliefs, customs, and other nonlegislated cultural practices?
7. Are the values embedded in human rights universally applicable, at all times and in all places?

Appendix A: Subjects

Appendix B: Genres

Appendix C: Countries

ACKNOWLEDGMENTS

*All possible care has been taken to trace ownership
and secure permission for each selection in this anthology.
The Great Books Foundation wishes to thank the
following authors, publishers, and representatives
for permission to reprint copyrighted material:*

Hortensia's Protest, from APPIAN: VOLUME IV—THE CIVIL WARS, by Appian. Loeb Classical Library Volume L 5, edited and translated by Horace White. Copyright © 1913 by the President and Fellows of Harvard College. Reprinted by permission of the publishers and the Trustees of the Loeb Classical Library, Cambridge, MA: Harvard University Press, 1913. The Loeb Classical Library® is a registered trademark of the President and Fellows of Harvard College.

Letter XLVII, from LETTERS FROM A STOIC, by Seneca. Selected and translated by Robin Campbell. Copyright © 1969 by Robin Alexander Campbell. Reprinted by permission of Penguin Books Ltd.

Magna Carta. Translation courtesy of the Avalon Project, Yale Law School, New Haven, CT.

Second Treatise of Government, from SECOND TREATISE OF GOVERNMENT, by John Locke. Edited and with an introduction by C. B. Macpherson. Introduction copyright © 1980 by C. B. Macpherson. Reprinted by permission of Hackett Publishing Company, Inc.

Declaration of the Rights of Man and of the Citizen. Translation courtesy of the Avalon Project, Yale Law School, New Haven, CT.

Independence v. Swaraj, from MAHATMA GANDHI: SELECTED POLITICAL WRITINGS (pp. 98–106), by Mahatma Gandhi. Edited by Dennis Dalton. Copyright © 1996 by Hackett Publishing Company, Inc. Reprinted by permission of the Navajivan Trust, India.

Ghandi's Followers Protest the Salt Tax, from I FOUND NO PEACE: THE JOURNAL OF A FOREIGN CORRESPONDENT, by Webb Miller. Copyright © 1936 by Webb Miller; renewed 1963 by Mrs. Webb Miller. Abridged and printed by permission of Simon & Schuster Adult Publishing Group.

The Stalin Epigram, by Osip Mandelstam. Translated by W. S. Merwin. Translation copyright © 1973 by W. S. Merwin. Reprinted by permission of the Wylie Agency LLC, on behalf of W. S. Merwin.

The Arrest of Osip Mandelstam, from HOPE AGAINST HOPE, by Nadezhda Mandelstam. Translated by Max Hayward. Translation copyright © 1970 by Atheneum Publishers. Reprinted by permission of Scribner, a division of Simon and Schuster, Inc.

I Will Bear Witness, from I WILL BEAR WITNESS: A DIARY OF THE NAZI YEARS, Vols. 1 and 2, by Victor Klemperer. Translated by Martin Chalmers. Copyright © 1998 and 1999 by Martin Chalmers. Reprinted by permission of Random House, Inc.

Harlem [2], from THE COLLECTED POEMS OF LANGSTON HUGHES, by Langston Hughes. Copyright © 1994 by the Estate of Langston Hughes. Reprinted by permission of Alfred A. Knopf, a division of Random House, Inc.

Survival in Auschwitz, from IF THIS IS A MAN (SURVIVAL IN AUSCHWITZ), by Primo Levi. Translated by Stuart Woolf. Copyright © 1959 by Orion Press, Inc. Copyright © 1958 by Giulio Einaudi editore S.P.A. Reprinted by permission of Viking Penguin, a division of Penguin Group (USA) Inc.

Letter from Birmingham Jail, by Martin Luther King Jr. Copyright © 1963 by Martin Luther King Jr.; renewed 1991 by Coretta Scott King. Reprinted by arrangement with the Estate of Martin Luther King Jr., courtesy of Writers House Inc. as agent for the proprietor, New York, NY.

The Rivonia Trial: Second Court Statement, from THE STRUGGLE IS MY LIFE, by Nelson Mandela. Copyright 1978, 1986, 1990 by the International Defense and Aid Fund. Copyright 1990 by Pathfinder Press. Reprinted by permission of Pathfinder Press.

Letter to Deng Xiaoping, from THE COURAGE TO STAND ALONE: LETTERS FROM PRISON AND OTHER WRITINGS, by Wei Jingsheng. Translated by Kristina M. Torgeson. Copyright © 1997 by Wei Jingsheng. Reprinted by permission of Viking Penguin, a division of Penguin Group (USA).

The Censors, from THE CENSORS, by Luisa Valenzuela. Copyright © 1988 by Luisa Valenzuela. Distributed by Consortium. Reprinted by permission of Curbstone Press.

We Say No, from WE SAY NO, by Eduardo Galeano. Copyright © 1992 by Eduardo Galeano. Original Spanish edition copyright © 1989 by Eduardo Galeano. Translation copyright © 1992 by Cedric Belfage. Published in English by W. W. Norton and Company, Inc. Reprinted by permission of Susan Bergholz Literary Services, New York.

Comrades, from JUMP AND OTHER STORIES, by Nadine Gordimer. Copyright © 1991 by Felix Licensing, B.V. Reprinted by permission of Farrar, Straus and Giroux, LLC.

The War and the Law, by Max Frankel, from the NEW YORK TIMES MAGAZINE, May 7, 1995. Copyright © 2001 by the New York Times Company. Reprinted by permission of the *New York Times*.

Safeguard Your Lives, from RED CHINA BLUES: MY LONG MARCH FROM MAO TO NOW, by Jan Wong. Copyright 1996 by Jan Wong. Reprinted by permission of Doubleday Canada.

Red Scarf Girl, from RED SCARF GIRL: A MEMOIR OF THE CULTURAL REVOLUTION, by Ji-li Jiang. Copyright © 1997 by Ji-li Jiang. Foreword copyright © 1997 by HarperCollins Publishers. Reprinted by permission of HarperCollins Publishers.

My Forbidden Face, from MY FORBIDDEN FACE: GROWING UP UNDER THE TALIBAN: A YOUNG WOMAN'S STORY, by Latifa. Translated by Linda Coverdale. Copyright © 2002 by Latifa. Reprinted by permission of Disney•Hyperion, an imprint of Disney Book Group LLC.

The Perplexities of the Rights of Man, from THE ORIGINS OF TOTALITARIANISM, by Hannah Arendt. Copyright © 1948, 1951, 1958, 1966, 1968, 1973 by Hannah Arendt; renewed 1976. Copyright renewed 1979 by Mary Mccarthy West. Copyright renewed 1986, 1994, 1996, 2001 by Lotte Kohler. Reprinted by permission of Houghton Mifflin Harcourt Publishing Company.